DISCARDED

THE TAILOR PROJECT

The Tailor Project

How 2,500 Holocaust Survivors
Found a New Life in Canada

ANDREA KNIGHT, PAULA DRAPER, AND NICOLE BRYCK

INTRODUCTION BY HAROLD TROPER

Second Story Press

Library and Archives Canada Cataloguing in Publication

Title: The tailor project : how 2,500 Holocaust survivors found a new life in Canada / Andrea
 Knight, Paula Draper, and Nicole Bryck.
Names: Knight, Andrea, author. | Draper, Paula, author. | Bryck, Nicole, author.
Identifiers: Canadiana (print) 20200209299 | Canadiana (ebook) 20200214047 | ISBN 9781772601442
 (softcover) | ISBN 9781772601459 (EPUB)
Subjects: LCSH: Holocaust survivors—Canada—Biography. | LCSH: Holocaust survivors' families—Canada.
 | LCSH: Jews—Canada—Biography. | LCSH: Tailors—Canada—Biography. | LCSH: World War,
 1939-1945—Jews—Rescue—Canada. | LCSH: Holocaust, Jewish (1939-1945)—Personal narratives.
Classification: LCC FC106.J5 K65 2020 | DDC 305.892/40971—dc23

First published in the USA in 2021

Cover photo: Jewish immigrants on board the SS *General S.D. Sturgis*, Halifax, NS, February 6, 1948.
Ontario Jewish Archives, item 628.

Printed and bound in Canada

*Second Story Press gratefully acknowledges the support of the Ontario Arts Council and the
Canada Council for the Arts for our publishing program. We acknowledge the financial support
of the Government of Canada through the Canada Book Fund.*

Published by
Second Story Press
20 Maud Street, Suite 401
Toronto, ON M5V 2M5
www.secondstorypress.ca

The Jew's connection with the clothing industry is by no means recent nor accidental...What tools could be less bulky and more easily carried by the wanderer than scissors and needles and thread?

—LOUIS ROSENBERG,
JEWISH STANDARD, AUGUST 1944

Contents

The Tailor Project

AUTHORS' ACKNOWLEDGEMENTS

At the heart of the Tailor Project are the inspiring stories of the tailors and their families. As noted on the website, this unique historical journey began with a search for tailors and/or their families to interview. We are indebted to the many families that came forward and shared their stories with us. Although this volume could only include a few families, we sincerely thank every person who showed us an intimate part of their family history. We thank those who welcomed us into their homes and provided us with the material they had to offer. Their stories, photographs, documents, and artifacts give life to the Tailor Project history.

We also thank the archives that worked with us, directing our research to important sources that we would not have found ourselves. These institutions were integral to the growth of this project, and to ensuring historical accuracy throughout the research. Their contributions have provided answers to many families and individuals who have had little access to their history until now. In particular, we are grateful to the archivists who gave freely of their time and expertise: Janice Rosen, archives director of the Alex Dworkin Canadian Jewish Archives; Donna Bernardo-Ceriz, managing director of the Ontario Jewish Archives, Blankenstein Family Heritage Centre, UJA Federation of Greater Toronto; Stan Carbone of the Jewish Heritage Centre of Western Canada; and Michael Schwartz of the Jewish Museum & Archives of BC. Special thanks go to Dr. Frank Bialystok, who shared his research materials from Library and Archives Canada for *Delayed Impact: The Holocaust and the Canadian Jewish Community*.

The 1948–1949 Garment Workers Scheme owes its beginnings to the Canadian Jewish Congress, the Jewish Labour Committee, and all the participating actors—firms, unions, and community organizations—who worked together to make the project possible. The five men who went to Europe to find tailors were an integral part of the story and special thanks go to the families of Sam Posluns, David Solomon, and Max Enkin, who provided valuable private historical documents and reminiscences.

Larry Enkin, Max Enkin's son, grew up hearing stories from his father about the Garment Workers Scheme. Sixty-five years later he asked the important questions: Where are those tailors today? What is their story? How did these survivors and their families contribute to Canada? Larry engaged Paul Klein and his staff at Impakt Corporation to undertake this challenging task. Tremendous credit is due to their unswerving devotion to the Tailor Project and we thank them for the opportunity to participate in this important and moving venture. Larry Enkin generously funded the project and its remarkable development. We are immensely grateful for his unyielding support and guidance.

Finally, we would also like to thank Margie Wolfe, publisher of Second Story Press, and her remarkable team, who made invaluable suggestions throughout the process of writing this book and without whom it would not have been published.

INTRODUCTION

THIS VOLUME introduces us to fifteen postwar immigrant workers—all Holocaust survivors—and their families. These fifteen individuals came to Canada under the umbrella of the Tailor Project, a government-sanctioned, postwar, labour importation scheme that brought approximately 2,100 European workers to take up jobs in the Canadian clothing manufacturing industry. Each of these fifteen stories is unique but, taken together, they are far more than the sum of their separate parts. On the one hand, they affirm the possibility of human resilience and the rebirth of hope in the face of catastrophic loss; on the other, they speak to how and why a communal Canadian Jewish sense of solidarity with the tattered remnant of postwar European Jews morphed into the Tailor Project—the first reversal of a decades-long prohibition against Jewish immigration in Canada. If far more restricted than its proponents had originally hoped, it is to the credit of those who worked to make the program happen that the Tailor Project pried open Canada's immigration door, if only a crack. That crack was wide enough to allow a first-of-its-kind resettlement of several thousand Holocaust survivors to Canada. And, although no one could know it at the time, the Tailor Project also had a more far-reaching impact than anyone could have imagined. Not only did the Tailor Project pave the way for the eventual removal of regulations restricting the admission of Jews into Canada, it was also among the first successful postwar hammer blows against racial, ethnic, and religious discrimination in Canadian immigration policy.

Few dreamed of an end to racial and ethnic selectivity in immigration when the Canadian government first reluctantly and half-heartedly authorized the Tailor Project. Until that time, the twin pillars entrenched in Canadian immigration policy were economic self-interest and ethnic and racial selectivity. It could even be argued that racial and ethnic selectivity trumped economic advantage. Certainly, this was true for non-Europeans. With little regard for the capital investment or talents of non-European immigrants, a bulwark of restrictive laws, regulations, and administrative procedures restricted their admissions. And in the immediate postwar years, the federal government was not about to make any changes to that policy. In 1947,

Prime Minister Mackenzie King reminded Parliament, that "With regard to the selection of immigrants, much has been said about discrimination. I wish to make quite clear that Canada is perfectly within her rights in selecting the persons whom we regard as desirable future citizens. It is not a 'fundamental human right' of any alien to enter Canada. It is a privilege."[1]

It was also a privilege then denied to many of European heritage as well. Starting before World War I and extending through the Great Depression and into the postwar period, would-be European arrivals were ranked in a descending order of ethnic or racial preference. In this racial sweepstakes, Jews were at the bottom. And who were favoured? Canada still regarded itself as the North American outpost of the British imperial aspirations and welcomed immigrants from Britain and the traditionally white dominions without restriction. It also courted white American settlers as "people of independent thought who understand the ways of this continent and its institutions."[2] Scandinavians and other Western Europeans, in the main Protestant, were also highly prized, their immigration encouraged. All others were "foreigners," their perceived racial and ethnic liability weighed against the degree of economic advantage these "foreigners" afforded Canada. At the turn of the last century that weight shifted as the Canadian economic outlook turned upward. After years of broken promises and frustrated hopes, Canada was suddenly swept up in an unprecedented surge of economic growth. It seemed that the world's appetite for Canadian exports—wheat, timber, metals—was insatiable and Canada's potential for expanded development immeasurable. Stretching westward out of the Ontario heartland, along the line of the completed transcontinental Canadian Pacific Railway, lay newly accessible interior forests, mining frontiers, and, most immediately, the vast agricultural hinterland of the Canadian Northwest, all ripe for development.

All that was missing was a population ready to work the land, dig the mines, and harvest the forests. A newly elected and development-minded government, seizing the economic moment, initiated an energetic program of immigrant recruitment designed to fill the agricultural expanse of the Canadian Prairies while assuring a ready pool of cheap labour for burgeoning mining and lumbering industries. The government initiatives actively sought traditionally desirable immigrants— those of British, American, and Western European stock—who dreamed of farming their own land on the Canadian Prairies. Immigration officials also welcomed those who were prepared to risk life and limb labouring in mines with lax safety standards or were prepared to endure the coarse life in the lumbering camps.

But for all the government's effort to bring in experienced and independent-minded farmers and labourers of desirable lineage, supply consistently fell far short of demand. With national prosperity thought to hang on population increase, the government reluctantly, but necessarily, reached down its ladder of racial preference to approve the recruitment of Central and Eastern European agricultural settlers and labourers who had previously been considered racially substandard. As the Canadian minister responsible for immigration explained in 1902, the government's litmus test for immigrant approval was simple: "The test we have to apply is this: Does the person intending to come to Canada intend to become an agriculturalist? If he does, we encourage him to come and give him every assistance we can."[3]

And come they did. Beaten into misery by overpopulation, economic deprivation, and state repression, hundreds of thousands turned their backs on decrepit and repressive regimes, packed up what little they had, and surged westward across Europe and on to the New World in search of a new beginning. For tens of thousands, that new beginning was in the Canadian West.

Among those who were swept up in the newly expanded Canadian immigration net were Jews spilling out of Romania and the Russian and Austro-Hungarian Empires. The Canadian Jewish population growth was dramatic. In 1891, the Canadian census counted only 6,503 Jews; ten years later, the number of Jews had increased nearly threefold to 16,717. Still more startling, between 1901 and 1911 the number of Jews in

Canada exploded, increasing to 75,838. But it was not just the increase in Jewish numbers that impressed itself on mainstream Canadians and their government. More significantly, and for many Canadians far more troubling, Jewish immigration—more than that of any other immigrant group—directly challenged the social and economic assumptions that grounded Canadian immigration policy. In the face of a Canadian immigration policy designed to expand Western agriculture, with few exceptions, Jewish arrivals demonstrated little inclination to farm. The same was true of Canada's mining and lumbering labour pool: Jews were absent. Instead, the vast majority of Jewish arrivals converged on Canada's cities. In 1911, ten years after the government initiated its program of agricultural settlement in Western Canada, the Jewish population had grown by 400 per cent but less than 6 per cent lived in rural Canada. By the 1921 census, it had dropped to 4 per cent. In contrast, more than 80 per cent of Ukrainians, almost 75 per cent of Scandinavians, and 70 per cent of Dutch and German residents were classed as rural. Indeed, no group in the census had a lower rural residency rate than Jews. What is more, few Jews, even those few in rural areas, were farmers or worked in extractive industries. The few Jews who lived in rural Canada were more likely to be small retailers, tradesmen, or artisans than agriculturalists or industrial labourers. In 1921, less than one in four of the few Jews living in rural areas was directly engaged in agriculture, forestry, or mining. It comes as no surprise, then, that in 1931 more than 80 per cent of Jews in Canada lived in Montreal, Toronto, or Winnipeg.

In a Canada where the Anglo-Canadian mainstream reluctantly agreed to the admission of foreign settlers on condition that they played the narrow economic roles assigned to them—farming the vast Canadian agricultural interior or working in extractive industries—Jews were obvious outliers. And if some in the Canadian mainstream accepted the increasing presence of Jews in cities with equanimity, many more came to regard the growing community of Yiddish-speaking foreigners and their children as a blight on the urban landscape and a threat to the national good. Jews were faulted for being clannish, clinging together in overcrowded inner-city neighbourhoods, given to politically subversive ideologies, and seemingly immune to the assimilationist efforts of Canadian gatekeepers, educators, and Protestant missionaries who promised salvation to those who would accept Christ as their saviour. As a result, whether newly arrived Jews found themselves consigned to long hours slaving on sewing machines or attempting to eke out a living in retail or the trades, they were collectively feared as corrosive of the established order, competitive with "real" Canadians, and subversive to the establishment of a Christian dominion from sea to sea. Following World War I, as immigration officials looked to scale back on foreign immigration, Jews caught the eye of officials more than any other group.

Of course, when it came to immigration, Canadian politicians and immigration officials had more to worry about than Jews. There was growing public unrest fed by economic uncertainty. A sharp business and trade slump following World War I brought with it both a decline in wages and a rise in unemployment. In Winnipeg, growing labour discontent exploded in a general strike that threatened the established political and economic elite. Canadian authorities lashed back against the strikers and their leadership, tapping into lingering wartime anti-foreign sentiment. Conjuring up images of the recent Russian Revolution, they declared the strike a crude plot by "foreigners" to impose radical and "alien" ideology on Canadians by force. These claims fed already growing accusations that foreign workers were stealing jobs from "real" Canadians. A call for immigration restrictions grew and the federal government listened. A series of cabinet-approved directives—orders-in-council—reduced the number of Central and Eastern Europe settlers, including Jews, entering Canada and by the mid-1920s, tighter passport and visa control barriers were in place. The government cut back on family reunifications by narrowing the list of family members eligible to enter Canada to first-degree relatives of people who were already in Canada. The wife, children, parents, and unmarried brothers and sisters of those in Canada were eligible to apply; married siblings, uncles, aunts, and cousins were not. Importantly, the government also shifted immigration health inspections, previously conducted at ports of arrival in Canada, to ports of exit in Europe. This move granted Canadian immigration authorities a medical cover to reject any would-be immigrant without access to appeal.

As far as Jewish immigration was concerned, the government had still more restrictive measures in mind. It made several additional refinements—as simple as they were effective—to restrict the admission of Jews to Canada as belonging to one of the "races that cannot be assimilated without social or economic loss to Canada."[4] Without fanfare, immigration officials worked out a ranking of all would-be settlers by their degree of similar "racial characteristics" to the Anglo-Canadian majority. To this end, European countries were separated into three groups: a Preferred Group, a Non-Preferred Group, and a catchall group called the Special Permit Group. The Preferred Group, made up of the countries of Northern and Western Europe, including Germany, was exempted from nearly all restrictive provisions of the new regulations except visa formalities. Their immigration continued to be welcomed. The Non-Preferred Group included people from Austria, Hungary, Czechoslovakia, Russia, Yugoslavia, Poland, Romania, and the Baltic states. As a support to Canadian

railway and Western land companies—then still heavily invested in ongoing land settlement—railway company agents were allowed to recruit agricultural immigrants from "Non-Preferred" countries if these would-be settlers could prove sufficient capital to buy land and, immediately on arrival in Canada, take up farming.

Immigration officials, however, were not about to allow Jews, except the now-narrowed list of first-degree relatives of people already in Canada, to enter—no matter what their country of origin. Immigration officials turned their racist consensus into administrative regulation, making Jewish immigration to Canada more difficult than that of others holding the same citizenship. Jews (excepting British subjects or those from the United States) were lumped into the Special Permit group with others regarded as racially suspect. This included those from Italy, Greece, Yugoslavia, Bulgaria, Syria, and Turkey. Because the new Fascist government in Italy had previously limited emigration of its citizens, and the number of immigrants from other Special Permit countries was never high, the Special Permit class served primarily to restrict the entry of Jews into Canada: Jews had acquired immigration ineligibility.

In the end, the impact of the newly applied Canadian immigration regulations turned the immigration law on its head. Rather than allow entry of all except prohibited groups, the regulations now prohibited everyone except specifically *permitted* groups. With the exception of the few Jews able to squeeze into Canada as immediate family of those already in Canada, a wall of exclusion had been built against Jews. There was only one tiny and unlikely exemption: A Jew could apply and hope to be granted a rarely issued cabinet-authorized entry permit. But hope was then a commodity in very short supply. Without the patronage of someone with enough political clout to apply pressure in Ottawa—and how many Jews had that?—there could be no permit. Jews seeking to leave Europe were best advised to look elsewhere. As one Toronto rabbi lamented, "Between the upper and the nether millstone, the Jew as usual will be crushed."[5]

For the next two decades, through depression and war and into the postwar period, as previously unimaginable horrors became a reality for European Jews, Canadian politicians and officials were unyielding in their defence of restrictions on immigration and to the immigration of Jews in particular. Appeals from the politically marginal Jewish community in Canada and the few Canadians who supported the notion that Canada should offer haven to refugees from Nazism were dismissed. The first crack in that wall of restriction was the Tailor Project. Coming as it did after more than two decades of ignoring every Jewish community appeal for immigration reform, the Tailor Project, no matter how limited in scope, is an achievement worth remembering and celebrating. It enabled a first group of several thousand Holocaust survivors and their families to begin new lives in Canada. It was also a first step toward opening Canada to the admission of Jews on the same terms as other Europeans and a key step toward the eventual elimination of racial and ethnic barriers to Canadian immigration.

Harold Troper
December 29, 2019

POSTWAR CANADA

In the long run there can be only one satisfactory solution—acceptance of the DPs [displaced persons] as immigrants by the newer, emptier lands, like Canada and the United States. It's likely that whenever the United Nations gets around to studying the problem, nations like ours will be asked to take a stipulated quota of these homeless people. (We are now taking a few with relatives here.)

Some Canadian officials think the smart thing for Canada would be to go into the DP camps now and pick out the most desirable immigrants we can find—men with skills that we can use. Then we could apply these selected immigrants to our quota when the time comes. Others say this scheme is good sense but poor politics. They glumly predict that Canada will simply ignore the problem as long as possible, and then take whatever half measure may be forced upon us at the time.[1]

WHEN WORLD WAR II ended in Europe, millions of people displaced by war and persecution were stranded in a decimated landscape. By 1947, those who had found their way back to their homelands had been replaced by tens of thousands fleeing the spreading oppression of Soviet occupation. As the above-quoted *Maclean's* article explained, the dispossessed refugees could not stay and they would not go home. Jewish survivors of the Holocaust, many who were now gathered in temporary camps in Germany and Austria, explained "We have nothing here. The whole country is saturated with Jewish blood and tears. It is as though you sentenced us to life imprisonment in a grave yard."[2] Canada, with its history of closed doors—particularly against Jews—remained an unlikely promised land. Yet the postwar world was no longer the grim, economically depressed one of the 1930s. If Canada was to progress on the world stage, it would need to revitalize its economy. It was becoming clear that the road to prosperity would have to be built with the help of immigrant workers. This would require a drastic overhaul of policies that had characterized the years of the Holocaust.

As the crisis of European Jewry escalated in the years leading up to World War II, Canadian Jewry and its representative agency, the Canadian Jewish Congress (CJC), lobbied quietly yet persistently for a humanitarian immigration policy. The community, constituting less than 1.5 per cent of the population, met failure at every turn. Anti-Jewish sentiment in the country was high and was reflected in the responses of both civil servants and politicians. Prime Minister Mackenzie King was wary that concessions regarding Jewish refugees could cost his party at the polls, especially in Quebec. He wrote in his private diary, "I fear we would have riots if we agreed to a policy that admitted numbers of Jews."[3] One of the few Jewish members of Parliament was A.A. Heaps from Winnipeg. Although they shared a friendly personal relationship, even Heaps was unable to convince King to alter the regulations. Clearly outraged, Heaps wrote, "The existing regulations are probably the most stringent to be found anywhere in the whole world. If refugees have no money they are barred because they are poor, and if they have fairly substantial sums, they are often refused admittance on the most flimsy pretext. All I say of existing regulations is that they are inhuman and anti-Christian."[4]

Any hope that Canadian Jews had for the rescue of their European brethren dissolved during the war years. Canadian officials obstructed large and small avenues of escape. Between 1933 and 1945 fewer than five thousand Jewish refugees were admitted to the country. Canada held the worst record of refugee admittance of any Western nation outside the theatre of war. As the war in Europe ended and servicemen returned, the first priority was to re-integrate them into the Canadian economy. Refugees were not on the agenda. Carine Wilson, the country's first female senator and chair of the Canadian National Committee on Refugees, pressed the immigration department. In January 1946, she outlined all the efforts that other Western countries had made to take in refugees, then concluded, "Surely… Canada will also want a position of equal leadership among her partners who have already taken positive action in these enterprises, motivated by the selfless desire to alleviate the hardships of those who are suffering so grievously. With our God-given resources and our fortunate economic circumstances, we dare say that it would be contrary to Canadian traditions of morality not to come to the rescue of the displaced and the homeless."[5] But pleas from refugee advocates continued to fall on deaf ears.

Canada's senate, beginning to look toward wartorn Europe as a possible source of much-needed cheap labour, re-constituted its committee on immigration and labour. The CJC seized their chance to plead for the surviving Jews of Europe. On July 3, 1946, CJC director Saul Hayes and demographer Louis Rosenberg presented their case. This was the first time they had been able to speak in public before a parliamentary committee and Hayes explained that although the Jewish community had diverse opinions on many issues, it was united as one in its submission. Surveying the history of the past twenty years, they had seen their "own flesh and blood persecuted, shamed and decimated for lack of a more sympathetic immigration policy in this country."[6] He outlined the outmoded policies of preference for agricultural workers and barring of many ethnic groups, asking that the country be protected from the "caprices or the race and religious prejudice of any official." Every other country had a better record of refugee admission during the war, Hayes explained, including the British rescuers at Dunkirk who found room for refugees aboard the small, civilian vessels that saved stranded British troops. The CJC appealed for a new immigration act free of racial discrimination. Hayes could not mask the bitter disappointment and frustration of his community.

> During the past decade a vast slaughter of our people has taken place; I emphasize, of our people, because although all European nations have suffered during the years of war… none has had the percentage of losses that the Jewish People have suffered. Over six million Jewish civilians have died violently…as a result of the preachings [sic] of Hitler and

of the latent spirit of anti-Semitism which permeates the continent of Europe. It is my duty to say that the number of these victims could have been very much smaller and very many of their lives could have been saved if such countries as Canada would have paid due

Saul Hayes, Director of the United Jewish Relief Agencies of Canada (UJRA) of the Canadian Jewish Congress, Montreal, date unknown.

heed to the requests and pleas of their kin and of Jewish citizens to grant a refuge to some of them while there was still time. It is a simple and truthful fact that because the applications made to the Immigration Branch on behalf of many of them were not favourably acted upon, their ashes and bones today lie in Buchenwald and soap had been made of their bodies instead of their being free and useful citizens in Canadian life today.[7]

Meanwhile, business leaders were arguing that peace could usher in an economic boom. Their opinions corresponded with the thinking of some members of King's government who were formulating a new vision for the country. Foremost among them was C.D. Howe, a former engineering professor and entrepreneur who became the wartime "Minister of Everything." Howe had played a central role in the war effort. One of his innovations was to recruit corporate executives as "dollar-a-year men" who helped run a variety of enterprises. One of these was Max Enkin, who would later lead the mission to bring garment workers out of the displaced persons (DP) camps. Howe, as postwar minister of reconstruction and supply, advocated for increased immigration and set his sights on the DPs. Getting the prime minister on his side, Howe installed a new administration at the immigration department.

Hugh Keenleyside was given control of policy with a mission to prioritize the opening of Canada's doors.

Opening the doors did not translate into an open immigration policy. While family reunification was permitted, King and his cabinet remained adamant on how Canada could select its new citizens. "The people of Canada do not wish," King wrote in his diary, "to make a fundamental alteration in the character of our population." He was well aware that there would be external pressure pointing to a moral obligation to take in refugees and opposing a continuation of blatant racism in the country's policies. He wrote, "there is going to be a great danger of the UN refusing the idea of justifiable rights of selected immigration with racial and other discriminations." The solution would be quotas based on country of origin and "racial composition." The goal would be reconstruction, not rescue.[8]

By 1947, a variety of labour schemes had permitted the first groups of DPs to enter Canada. Most signed lengthy contracts to work in lumber camps and on farms, in mines, railroads, and construction, and as domestics. Recruiters and immigration officials in Europe observed Canada's ethnically selective code. Jews were still considered undesirable.

MAX ENKIN (1900–1990)

MAX ENKIN'S FUNERAL at Holy Blossom Temple in Toronto in 1990 was filled with tributes to its Honorary Life President. Rabbi Emeritus Gunther Plaut, a close friend, renowned Jewish scholar, and community leader, eloquently assessed Enkin's character and his remarkable life:

> He was small in stature, but large in vision. He did not pursue honour, but honours pursued him. He was a Jew to the core, but—or because of it—non-Jews were attracted to him…. His reputation for unbending integrity, the esteem in which his co-workers as well as his competitors held him in the fashion field, his many honours, among them the Order of the British Empire and the Order of Canada. These were signposts of a career to which any man would point with justifiable pride—except that Max Enkin never pointed to himself. He was self-made yet utterly modest. His greatest asset was not material wealth, but a good and noble heart. He had above all, a way of looking at life's problems from a religious perspective. He considered ethics the heart of Reform Judaism, and many was the time when he would ask me: "What does Judaism require of me in this situation?" In a way that was the secret of Max Enkin's influence: he asked Jewish questions.[1]

Miriam and Morris Enkin arrived in Montreal in 1906 when Max was six years old. The family had fled Vitebsk in Belarus, where Jews had lived since the sixteenth century. They fled poverty and pogroms, joining the masses of Eastern European Jews looking for new homes in North America. Morris was a carpenter but felt his prospects would improve if he worked for the Canadian Pacific Railway. However, an industrial accident left him disabled, so he supported his family by running a small grocery store. Max always remembered the suffering that his father's job-related injury caused his family at a time when there was no workmen's compensation, unemployment insurance, or medicare. Max was only able to finish eight years of schooling before he

Max Enkin, along with Sam Herbst and Sam Posluns, overseeing the tailoring tests of applicants from Bergen-Belsen. In the back row, left to right are Sam Herbst, Max Enkin, and Sam Posluns.

had to work to help his family. Yet his love of learning stayed with him and he was an avid reader all his life.

Enkin left Montreal for Arnprior, Ontario, near Ottawa, where he met and married his first wife, Pearl. Now in his twenties, Max entered the clothing business in Toronto and soon rose to general manager at the Warren K. Cook Company, a manufacturer of men's clothing. The 1920s were a time in men's fashion, Max recalled, when "you could have any colour and fabric choice you wanted as long as it was blue or gray serge."[2] He worked hard to grow the company, but upon his return from his work with the Garment Workers Commission in Europe, Enkin's relations with his employer became strained. In 1950, he purchased a struggling company in Hamilton, Ontario—Coppley, Noyes & Randall Ltd. Enkin built the company of sixty into one of the largest manufacturers of quality men's clothing in Canada with more than six hundred employees. It was widely known as Cambridge Clothes. Max drove himself to his offices until he was eighty and kept up a full daily work schedule well into his ninth decade.

The early years of Enkin's manufacturing career coincided with the Depression and the often-violent struggle between the growing unions, pressing management for improvements in working conditions and fair wages. Max was a firm believer in respectful negotiation, fairness, and conciliation. He recalled that the first time he was threatened with a strike, his response was, "Why bother? Let's sit down and talk now rather than later." He was proud that there was never one strike in all the decades he ran his companies.

Although he lost his wife, Pearl, to cancer and was left to raise two young sons, Murray and Larry, Enkin expanded his activities in the clothing industry. He was instrumental in the creation of a welfare and pension fund for the Amalgamated Clothing Workers. He also helped create the Industrial Standards Act for the Men's Clothing Industry in Ontario, was founding chair of the advisory board of the textile and clothing industry for the federal department of industry trade and commerce, and chairman of the Men's Clothing Manufacturers' Association of Ontario. It was due to Enkin's reputation in supporting workers' rights that he was chosen as the chair of the Garment Workers Commission to the DP camps.

The plight of European Jewry had moved Enkin to activism long before the outbreak of war. His work with government gave him access to officials at various levels, and he did not shy away from knocking on the doors of provincial and federal officials to fight restrictive antisemitic immigration policies. In 1942, Enkin was named deputy administrator for the textile industry on the Wartime Prices and Trade Board, the board that controlled Canada's economy. His task was to find textiles for the civilian population and Max made many perilous trips to the UK. Once, on a small Norwegian freighter, he recalled wondering what he was doing on a violent ocean infested with German submarines. "I answered then as I always answer. I felt I was paying my dues. You get, you've got to give. I had two young sons. This was my way of serving them and my country. I was a Jew and I was imbued with anti-Hitlerism." Enkin was awarded the OBE, the Order of the British Empire, for his wartime services.

At the end of the war Max married Jeanette Gardner of Winnipeg, after which he embarked on a mission that would be the first of many humanitarian endeavours. What Enkin experienced in the DP camps moved him deeply. A journalist who interviewed him upon his return remarked how Max, "ordinarily a jolly, optimistic man" was "overtaken by gloomy despair when he thinks of his recent trip" and the survivors they left behind. "I feel like a public executioner when I think of it. You could pick one man or woman out of every 20 or 30. To that one you could say, 'You will have a chance to rebuild your life.' The others you could only send back to their crowded, unheated quarters, to their starvation diet and to their idleness and despair."[3]

Enkin set out to educate Canadians about the conditions he'd witnessed in Europe. He reminded them of the terrible toll the war years had taken. "Aside from the loss of their loved ones and the loss of all their material possessions," Enkin wrote, "there were the harrowing experiences of personal survival under the most indescribable and unbelievable situations. All these people want now is the chance to rebuild their lives. They don't want pity, sympathy, or charity. They have somehow maintained a unique dignity. Having gone through the crucible of suffering, they have developed a philosophy that we perhaps cannot understand."

Enkin was more blunt speaking to his fellow Canadian Jews. "I don't know whether I have transmitted to you the poignancy and anguish that we have felt in visiting and working and talking to some five thousand people," Max admonished his audience. "I am beginning to doubt if many know or appreciate how these people find themselves there, who they are, and what we owe them if we are to justifiably uphold our own respect and genuinely acknowledge that we are our brothers' keeper." His immediate goal was to assure that housing was available for the garment workers when they arrived, particularly for the families. "The challenge to redeem our conscience is given us now in the manner that we receive the trickle of DPs who are coming to Canada." As Enkin reminded them,

Most of us are the sons and daughters of immigrants to this country. Your fathers and mothers did not land in homes with tiled bathrooms, large recreation rooms and innumerable bedrooms. They most likely were housed by friends who helped them establish themselves. Hospitality and looking after the homeless is or was an age-old tradition of our people. Let us copy and follow their example.[4]

The garment workers would be the first of several groups of Jewish workers in various industries to be allowed into Canada. Enkin understood that after their contracts expired, many would not remain in those trades. He was instrumental in founding Toronto's Jewish Vocational Service (JVS), an agency conceived to help Holocaust survivors and returning Jewish servicemen find employment. Enkin continued to be active in the manufacturing industry while pursuing his commitment to social justice and inter-faith harmony. He served for twenty-five years as national treasurer of the Canadian Council of Christians and Jews, was president and trustee not only of his synagogue, but also of the Canadian Council of Reform Congregations. Enkin served as trustee, or on boards, of many Jewish organizations and hospitals and was honoured in Israel and in Canada, receiving the Order of Canada in 1983. In his own words, Max Enkin was a "Tough realist, incurable and eternal optimist, a believer in the ultimate power of good."

C O P Y

HANNOVER, December 12, 1947.

Mr. Saul Hayes,
Executive Director,
Canadian Jewish Congress,
1121 St. Catherine St. West,
Montreal, Que.,
Canada.

Dear Mr. Hayes:

After spending 3 weeks in the American and British Zones of Germany,
I feel called upon to write this letter to you, and through you, to
the leadership of the Congress before I leave for Poland.

During my stay I have visited a number of Jewish D.P. camps, met and
discussed the migration and other problems affecting the Jewish D.P.'s,
with leaders of the Joint, HIAS, Central Committee of Liberated Jews,
Spokesmen for the Jewish Agency, scores of officials of I.RO., from
the top levels down and of course with the people affected. In
addition I have contacted and have spoken to a large number of Canadian
officials who are here and who are in charge of the Canadian Immigration projects. I have also met Mr. Matthew Ramm and Miss Ethel Ostry
who are the direct representatives of the Congress here. From all
these contacts, observations and discussions I have come to the
following conclusions:

1. That there is a very definite anti-Jewish bias in the Canadian
Immigration policies and in their application on the spot. This
opinion is practically universal. Top I.R.O. people share it with
Jewish organizational representatives. While in some cases it is
concealed, discrimination is brazen and unashamed in others. Here
are a few examples:

a) In the American Zone all cases of Jewish applicants for the Lumber
project, had their visas taken away from them after they had gone
through all tests, screened, etc. etc. There's revulsion against
this particular case on all sides.

b) Of all the Jewish girls who applied for the Domestics project in
the U. S. Zone, all but one were rejected and that one was accepted
only because she stated that she was Polish.

c) In the Close Relative scheme there are scores of D.P.'s for whom
approval was secured by relatives in Canada, who are awaiting for
almost a year to be called by the Canadian officials here. Whether
Ottawa fails to send their numbers or whether the officials here fail
to call them I cannot say, but I am inclined to think that much of
the delay is caused right in Ottawa, where, in my opinion, an attempt
is being made to keep the number of Jewish close relatives down to a
certain percentage.

kept to a percentage level.

J.B. Salsberg MPP
to Saul Hayes,
12 December 1947.

THE BULK LABOUR SCHEMES

THE FIRST SIZEABLE GROUP of postwar immigrants admitted to Canada came from Britain in 1946. Repatriated German prisoners of war who had been assigned to work on Canada's farms and in lumber camps were swapped for four thousand Poles who had fought for the Allied cause in General Anders' Army. The Polish soldiers were unwilling to return home and Canada was in desperate need of unmarried men to perform "heavy labour." It had been decades since Canadian immigration officials had worked to admit applicants rather than bar them. Although their instructions were to screen solely for "subversives," they made it clear to the Polish authorities that Jews would be refused. Jewish soldiers were discouraged from applying for what was, in practice, a contract labour scheme for single men. When the first group of 1,700 arrived in Canada, it included a sole Jew.[1] There were only three Jews among the 2,900 who had arrived by 1947.[2] As demands for both unskilled and skilled labour grew, cabinet looked to model other programs on this first success. Officials on the ground in Europe would prove no less stringent in perpetuating ingrained prejudices when these labour schemes were implemented.

By 1947, Canada had increased its quota to admit twenty thousand DPs by the middle of the following year. Some would be close relatives, sponsored by their families who pledged to support them, but most would be recruited from the DP camps for bulk labour programs. The focus on the need for labour, especially in mines and forests, deflected public attention from this stark alteration of immigration policy. Procedures were put in place whereby different industries could apply for workers. They would guarantee jobs, usually for a year, and sign government contracts assuring they would abide by agreed upon wages. Employers would provide housing and basic needs. Selection teams comprised of both industry and department of labour officials would be sent to the camps to select qualified workers. The early program was soon expanded to include specialized agricultural workers, particularly for sugar beet production, and women who could qualify as domestic workers and hospital workers. Although these schemes were in principle open to everyone in the camps, the reality was that ethnic stereotypes restricted many from these programs. Balts and Estonians were preferred for forestry. Ukrainians would be recruited to gain government support from Ukrainian Canadians. Civil servants made it clear they believed that Northern European women would make the best workers. "Jews aren't willing to be domestics," one female consultant in the labour department explained. "It is not their forte."[3]

Young, unmarried Jewish survivors were more than willing to find a way out of the camps by applying for Canadian labour schemes. Many Jewish women had experience in nursing care in hospitals after liberation. Most were rejected outright; those who were initially approved found their security clearances retracted after cables were received from Ottawa drawing a line against Jews. None of this was announced publicly, though it was clearly noted by shocked International Refugee Organization (IRO) officials. Canadian officers employed a level of subterfuge to exclude Jews: they recorded applicants based on their place of birth. If most Jews were rejected, it would not appear in the records. Edith Ferguson, a Toronto social worker helping out in the DP camps, told *Saturday Night* magazine that she witnessed Canadian selection teams blatantly discriminating against Jews on instructions from Ottawa. She urged Canadians to pressure the government to admit more Holocaust survivors.[4]

Joe Salsberg, a former union leader and the only Communist member of the Ontario legislature, travelled to Europe in the fall of 1947 on a private fact-finding mission.[5] His observations would confirm what the Jewish community was hearing from other sources. He returned to the Polish hometown he had last visited in August 1939 to discover that most of his community had perished in the gas chambers of Treblinka. His grandmother had been "taken away in a cart—she was a little thing and far too old to walk—and they shot her on the side of the road. Nobody knows where she's buried…. I left town that night in an extremely emotional disposition. It was the first time I've ever lost control. I cried like a child." Salsberg spent a month surveying the DP camps in Germany. He published his observations in the Canadian Jewish press, pleading with readers to write to their surviving relatives and friends in the camps who felt alone and abandoned. He wrote that he "was put to shame by the justified complaints and accusations which the Jews in the detestable camps levelled against their relatives abroad for their failure to write to them."[6]

Salsberg also collected evidence of Canada's antisemitic screening procedures, which he reported in a detailed letter to Saul Hayes, explaining, "while in some cases it is concealed, discrimination is brazen and unashamed in others." He had conferred with IRO officials and representatives of Jewish aid organizations who all shared the same opinion. And he gave Hayes examples. In one case, eleven Jewish men who had passed all the tests and screening for the forestry program had their visas taken from them at the last minute. In another, he described how every Jewish woman in one camp who applied for the domestic scheme was rejected except for one, who listed herself as a Polish Christian. Salsberg wrote that the vice consuls "insist on the listing of Jewish immigrants as of the 'Hebrew' race. They showed me forms on which they scratched out the 'White' designation and imposed 'Hebrew' instead." Salsberg was reluctant to point his finger at the people implementing policies that, he believed, originated in Ottawa "where policies are made and from where instructions are issued." He did point at the security officers, whose actions he found "positively astounding." Regulations barred members of the Nazi SS—war criminals who were not only Germans but also included members of other ethnic groups who had allied themselves with the Nazis—from admission to Canada. Salsberg described how a physician had prevented a group of a dozen men with SS tattoos in their armpits from boarding a ship to Canada only to see them screened and approved by security. "On the other hand," Salsberg noted, "a Canadian security officer questions a Jewish child 'What were your parents doing in Auschwitz—and where did you get the money to come from Auschwitz to here!'" Salsberg concluded, "The battle for the admittance of Jewish D.P.s to Canada is a battle in the full sense of the word. It has to be carried on from the top levels down to the docks where the immigrant is placed on board ship,

and it is a battle all the way down. There is a specific job which Congress and other must do in Ottawa, and there is an enormous task right here."[7]

The contents of Joe Salsberg's report came as no surprise to the Canadian Jewish Congress (CJC). It only confirmed what they already knew. While Hayes and Sam Bronfman were travelling from Montreal to Ottawa to diligently press the case for the admission of survivors, members of the clothing industry in Canada were contemplating the bulk labour program as a means of bringing large groups of survivors to Canada. By the time Salsberg left Germany, the garment workers scheme was well underway.

Bergen–Belsen DP Camp. Former officers' quarters used as accommodation for survivors.

THE DISPLACED PERSONS CAMPS

*Wherever I went, I always
felt myself in the presence
of a truly great people.*

—SAM POSLUNS

DURING THE FIRST MONTHS after the war, many Jewish survivors had ventured back to their homes with hopes of finding loved ones only to return alone. The Soviets slowly opened their borders to release Polish Jews who had fled east to escape the Nazis. In 1946, escalating anti-Jewish pogroms pushed most remaining Jews out of Poland. Between 1945 and 1948, some 250,000 stateless Holocaust survivors found their way into areas of Europe controlled by British, American, and French occupation forces. At first, the Allied officials treated Jews as citizens of their prewar countries. Axis nationals were still considered enemies and not entitled to special care. The first improvised displaced persons (DP) camps like Dachau, Bergen-Belsen, Feldafing, and Landsberg were located on the sites of former concentration camps. Other camps had been created out of warehouses, bombed-out railway stations, schools,

movie theatres, stables, and even ships at anchor. They contained a volatile mix of Jews and non-Jews, including Nazi collaborators and concentration camp guards. Barbed wire and military sentries surrounded some of the camps. Jewish agencies and Jewish DP leaders spoke out against these conditions. A British official responded that, unlike the Nazis, they would not treat Jews "as a separate national category." General Dwight D. Eisenhower proclaimed that the Americans would make "no differentiation in treatment of displaced persons."[1] Negative reports and publications describing the abominable state of affairs in the early camps prompted the new US president, Harry S. Truman, to find solutions. Truman gave the task of investigating the conditions of the DP camps to law school dean Earl Harrison, whose report concluded, "We appear to be treating the Jews as the Nazis treated them except that we do not exterminate them." He illustrated the need for a significant improvement in living conditions and a new approach confirming "their status as Jews."

"While admittedly it is not normally desirable to set aside particular racial or religious groups from their

Bergen-Belsen concentration camp site, 1948.

nationality categories," Harrison wrote, "the plain truth is that this was done for so long by the Nazis that a group has been created which has special needs." As a result, by 1946 camps were either exclusively Jewish or partitioned between groups. Food rations were raised for survivors and camp residents were able to administer their own affairs. While living conditions in the DP camps improved, they remained way stations to nowhere.

More than one-quarter of those languishing in the DP camps were Jews; most were Eastern European. They had survived the concentration and death camps, in hiding, in partisan units, passing on false papers, or as refugees in the Soviet Union. Many were Zionists, yet British Mandate Palestine remained tightly closed to legal immigration. The sad irony was that the safest place in Europe for them now was in the DP camps of Germany, Austria, and Italy. Survivors focused on rebuilding their health, learning new job skills, searching for new homes, and creating new personal bonds. Few Jewish children had survived and, hoping to rebuild their families, the DPs married quickly; the camps were soon filled with babies and toddlers. Children born in the DP camps were treasured as miracles, as "messiah children," or *Maschiachskinder*.[2] Max Enkin, who led the Canadian garment workers selection team, noted how the "little children [were] truly worshipped…you could just see the hunger of love and affection."[3] The birth rate in the DP camps was the highest in postwar Europe.

By 1947, administration of the DP camps had been moved from the United Nations Relief and Rehabilitation Administration (UNRRA) to the newly formed International Refugee Organization (IRO). Jewish organizations were given free rein to set up religious institutions, agricultural and academic schools, and vocational training as the camps were transformed into small communities. The main Jewish agency working within the camps was the American Jewish Joint Distribution Committee (JDC). Since its inception in 1914 the JDC had become the primary source of relief, rescue, and resettlement for Jews in peril. The organization provided supplementary food rations in the camps, as well as clothing, religious materials, and assistance with the various emigration programs that brought survivors out of the camps.

Although a semblance of normative life resumed, visitors to the camps were struck by the continued hardship and despair they encountered. Canada sent social workers, welfare administrators, and medical personnel as part of their United Nations obligations. Winnipeg Jewish social worker, Ethel Ostry Genkind, was sent by the Canadian Jewish Congress (CJC) to help with the selection of orphans—the first group of survivors permitted entry to Canada under CJC sponsorship. She wrote about meeting survivors in a camp near Salzburg,

the "sunken-eyed ragged adults and children with outstretched arms, begging hands, and rickety bare legs, their chest bones sticking out from thin tattered bits of clothing."[4] The 1946 *Maclean's* article "They won't go home" described DP living quarters:

These dwellings make you think of stables not of homes. Great barnlike buildings with cots all in a row, some of them with whole families, men, women and children, all living together without so much as a mosquito netting between one family's beds and the next.

Small wonder that in dwellings like stables human beings should look like cattle. They sit by the hour, playing cards for tiny stakes or none, writing interminable letters, talking interminable gossip, or just lying on their beds looking at the ceiling. One look at them is enough, better than a hundred statistical reports, to show the nature of this difficult problem—the problem of caring for landless, homeless, hopeless people without letting them rot…. What will become of them, nobody seems to know.[5]

The five men who visited the camps to select garment workers in the autumn of 1947 found conditions had not improved. Bernard Shane wrote of "poorly constructed DP camps, inadequately built, poorly heated, and immensely overpopulated." One Austrian camp was composed of wooden shacks "that looked more like chicken coops than fit for human habitation." Shane found the hospital filled with DPs who looked "old, harried and drawn. The meagre diet of 1800 calories daily are no match for the bitter cold and winds that blow through the Tyrolean Alps."[6] Max Enkin encountered

frustration, disappointment and disillusionment. I saw malnutrition, abominable housing and the lack of everything that man in humble dignity is entitled to. I saw how mankind gone mad has uprooted millions and left a toll of wreckage in human lives that may never be rebuilt. I saw a dream of human life that only a gifted fiction writer might be able to describe to you, and even then could not even tell the whole story, because in the whole history of mankind never has such carnage and spoliation been executed in so vast a scale.[7]

Around the same time as the Garment Workers Commission was in Europe, philanthropist Allan Bronfman visited the camps in the American sector and reported back to Saul Hayes, the CJC's director in Montreal. Bronfman's brother Sam was president of the CJC. In the Düppel camp, Bronfman found "ramshackle apartment or barrack buildings three stories high with 5, 6, 7 and as many as 8 occupants in each room." Speaking Yiddish with some of the families, he noted that most of the groups consisted of "a grandmother, father and mother and two or more children—all in one room, where they sleep, eat, cook, wash clothes and do all their housekeeping. The young fathers and mothers are cheerful enough, but the older folks…are very sad of countenance indeed." Bronfman also met with military and JDC officials and even paid a formal visit to the Vatican to receive an expression of support for DP emigration from Pope Pius XII. He was impressed by the tremendous sympathy he encountered from JDC officials and remarked on the frustration of the military that there was no resolution of the DP problem in sight. It seemed to them that the camps might remain indefinitely. In his report Bronfman underlined the urgent need for countries like Canada to offer homes to the DPs, wondering, "how long can people who are idle, with no activity or interest to look forward to…be expected to remain placid and quiet?" He concluded that only the members of the United Nations could resolve this "great and tragic human problem."[8]

SAM POSLUNS (1910–1994)

WHEN SAM'S PARENTS, Abraham Poslaniec and Sheindel Saltzman, arrived in Canada, the immigration officer recorded their family name as Posluns, and so it remained. This was a common experience for immigrants in the late nineteenth and early twentieth centuries. Canada at the time was not yet a multicultural society—immigrants were expected to assimilate. The Posluns raised their seven children in Toronto, where Sam, the youngest, was born in 1910. Abraham began his career as a clothing worker at the T. Eaton Company and in 1914 he established the Superior Cloak Company with Sam's brother Joseph. They began in a tiny garage, filling orders for Eaton's and other large stores. All four of the Posluns sons eventually became involved in elements of the clothing business.

Tragedy struck the family in 1922 when Abraham was killed in a traffic accident, shortly before Sam's bar mitzvah. Sam was, however, able to complete his education and following high school, his family supported his studies in clothing design in New York City. He went on to develop methods for the mass production of women's coats. Sam returned to Toronto where he married Rebecca Brenzel in 1930 and they had four children. By 1936, Sam and two partners were running Popular Cloak, which manufactured women's outerwear. Its office and showroom were in Toronto; the factory was in Brantford, Ontario. Sam was in charge of the office and responsible for design, sales, and record keeping.

While his older brothers took over Superior Cloak, which encountered some significant labour disputes in the mid-1930s, Sam was a strong supporter of the unions. He was on friendly terms with David Dubinsky, the New York-based international president of the International Ladies' Garment Workers' Union (ILGWU). When, one year, the union asked Popular Cloak for a nickel an hour raise, Sam's response was that the company could afford ten cents. Dubinsky, however, countered that the ILGWU needed to show their power, so they arranged for a short strike at a convenient time in the manufacturing cycle, and then agreed on a nickel raise that year and another nickel the following year.

Popular Cloak was also known for its ethical stance toward the retailers it was dependent on for sales. The mammoth department store chain, Eaton's, used its

Samuel Posluns, in the 1940s.

Sam Posluns travel permit, dated October 18, 1947, allowing him to move around postwar Germany to recruit tailors.

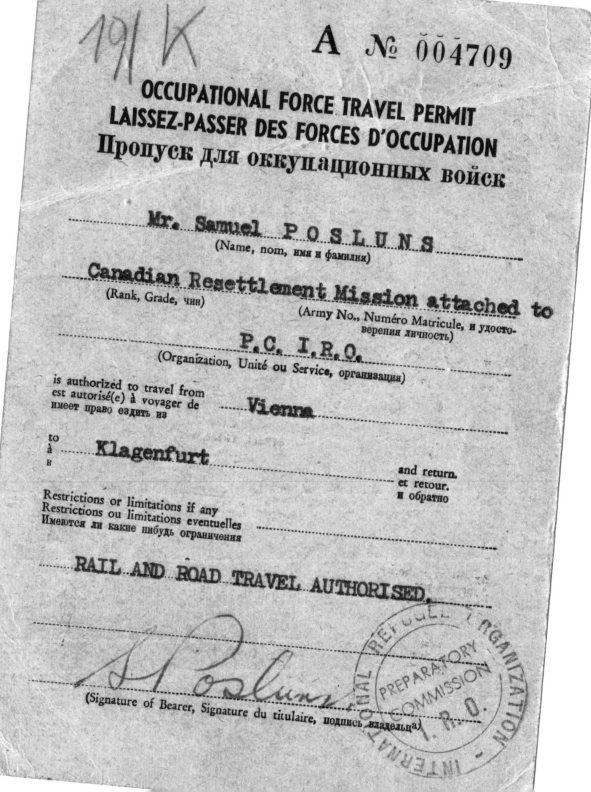

191 K

A № 004709

OCCUPATIONAL FORCE TRAVEL PERMIT
LAISSEZ-PASSER DES FORCES D'OCCUPATION
Пропуск для оккупационных войск

Mr. Samuel POSLUNS
(Name, nom, имя и фамилия)

Canadian Resettlement Mission attached to
(Rank, Grade, чин)   (Army No., Numéro Matricule, и удостоверения личность)

P.C. I.R.O.
(Organization, Unité ou Service, организация)

is authorized to travel from
est autorisé(e) à voyager de   Vienna
имеет право ездить из

to
à   Klagenfurt   and return.
в   et retour.
                              и обратно

Restrictions or limitations if any
Restrictions ou limitations eventuelles
Имеются ли какие нибудь ограничения

RAIL AND ROAD TRAVEL AUTHORISED.

(Signature of Bearer, Signature du titulaire, подпись владельца)

INTERNATIONAL REFUGEE ORGANIZATION - PREPARATORY COMMISSION - I.R.O.

clout to demand lower prices from manufacturers and kickbacks for their buyers, but Posluns maintained a "one price" policy. The small-town storeowner paid the same price for their coats as the big-city retailers. As a result, Eaton's refused to buy from Popular Cloak for many years. Although the company's bottom line was affected by this, Sam stood his ground. Eventually, Eaton's relented.

Posluns was twenty-nine when the war began and, although he had young children, he signed up for active duty. He worked his way up to sergeant in the army and then flying officer in the Royal Canadian Air Force. He was stationed in Trenton and was not deployed overseas. He also became involved in the Air Cadets and after the war helped former cadets find employment.

A devoted advocate of social justice, Posluns was elected president of the United Jewish Welfare Fund in 1947. Once he was selected to represent the women's clothing manufacturers on the Garment Workers Commission, Sam used his personal relationships with other clothing manufacturers to sign them up for the Tailor Project. Soon after his return to Canada, Posluns spoke publicly about what he had seen and how it had changed him. He told a meeting of the manufacturers' association that he had been proud to be their representative "on this memorable undertaking," yet his trip had seemed like a "terrific nightmare."[1] "How can one understand," Sam explained, "how can one put into words

when words have not yet been written into the English language to express the sufferings and the mass slaughtering of a people?" Although he felt it was not his place to detail the devastating stories of survival he had heard from survivors, Sam was determined to impress upon his Canadian audience that understanding the DPs' attitudes and mentality required sympathy. "I know that some of you might be worried as to whether people who have suffered and endured as they have can be normal again and whether they can ever fit into our way of life," Sam told them. "Do not think for a moment that these are a discouraged or a degenerate people. The fact that they are still alive is proof to the contrary. They are mentally alert, intellectual, and good craftsmen, with a willingness to work."

Posluns' forceful address lambasted the treatment that Jewish DPs had endured during "two and a half years of so-called liberation." He pointed out that other countries had barred Jews from their immigration projects. "Therefore you can well imagine what this project meant to our people who still languish in the DP camps, the lift it has given them and a new hope that must come from the realization that after all this time they still have not been forgotten."

The selection team had found the screening process to be "heartbreaking" and Sam pressed the group to understand that their project would "give at least a few the right to live as you or I." He reminded them that they were involved in a humanitarian endeavour. "Your repayment should not come from the increased production but from the inner satisfaction that I know it will give in having given a new hope to a small segment of a very, very large problem." He asked them to open both their homes and their hearts to the DP families. And he was blunt: "Are we to admit now that all the aid we have spoken of and all the tears we have shed and all the speaking we have done is a mockery? Are we to admit that we are hypocrites and that after all, we are only trying to ease our own consciences and not trying to help anyone? Here is a real opportunity to do something that is really tangible." Sam had been deeply touched by what he had witnessed and he understood that the survivors would come with unique needs, "the need for love, and warmth, and friendship, which must be forthcoming from us, is needed as badly as the accommodations themselves."

Six months later, when many of the DPs had arrived and were settling into Toronto, Sam delivered another impassioned speech. He detailed the difficult and crowded living conditions in the camps and reminded his audience that all the survivors wanted was to be free and to emigrate. "Wherever I went," Posluns told them, "I always felt myself in the presence of a truly great people" for whom he had "developed a deep affection and admiration."

Sam's work with the mission to the DP camps had a profound impact on his future. He became devoted to Jewish education and was the first president and founding chair of the Board of Jewish Education, where he remained active for decades. He led Beth Tzedec Synagogue as its president and was also a founding board member of the North York General Hospital. Throughout his life, Sam struggled with increasingly profound hearing loss. He learned to lip-read in order to participate fully in his business and volunteer endeavours. Posluns was also an avid gardener. In 1949, he moved his family to a semi-rural home where he relished growing produce and flowers. Sam was renowned for sending truckloads of gladioli to Mt. Sinai and Baycrest hospitals to cheer up the patients. Sam Posluns died in Toronto in 1994.

IRVING LEIBGOTT

My father was a tailor, his brothers were all tailors, but I told my father, "I don't want to be a tailor." When the war broke out, I didn't have a choice. I knew how to sew, we sewed uniforms, so I didn't starve…. I was lucky.

I WAS FIFTEEN when the war started, so you could say that I grew up during the war. I was born Yechil Leibgott on February 25, 1924, in the small city of Płock—in Yiddish, we called it Plotsk—which had a Jewish population of about nine thousand. Jews made up roughly a quarter of the town's population. Before the Germans invaded Poland in 1939, I apprenticed with my father, Avraham Leibgott, learning the tailoring trade. My mother, Chaya, was a homemaker. They had two children—me and my sister, Sonia.

I was able to continue working as a tailor with my father at the beginning of the war, when the Germans first came in. Then they closed down all the little tailor shops and took the tailors who had been working for themselves to a factory where everyone had to work for the Germans. We made German uniforms and fixed ones that needed fixing. In those early days, I lived in various ghettos. As soon as the Germans occupied Poland, they set up large administrative districts in central Poland and annexed them to the Third Reich. Płock and its surrounding area became part of administrative region of Zichenau (in Polish, Ciechanów). The ghetto in Płock was established early in 1940, but in the winter of 1941, they liquidated the ghetto and sent most of the Jews to the Treblinka death camp. The younger people who could work were sent to forced labour camps.

I was in a few different forced labour camps and concentration camps after that. In Starachowice, I had to work in the mines and in a munitions factory; in another camp I worked in a sawmill. So in every place, we did different things; whatever they told us to do. We had to work hard and we had practically no food—maybe a slice of bread a day. We had to work twelve hours a day. I was lucky to survive. In 1944, the Germans closed—liquidated—the labour camp in Starachowice, and I was transported to Auschwitz. From there, right

Irving Leibgott (right) with his sister, Sonia, and her husband, Chaim Ash, in Kaunitz, Germany, 1945–1947.

at the end of the war, I was sent to Dachau, which is in southern Germany, not far from Munich.

In the spring of 1945, I was liberated by the US army. I stayed in the Feldafing DP camp run by the Americans for a couple days, but I wanted to look for my sister, Sonia. She had gotten married in Płock in 1940 and, although her husband and I were able to stay together all through various camps, we were separated from Sonia as soon as we were taken out of the ghetto. We had no idea if she'd survived.

I'd heard that some women had been liberated not far from Bergen-Belsen, in the northern part of Germany, where they'd been working in some kind of munitions factory. I left my brother-in-law in Feldafing and started travelling around, looking for Sonia. I went to Bergen-Belsen, where I met some women who turned out to be friends of my sister; they'd been working together in one of the camps. When the Allies were getting close, the Germans had marched the women away and then just abandoned them there, in the little village of Kaunitz. It wasn't much more than a church, a tavern, and a bunch of farmers, but the women had stayed there. They had been liberated by the Americans, but the Americans and the British and the French divided Germany into zones, and the British had ended up taking over the part where the women were liberated. So I went to Kaunitz and found my sister there. She and some of the other women were living like a family, and I moved in with

them. They had a kitchen, they had milk—it was nothing like being in a camp. The British were supplying us with food, clothing; whatever we needed.

I travelled back to Feldafing and brought my brother-in-law to Kaunitz, so he and Sonia could be reunited there. We ended up staying in Kaunitz for three years, just waiting to leave Germany. It was terrible. The British still provided us with food, but we had nothing to do. It was just a waste of time. Well, that's what it was like after the war. Living in the village wasn't really like living in a camp. There were barracks, but there were also houses. The Germans had empty rooms, so we could spread out and live with the Germans in their houses. But all we did all day was sit around playing cards, riding bikes, playing soccer, kicking around a ball, and sometimes going for walks. We also babysat the kids that were born there. Everybody got so excited when babies were born—the first after the war. Everybody liked to help with the babysitting. Everybody. My nephew was born while we were living in Kaunitz.

I had a girlfriend in Kaunitz, but she went to Israel. I was thinking of going, too, but my sister put up such a fuss. We were the only ones in our family to survive the war—nobody else. We were both hoping to go to the United States, and she didn't want us to split up. She told me not to go to Israel.

It was while we were living in Kaunitz that I heard about the call for tailors. There were posters advertising

Irving Leibgott doing tricks on a bicycle in postwar Kaunitz, Germany, 1946–1947.

that people from Canada were looking for tailors. The Canadian government and the unions needed tailors, so they went to the DP camps and other places where refugees had gathered looking for them. I saw the poster and applied. I remember that when they came to interview us, they asked us to show them if we could sew. I think the sewing test was to sew on a button. It was easy—I even showed a friend of mine how to thread a needle and he went as a tailor. It was very easy. But they had a quota of how many people they could take.

Once we'd passed the sewing test, we had to go through a medical exam. If somebody had something wrong with them, especially with their lungs, then they wouldn't give them a pass to travel. There were some people who had to stay behind in Germany after the war.

So that's how I came to Canada. We had also applied to go the US because I had an uncle in Brooklyn, but there was a five-year wait for a visa, and the work in Canada came up before that. We waited three years in Kaunitz before getting the chance to go to Canada. Nobody wanted to take us in. My sister said, "You're a tailor, you know how to sew. Go to Canada. Then, maybe from Canada, it's going to be easier to go to the United States." So that's what I did.

The Canadians arranged jobs for us and found us rooms for a month. And they made it clear that they didn't want us to depend on the government for relief.

After a year or so, I was able to bring Sonia and her husband to Canada. They did end up going to the United States, but after I got married—I met my wife, Mary, in Canada—Mary didn't want to hear anything about leaving. My nephews are still in the United States.

I don't remember that much about the boat trip to Canada except that it wasn't a particularly nice boat. It was the USS *General S.D. Sturgis*—a troop transport ship. I read that it had been a cattle boat and was converted so it could be used for transporting American troops. Then they used it for us. We all felt good that we were leaving Germany, but most people were really sick on board. I wasn't, so I could walk around, but most people could only lie around with their blankets covered in vomit. We slept on bunks. There were no private rooms. When my sister came over a year later, they were on a much nicer boat with separate cabins. We just had a whole bunch of bunks. The food was nothing special, but most people were too sick to eat anyway. It wasn't a nice boat at all. Men and women weren't separated on the ship, either. There were some couples who lived together, and I remember a girl sleeping near me who didn't like her bunk. It was shaking so much, and she was so ill. I switched bunks with her to see if it was better for her.

I didn't know anybody when we started out from Kaunitz, but I met someone just before we went on the boat who became a lifelong friend. He actually became my business partner. We ended up opening a valet tailoring service and worked together in Montreal for forty years.

As soon as the ship docked in Halifax, we got on a train to Montreal. And as soon as we got to Montreal, they started separating us. I didn't have a choice about where I would go. Many people were sent to Toronto and a few families even went to Winnipeg. I had heard of Toronto because when I was in school I collected stamps from a neighbour of mine who got letters from Toronto. I'd never heard of Montreal before the war, but I was on the list of people who were supposed to stay in Montreal. I went over to the people who were arranging everything and told them that I wanted to go to Toronto. They said, "Okay, go to Toronto." But everything had been arranged for me in Montreal—I had a job and a room there. If I wanted to go to Toronto, I'd be on my own. I was free to go, but how could I? I didn't have a penny to my name. So I stayed in Montreal. As it turned out, there were more tailors there than in Toronto then.

There was no one to greet me in Montreal—actually, my greeting was terrible. As I said, they'd arranged rooms for us, and people were picking us up and taking us to the rooms where we were supposed to stay for a month. I think the rooms had been arranged by someone from the Canadian Jewish Congress (CJC) or from the Jewish Immigrant Aid Society (JIAS), or maybe it was someone from the union—I'm not sure. I just remember that when I got to my room it was a Friday night. I was standing downstairs with my little bag and there was a woman upstairs who started complaining right away. I didn't understand most of what she was saying—she was speaking half in Jewish [Yiddish] and half in English—but she was complaining that she wasn't getting enough money for the room. That was my welcome.

There had been a few other guys in the car with me on the drive to the room and I'd taken the address of my friend. I slept one night at the place I was supposed to stay and, the next day, I went to where my friend was staying. The family who lived there said they had room for another person and I could share their son's room because it had two beds. So, I moved in with them instead. All I'd brought with me was some clothing. I didn't have much. I think I was given ten dollars when I arrived. That's the welcome I had to Canada.

I ended up staying with that family for a couple years, paying them for room and board. The son was my age and we became friends, going out places together. I stayed friends with the whole family for years. When I arrived, I only spoke Jewish and Polish. I learned English speaking to the family. They had come from Russia years ago, and they spoke Jewish. Their son didn't speak Jewish, though, so I slowly started picking up little bits of English. I never did learn French even though I started to take lessons at the library. Later, we

had some French customers who came to our shop, but they all spoke English.

As I said, I arrived on a Friday and on Monday morning, somebody picked me up and took me to the factory. I started work straight away in a men's clothing factory making suits, jackets, and coats. The factory wasn't very nice. It was like a jungle. People were fighting with each other for better jobs. I didn't like the tone, but I had no choice. Sometimes in the factory, two guys would be doing the same job, so I started to do the same job, too. They didn't like it because sometimes, when we were a little busy, they could work a couple hours a week overtime, getting paid double time. When I started to work on the same jobs, there was no overtime for them and they didn't like that at all. So they'd give me the worst work bundles to do. Some cloths are easier to work with than others. They'd give me the worst things, and the foreman even helped them.

This went on for a couple of weeks. By the third week, I could see that they didn't like me doing their jobs. I went to the foreman and I asked him to give me something else to do, that I didn't want to fight with them. But he said that there was nothing else. So I told him, "You know what? Just give me anything." I even asked him to give me piecework. Anything that meant that I wouldn't be taking work away from the others. I was supposed to be working for twenty-five dollars a week, but the foreman said if he put me on piecework,

I wouldn't be able to make my full wage. I replied that it was up to me. I'd just take whatever I made. In the end, they put me on another operation with some other guys, doing the same thing. So the first week, I did make twenty-five dollars.

The first year, I just saved every penny to bring over my sister and brother-in-law and their kid. After my year was up, I quit the factory. I just couldn't stand it there with all the guys fighting, really fighting. Most of the people working there were Jewish and in the beginning, the foreman and everyone else spoke Jewish, although there were some French guys too, and a few Italians.

My partner and I bought a little valet tailoring service. We started with a very small store on a little street off Saint Lawrence, and at first we had a hard time making a living. We had to start off cleaning clothes and doing small repairs. Then we started to do custom tailoring; to make suits to measure along with a few repairs. Eventually, it all worked out. We bought another shop on the same street and were at that place for five years. Then, we moved to another street for about another ten years, until they knocked that building down. That's when we moved to the last location, where we were for twenty-odd years. So it worked out better and better over the years. We didn't become rich, but we were making a better living and had a better life than I would have had in the factory.

Mary and I met in Montreal and got married in 1953. I'd known her for about two years by then, so we must have met in either 1950 or 1951. She was seven years younger than me and worked as a bookkeeper. She was born in Poland, but the family had come before the war, when she was two or three years old. This is how we met: a friend of mine came over as a tailor but didn't actually work as a tailor when he got here. He worked for my wife's father. They worked at home, in the father's house, and he had five daughters. My friend was already married when he came to Canada, so he was after me to get married—he couldn't stand it that I was still single. There were all the daughters, so my friend introduced me to them. I started going out with Mary, and then we got married. When I came here, I had still wanted to go to the United States, but she wouldn't hear of it. What can I tell you?

But I can't complain. It's been very nice here, and I worked hard. Slowly things got better. My business partner and I bought a little duplex; I lived downstairs and he lived upstairs. Then, when we sold the duplex, I bought a little house. The only complaint I do have about coming to Canada is that I didn't like that factory. And we really weren't given any opportunities at all. We came here and then we were on our own. They brought us over, gave us a job and a room, and the rest was up to us. I quit one factory, went to another, and then I quit again after a few months. The first year I worked at a factory, I just saved up the money that I needed to bring my sister and her family over.

So I can't complain. This is a good country. I personally didn't experience a lot of antisemitism here, but it was going on. It was going on all the time. Nobody likes the Jews. I remember in Poland, before the war, there were antisemites. They used to stand on the corners by the Jewish stores with signs telling people not to buy from Jews, that the Jews should go to Palestine. But I didn't see that here.

Mary and I had three children, two boys and a girl, and the boys still live in Montreal; my daughter moved to Toronto. The oldest, Jeffrey, born in 1955, became an engineer. Karen, born in 1959, is a speech pathologist, and Brian, the youngest, born in 1962, is a house inspector. Jeffrey has three children, Karen also has three children, and Brian has two children. They are doing interesting work and we are blessed to have eight wonderful grandchildren and six great-grandchildren.

When I finally retired and closed the store, I took one of the sewing machines home. I still use it if I need to fix something for myself.

THROUGH THE EYE OF A NEEDLE

JEWISH ENTREPRENEURS first introduced the factory-based "ready-to-wear" clothing industry into Canada at the end of the nineteenth century. By the 1930s, participants in Canada's clothing and textile industries—owners, workers, and unions—were predominantly Jewish immigrants. About 10 per cent of Jews in the "schmatta business" were owners and 90 per cent were workers. In the women's ready-made clothing industry, Jewish men comprised 60 per cent of the workforce and Jewish women and girls, 40 per cent. Many of them had been politicized in Eastern Europe and they were drawn to the trade union movement. Jewish workers founded the Amalgamated Clothing Workers' Union (Amalgamated) and the International Ladies' Garment Workers' Union (ILGWU) in the US, but active branches of these unions also dominated labour relations in Canada's big cities. As war approached, shifts in the industry saw a movement toward the incorporation of smaller workshops into the larger factories, and the replacement of male workers by cheap, non-union labour, particularly rural and immigrant women in Quebec.[1]

Demand for both men's and women's clothing exploded between the wars, but mass production was an inherently risky business. It was cheap and easy to start up a company, but a gamble to maintain success. Public tastes could be fickle, so manufacturers and retailers could either sell out of a popular fashion or be stuck with racks of unsaleable styles. Predatory buying practices by large department stores also forced cost-cutting measures on producers, who suppressed wages.[2] The economics of the clothing trade was further complicated by the very close—often familial—relationships between workers and owners. Many manufacturers had begun as workers themselves, which was a unique aspect of Canada's garment industry. In the particularly volatile Toronto labour environment, for example, class struggle and worker militancy was high. The garment unions dominated the social, cultural, and political life of Jewish workers, yet family and community ties between Jewish workers and manufacturers sometimes dampened worker militancy or motivated concessions by employers.

Union leaders understood the unstable nature of

Montreal garment workers c. 1944.

this labour-intensive industry. In their fight for better wages and working conditions, they realized that they could not press too hard. If concessions placed an employer at a competitive disadvantage, another company paying its employees less could put the unionized company out of business and its workers out on the street.[3] The Depression, in particular, put conditions for all workers under considerable strain and the mid-1930s saw a series of massive strikes. Their resolution would serve to align conditions among the major manufacturers of men's and women's wear. Ontario and Quebec's provincial governments enacted legislation to ensure that collective agreements would be honoured throughout the clothing industry.

Montreal, Toronto, and Winnipeg were the centres of Canada's garment industry. Factories were sometimes located in smaller communities, while the offices, showrooms, and cutting rooms were concentrated in large buildings close to the big city buyers. Winnipeg's garment centre was the area northwest of the Portage and Main intersection. In Toronto, several blocks—bordered by Adelaide and King Streets, and running up to College Street between University and Spadina Avenues—were filled with factory buildings as high as fourteen stories. In Montreal, the large garment industry buildings clustered at the rue de Bleury–Sainte-Catherine intersection, around Phillips Square, on rue Peel, and ran up boulevard Saint-Laurent (known as "the Main") to rue

Sherbrooke. Each building housed dozens of shops and several hundred workers.[4] Factories and businesses were also close to the traditional areas of Jewish settlement. Indeed, for several reasons, it seemed that the clothing business was synonymous with Canadian Jewry. Jewish immigrants brought their tailoring skills with them—in their old and new countries, many occupations were barred to Jews—and their options were limited.

Wartime, following immediately on the heels of the Depression, did not improve opportunities for Jewish blue- or white-collar workers in Canada. The Canadian Jewish Congress (CJC) was fighting on several battlefronts at the time—they were not only doing as much as they could to aid and rescue European Jews, but also to oppose racial and religious discrimination, particularly antisemitism, in Canadian hiring practices. While Jewish workers were sometimes refused positions in the garment industries due to their perceived militancy or an employer's low-wage practices, the mostly Jewish manufacturers welcomed their skills and work ethic. Canadian companies, on the other hand—whether they were state or privately owned—could require applicants to state their race and religion, then refuse employment on racial grounds without consequence.[5] The Joint Public Relations Committee (JPRC) of the CJC surveyed Canadian Jews who had experienced job discrimination and one typical example they found was that of a trained machinist who was refused a job at a

Toronto shop. He was told the job was filled, only to note continued advertisements for the same position. A young woman asked outright if a "Jewish girl would be employed" before she went for an interview at another shop. The prospective employers replied that "they had never done so and had no intentions of hiring them in the future, and therefore, [she] should not bother coming down to see them."[6] In Winnipeg and other big cities, Eaton's department store did employ Jewish women, but only in the mail-order department, out of sight of customers.[7] In order to combat widespread discrimination, the JPRC joined forces with unionized labour in 1947, a relationship that would play out in the battle to bring survivors to Canada.

The Canadian Jewish Labour Committee (JLC), created in 1936 as a trade union umbrella group, also played a key role in the struggle for human rights in Canada. At its peak it claimed fifty thousand members and was closely aligned with the Cooperative Commonwealth Federation (CCF), the precursor of the New Democratic Party.[8] Their original mandate was to provide refugee relief, but as the war ended, the JLC turned its resources toward both aiding survivors in Europe and fighting discrimination at home, particularly within the union movement. In 1946, they hired Kalmen Kaplansky as director. Kaplansky had emigrated from Poland at the age of seventeen and, after his academic dreams were quashed by McGill University's

Jewish quota, he worked as a printer in Montreal. Kaplansky travelled to Bialystok in the summer of 1939 in an unsuccessful attempt to persuade his family to join him in Canada. The passenger ship returning him to Montreal was the first British ship attacked by the Germans at the outbreak of war and he narrowly survived. He then served three years in the Canadian army. Once he was appointed director of the JLC, Kaplansky enhanced and expanded on their wartime work with union leaders, leading him to become known as the "grandfather of the Canadian human rights movement."[9] His good working terms with both the union leadership and government officials would enhance the JLC's participation in the development of the bulk labour schemes. Unions had to be assured that the DPs would not flood the job market, while manufacturers and government needed their own guarantees that the newcomers could be absorbed without causing worker unrest. The president of the JLC, Bernard Shane, along with Kaplansky, was to be instrumental in the creation of the garment workers bulk labour scheme. He also served as one of the five members of the selection team that travelled to the DP camps.

MENDEL BEKIER

Based on interviews with his daughter, Ziny Kirshenbaum.

Jews weren't being allowed in anywhere after the war. Nazis they let in to the US, France, etc. Canada neither. Unions in Canada said they needed tailors, so delegates came to the camp to say Canada needed a few hundred tailors. I wasn't a tailor, but the Jewish Labor Committee in the US knew me. I had friends there. One guy named Shane came from Montreal—he was head of one of the tailor unions. He came with a list of names given to him by the Committee, of people they wanted to get out who may not be tailors. I was on the list. So I came to Canada as a tailor. Otherwise Jews weren't allowed into Canada.

—MENDEL BEKIER[1]

MY PARENTS TALKED about the Holocaust all the time. As long as I can remember, I used to tell my friends that when other children were told bedtime stories and nursery rhymes, we learned about the Holocaust. My father's father, Michael Bekier, died before the war, in 1935, but his mother, Zelda, and the rest of his family died in the Holocaust. My father escaped with his girlfriend, Mania, and some friends and they spent the war in the Soviet Union. The rest of the family ended up being sent to various concentration camps; my father didn't even know when or where most of his family were killed, although he did hear that at some point they were all sent to Treblinka. Except for one cousin, my father was the only one left after the war.

My father, Max Mendel Baker (originally Bekier), was born on October 10, 1913, in Grójec, Poland—in Yiddish they called it Gritze. He had two sisters and four brothers and came from a very large extended family. His father owned a bakery where they made all kinds of bread and buns and the challah that Jewish women bought for Shabbos. Every Thursday was market day in Grójec. All the Poles would come from the surrounding

Mendel Bekier at
twenty-four, 1937.

rural areas and the Jews, who were mostly poorer than the Poles, would bring their goods to the marketplace to sell.

My father's two older brothers went to work in the bakery, but he didn't want to be a baker. I don't know if he especially wanted to be a shoemaker but after his bar mitzvah, that's what he decided to apprentice in. It took him four years to qualify. When he was nineteen, he and two of his friends put their money together, bought a couple of machines, and opened their own little shoemaking shop. They rented a room from my father's uncle just two doors down from the bakery. My father was a *komashin* maker, which means that he specialized in making the tops of shoes, the uppers. That was its own thing.

When the Nazis first came to Grójec—only two weeks after the invasion began in 1939—being bakers saved my father's family for a while. At first, the Germans allowed bakers to keep working—so even though my father was a shoemaker, he put on his white apron and went back to the bakery. A few days later, though, the Germans decided to close all but three Jewish and three Polish bakeries—Jews weren't allowed to buy from the Poles and the Poles weren't allowed to buy from the Jews—and they forced my grandfather to close the family bakery. Not long after, while my father was standing in front of the closed-down shop, a German officer stopped his truck and asked, "Are you the baker here?" When my father said yes, the officer told him that he needed 250 pieces of apple kuchen and asked if my father could make it. He said that he could if he had the ingredients. The officer soon returned with a sack of flour, two baskets of apples, and sugar—we could have baked a thousand pieces! When the officer came back to pick them up, we gave him a piece to taste with a cup of coffee and he said it was "Wunderbar!" (Wonderful!) From that day on, the bakery was allowed to reopen, but we could only bake for the Germans.

That German officer, my father said, was not vicious like the others—he was a mensch. After a few days of coming to pick up his daily order of buns, he bought six or eight loaves of German military bread and told my grandmother to give it to the poor Jews. He did this every day for two weeks. It turned out that he was a teacher who had been drafted into the military. Just before he was shipped out of our town, he came by the bakery and told my father, "Herr Bekier, pack up and get out—the Germans are about to make things very bad for the Jews." When he heard this, my father realized that they had to escape. Two weeks later, he fled across the border between Poland and the Soviet Union with his brothers and Mania (who later became his wife and my mother). In December 1939, they got a letter from home saying that everything was okay and they were needed to work in the bakery. So two of his brothers, Herschel and Itcha, went back; they ended up being killed. My father and his two other brothers, Avrum and Moishe, didn't want to go, so they stayed in the Soviet Union with Mania. At some point they were all arrested and separated and sent to various labour camps. He and my mother weren't reunited until they were back in Poland after the war.

My father returned to Poland in 1946. The train cars full of Christian Poles were marked with crosses and the words "Here travel Poles," so people knew that the remaining train car was full of returning Jews and construction workers along the tracks threw rocks at them. That was his first welcome back to Poland. He made his way to Grójec, where he was hardly greeted with loving arms—not at all, that is—and was basically chased out of town. He and Mania found each other in Lodz and got married, but it was too dangerous for them to stay in Poland, so they went first to Austria and then to Germany. My father always said he would rather visit Germany than visit Poland, ever. They ended up in the Wetzlar DP camp near Frankfurt, where there were three thousand Jewish refugees from all over Europe.

My parents spent two years in Wetzlar. It was a former army camp and they had to live in military barracks. My father talked about the DP camp a lot. They were given all the basic necessities there. It didn't sound great, but compared to what they were coming out of, it didn't sound terrible. They were given a small allowance for things like food, coffee, and cigarettes. For anything extra, they were allowed to make money chopping wood for the stoves that heated the barracks.

I remember my father also talking about leading a sit-down strike in the camps. There were various translators brought in to help with the interviews for people who wanted to go this country or that country. Somehow, they found out that a Lithuanian, who was an antisemite, wasn't translating correctly and was trying to undermine the Jewish refugees applying for visas. The DPs demanded to see the transcripts so the translators could be held accountable and held a sit-down strike in the camps to force the authorities to deal with the matter.

Both my parents told me that they had originally talked about going to New York, going to the States—although I don't think they cared where they went. But they didn't want to go to Palestine. One of the survivors from the group of friends who had fled to Russia with my father moved to Israel. My parents didn't want to go there because the war of independence had already broken out by then and I think my father was done with war. He chose to come to Canada because of the Tailor Project. That came up while they were in the Wetzlar DP camp.

My father said that the Tailor Project people found him. Delegates for the project came to the camp saying that Canada needed hundreds of tailors. My father was a shoemaker, not a tailor, but the Jewish Labor

Committee in the US apparently knew him through the Bund (the General Jewish Labour Bund political party), where he'd been a member since he was seventeen. People had to register when they got to the camps. That's how people found their relatives, but it also helped the Tailor Project delegates find him. There was one man named Bernard Shane, head of one of the tailor unions, who had come from Montreal. He arrived in the Wetzlar camp with a list of names given from the committee, a list of people they wanted to help get out—even people who were not tailors—and my father was on that list. They told him that this was how they were going to get him out: he would have to pretend he was a tailor.

The delegates put a stunt tailor in my father's place, that is, someone who could take the sewing test in his place. He told us about that a long time ago and I used to tease him that I was going to tell the government and have him deported. He didn't seem the least bit worried, though. I don't know if the person who took the test for my father was somebody within the camp or somebody they brought in, but somebody took the test for him. He didn't know who it was. Or if he did, he didn't tell me. He just said they got a guy to take the test for him. Don't forget that this was before the digital age—it was much easier to get away with that kind of thing then. In any event, his exit visa was stamped "garment worker." I don't think that the people in charge were that strict.

I have letters of reference from people saying that they knew him, saying things like, "I know Mendel Baker. I grew up with him and he's not a criminal." That kind of thing. I don't know if the letters were for Canada or for when they were trying for the States.

When they arrived in Toronto, the Canadian Jewish Congress (CJC) found them a basement apartment and the landlord of the home got her friends together and threw them a wedding shower, because they had gotten married before they came over. They got the necessities they needed to get them started. My brother was born when they were living in that basement apartment and he slept in a laundry basket. That was his crib.

The Tailor Project set my father up with a job at Tip Top Tailors when he first came to Toronto. Both he and my mother started working there—my mother already knew how to sew. My father very quickly found a job as a shoemaker, but they wouldn't let him go. I have a letter from the minister of labour, MacNamara, that seems so arrogant. It just says something like "No, no. You should be grateful that we let you in here. How nervy of you to think you're going to leave the job before the year is up. Well, you're not going to leave." The letter's tone is the way you would talk to a naughty child. But eventually, my father did leave—after his time was up. I have his release paper. He spent the rest of his life working as a shoemaker. He worked in a shoe factory in Toronto for forty-three years.

Imm. 183.

IMMIGRATION IDENTIFICATION CARD

THIS CARD MUST BE SHOWN TO THE EXAMINING OFFICER AT PORT OF ARRIVAL

Name of passenger..........BEKIER✱   MENDEL..........

Name of ship..........U.S.A.T. "GEN. S.D. STURGIS"..........

Name appears on Return, sheet..........28..........line..........6..........

Medical Examination Stamp | Civil Examination Stamp

LANDED Immigrant

CANADA IMMIGRATION
OCT 16 1948
HALIFAX, - N. S.

(See back)

Mendel Bekier's Garment Worker visa, including an official stamp indicating he and his wife, Mania, had passed their medical inspections before leaving Europe. They arrived in Halifax on October 16, 1948.

After my parents had worked for a couple of years, they borrowed money from all of their friends and bought a house. They bought a house on Beatrice Street and rented out every room until they could pay it off. That's how they finally got to own a house. My brother, Michael, was born in 1953 and I was born in 1957; we each have two children.

My father spent his life actively promoting Jewish culture. He talked about a Jewish author, a great historian named Simon Dubnow, who, during the war called out to all Jews to record everything so the world would know what was being done to them. My father was not a religious man—he lost that in the Holocaust—but he was a very strong proponent of Yiddishkeit and Jewish culture. Later, in Canada, he was the president of the Toronto Chapter for the Workmen's Circle and they brought in lecturers and had meetings and presentations. He had an entire Yiddish library that we donated to the University of Toronto library.

As I said, my father joined the Bund—which he called a Jewish socialist youth organization—as a young man. Whenever I talk to people about it, they say, "Yeah, they were Jewish Communists," but the Bund helped him when he first went to the Soviet Union and later when he became part of the Tailor Project. He told me that he first joined because he knew it was important to be part of a Jewish organization and the Bund Youth were intelligent and informed. There were lectures every Shabbos and they brought in writers from Warsaw. My father was pretty active in the Bund—he sang in the choir and performed in the drama troupe. He didn't really talk a lot about it, but he was very proud of the fact that before the war he was a member of the Bund Youth and they were very educated.

People here came together because they had lost all of their family members. They didn't have family. So a lot of people got together in little social groups from the cities where they were originally from. My parents also had the Gritzer Society—made up of all of the survivors from his hometown—but the Workmen's Circle was really an education and social organization that propagated Yiddish culture and history and literature. They brought in Yiddish singers and mainstream politicians to speak. It was a way to keep the Jewish community active.

My father was grateful to be living in Canada. There might still be antisemitism here, but Jews live freely. He gave thanks that we live good lives.

CONGRESS BULLETIN

OCTOBER 7, 1948

MONTREAL

VOL. 5 — No. 7

Congress at Work

Immigration: Canadian Jewry's Greatest Undertaking

AN EDITORIAL

Quietly, with a minimum of publicity, the Canadian Jewish Congress is in the midst of one of its most extensive and important activities in the history of Canadian Jewry:

The Congress is helping to bring into Canada and to settle thousands and thousands of Jewish refugees from Europe.

After many years during which the gates of Canada were effectively barred to refugee immigrants we are now at a stage where the repeated petitions and demands of Canadian Jewry and of thousands of humanitarian Canadians of all creeds are being met.

The Congress request that the Government regulations on the admission of relatives of Canadians be liberalized has been put into effect.

The Congress has been permitted to bring one thousand Jewish war orphans into the country and is now asking for an extension of this privilege to another 200-odd young Jews in Europe.

The Congress suggestion that tailors, milliners, furriers, and other tradesmen among whom there are many Jews be admitted as industrial groups is now being carried out.

The Congress has also undertaken great responsibilities:

In many cases Congress has given pledges to the Government.

Congress has to pay a considerable portion of the transportation costs.

Congress pays for the reception and the settlement of the new arrivals. Household equipment, furniture, clothing, in some cases medical bills, are to a large extent paid for by Congress. (In many cases these are given to the refugees by other Jewish institutions, such as the Jewish Immigrant Aid Society of Canada, which are cooperating with the Congress, but the Congress in the final analysis pays the bills.)

Congress may be expected to continue

ANNUAL DRIVES

HALIFAX: Leo Lania is addressing the local community at the Robie Street Synagogue on Sunday evening, October 10, in connection with the current annual Canadian Jewish Congress and the

Excerpt from an editorial in the Canadian Jewish Congress *Bulletin*, October 7, 1948.

THE GARMENT WORKERS BULK LABOUR PROGRAM

THE HORRIFYING NEWS of the Kielce pogrom in Poland in July 1946 shocked Canadian Jewry. The murder of forty-two and wounding of fifty concentration camp survivors by their neighbours prompted a massive exodus from Poland. Jews who had emerged from hiding and passing or had been among the few who returned from the camps, were joined by tens of thousands who had escaped the Nazis by fleeing to the Soviet Union. Bernard Shane and the Jewish Labour Committee (JLC) urgently requested that the Canadian Jewish Congress (CJC) work together with them to create nationwide petitions pressing the government to specifically admit "homeless Jews and thus save them from certain death." Shane wrote that the attacks on Jews across Eastern Europe proved "beyond a doubt that the position of the Jewish remnant in that part of the world is untenable." He was blunt about Canada's "apparent indifference." The JLC memorandum railed against a world in which a Jew's "life, his fate and his rights to life have ceased to be on the conscience of men." They proposed a six-week publicity campaign followed by the presentation of the petitions to Parliament by a group of Jews and "leading non-Jews." Hayes conferred with Jewish and gentile refugee aid agencies and all agreed that such an approach would not only take too long, but that focusing solely on Jews would be counterproductive.[1] The JLC would not give up so easily.

The bulk labour programs initiated by the Canadian government had not gone unnoticed by the JLC, by Jewish clothing manufacturers, or by the CJC. The organized Jewish community had pursued almost two decades of quiet diplomacy in their rescue attempts with very little to show for it. Garment workers and manufacturers had even closer ties to the victims of the Holocaust than the members of the Canadian Jewish establishment. Most were struggling with the enormity of the loss of their close relatives and former communities. All three groups saw the bulk labour schemes as a model for the entry of at least a portion of the surviving remnant.[2] They were very aware that the government, its agencies, and Canadian employers were discriminating against Jews because they were not considered appropriate for work as loggers, farmers, miners, domestics, or nurses. But what if, as Troper and Abella pointed out in *None is Too Many*, "economic selectivity in fact favoured Jewish workers? When an industry did *not* object to Jewish labour?"[3]

When Sam Bronfman and Saul Hayes met with the prime minister and cabinet members in February 1947, they suggested that the needle trades had specific shortages that could be remedied by what was clearly a specifically Jewish solution. Once again, King was noncommittal. Meanwhile, in Toronto, clothing manufacturers were in discussions with union leaders to put together their own presentation to government. One of the manufacturers, Sam Posluns, got in touch with Hayes, who persuaded him that a coordinated national effort was necessary. Hayes called a meeting with the Montreal manufacturers and representatives of the International Ladies' Garment Workers' Union (ILGWU) and the JLC.

By March, Toronto, Montreal, and Winnipeg were on board and a campaign to recruit participation from clothing companies across the country began.[4] Letters flooded into Ottawa from manufacturers like Toronto's Tip Top Tailors—David Dunkelman, founder of the men's wear company, wrote to the minister of labour, "We are having tremendous difficulty securing tailors for our industry." He said that although they were providing training, young people were just not interested.[5] Kaplansky and the JLC worked hard to convince hesitant trade unions that "immigrants should be admitted on the economic absorptive capacity of the country, not on the basis of their race, colour, [or] religion."[6] Briefs coordinated between the men's and women's garment industries were presented to the government in March. They described the importance of clothing manufacturing to the economy, pointed to the highly skilled and mostly immigrant workers, and how they had been "informed that there are presently in Displaced Persons Camps in Europe, persons of the necessary skills who have been born into this industry and who are urgently required to replace outgoing employees who are irreplaceable in the Dominion of Canada." They kept their request modest, asking for five hundred "new entrants" to be divided between the three manufacturing cities.[7]

Although Hayes worked as a matchmaker for the program, drafting a brief that was incorporated into the final industry presentation and coaching the delegation on their dealings with government, the CJC remained behind the scenes. When the labour-management team went to Ottawa in May, they presented an industry united in their need for DP workers. There was no special pleading for any specific ethnic group, though to all involved the Jewish nature of the workers they were requesting was implicit. The hopes of the community were anxiously resting on their shoulders. This time, the request was for two thousand workers and their families. The delegation agreed to guarantee that the costs for selection, transportation, and settlement would be borne by the industry. In truth, these costs were to be shared by employers and the agencies of the CJC and Jewish Immigrant Aid Society (JIAS), but these were details Ottawa did not need to know. The team left Ottawa confident that their request had been given a fair hearing. Several weeks later, when cabinet met to decide on bulk labour schemes, the admission of two thousand "craftsmen for the clothing industry" was approved. This would be the first bulk labour project conducted as a joint endeavour between trade unions and employers in a specific industry. And it would also set a precedent by allowing some workers to bring their wives and children.

Industry leaders immediately went to work corralling employers of all faiths to produce formal requisitions for two thousand DPs. In some cases, manufacturers were assigned numbers that they were expected to accept, whether they needed them or not. As he was about to leave for Europe as part of the selection team, Toronto manufacturer Max Enkin wrote a personal appeal to a colleague emphasizing the humanitarian nature of the project. "We are given a great privilege of saving people," he wrote, "and I know that you would not want it on your conscience to have not participated in such a scheme." Enkin recalled that, "Whatever little resistance existed was soon shamed away, however, when one firm, the principal owners of which were Gentiles, signed up for 150 workers—all

of whom they could well have done without."[8] By mid-July employers had signed pledges to take on DPs for twelve-month contracts and assure them union wages and working conditions no less favourable than those "prevailing in the locality for comparable classifications of employment." Upon arrival, the new employee would have to countersign the same document, pledging to "perform the duties of his employment faithfully" and to reimburse the employer or their representative association for the cost of transportation from the port of arrival by wage deductions "not to exceed 10% of the wages in any pay period." These contracts were part of a three-way agreement that included the ministry of labour. Termination of employment during the first year would have to be government-approved.[9]

The parameters of candidate selection were determined by the labour department. After they were chosen for the program, DPs would then have to pass immigration, security, and health screenings. So the final determination of exactly how many cutters, finishers, seamstresses, and other skilled workers would actually arrive in Canada was impossible to predict. The restrictions given to the selection team related to the age, marital status, and size of families. The survivors could be between eighteen and fifty-five years old, single or married, with two or fewer children under the age of eighteen. In all families it would be the father who would qualify for the program. Widows with children were not to be considered. The suggested ratio was 25 per cent single men and women, 25 per cent married with no children, and 50 per cent married with children. In cases where both parents qualified as workers, they were restricted to only one child. Fathers of the larger families would be expected to be highly skilled "so that the earning capacity will be such as to maintain the family." Every member of the family would have to be in good health or they would all be disqualified—"fingers missing, defective eyes, or hearing deficiencies" were cause for rejections. Eyeglasses were acceptable. Finally, and this was emphasized, the tailors should be "types of individuals who will respond to the Canadian way of life and will readily fit into the Canadian economy."[10] How these rules played out during the program—what exceptions were made and how many DPs slipped through the cracks who were not remotely tailors or seamstresses—is impossible to calculate. What was clear to everyone involved in the needle worker project was this was a humanitarian effort. There would be non-Jews included in the groups, however they envisioned that 90 per cent of those selected would be Jewish Holocaust survivors. At least that was the unspoken agenda.

BERNARD SHANE (1890–1975)

BERNARD SHANE (OLSCHANSKY) arrived in Philadelphia when he was sixteen and, like many of the Russian Jews who came before him, took a job in a tailor workshop. He soon entered the International Ladies' Garment Workers' Union (ILGWU) where he spent the next sixty years as a worker, labour organizer, and union leader in both the United States and Canada. His obituary in the Canadian Yiddish-language newspaper, the *Keneder Adler* (the Canadian Eagle), noted that "early on the leaders of the International recognized in the young and ambitious Bernard a talent for organizing, honesty, and loyalty to the workers' cause." His "fine relationship with people," the piece continued, enabled his rise "from rung to rung in the labour movement and the union leadership." Shane was described as a moderate who supported workers' rights against the often-violent tactics of their employers, while fighting left-wing elements inside the union who promoted the interwar Soviet model of class struggle. "Shane peacefully, systematically, and tactfully fought all obstacles, winning for the workers in the garment industry and significantly improving their economic situation and establishing an admirable relationship between employers and the workers in their union."[1]

Shane first came to Canada in 1929 to organize garment workers in Toronto. After two years there he was sent to Chicago to work with dressmakers, and then, in 1934, Bernard arrived in Montreal to take charge of the ILGWU. The successful unionization campaign in Toronto in the 1920s led much of the clothing industry to move to Montreal where seamstresses worked as long as eighty-hour weeks in sweatshop conditions, earning fifteen cents a dress—barely ten dollars a week.[2] Most of these female workers were French-Canadian, but they included many immigrants, particularly Jews. Shane encountered the unique challenges of ethnic tensions, the economic depression, the anti-communist and anti-union policies of the Quebec government led by Maurice Duplessis, and obstruction from the powerful Catholic Church. Shane called on his American-Jewish colleague, Rose Pesotta, to work with the female workers. In 1937, aided by Canadian-Jewish activist Lea Roback, who was fluent in French, Shane and Pesotta succeeded in organizing a massive strike that lasted two

Bernard Shane in 1967.

weeks. This was one of the first—and, with five thousand workers, most noteworthy—strikes to improve women's working conditions in Canada. During his time with the Canadian ILGWU Shane won workers in Montreal shortened hours and work weeks, paid vacations, and other welfare benefits.

Shane remained in Montreal where he became one of the founders of the Canadian Jewish Labour Committee (JLC), and its treasurer. During World War II, the JLC established a standing committee against racial intolerance, the aim of which was to fight racism, particularly antisemitism, within the unions. As soon as the war was over, particularly after the 1946 pogrom in Kielce, Shane and the other leaders of the committee worked to open the doors of organized labour and the immigration department to DPs. When it was time for the JLC to select a representative to join the commission, Shane was the clear choice.

Upon his return from Europe, Shane wrote a series of articles detailing his experiences in the DP camps. They were published in Yiddish in the *Keneder Adler* and in English in the *Canadian Jewish Chronicle*, entitled "In search of tailors: Impressions gained during a recent two-month journey through the continent." In the very first camp they visited—Bucholtz, near Hanover, Germany—the commission worked for five days and approved five hundred applicants. All five of the men on the commission "realized the heavy responsibility which this mission placed upon us. Before us appeared helpless, dispirited human beings who saw in our mission a spark of hope for their liberation from their present misery. They looked upon their present situation as a death-sentence and at us as saviours in whose power it was to liberate them and give them a new lease on life." In the midst of so many survivors seeking a way to emigrate, Shane reflected on how much their commitment to adhere to government restrictions weighed on them. "We were there to get tailors and tough as it was on us personally, we often had to suppress our feelings, swallow hard and follow regulations."[3]

Shane left Europe "with mixed feelings." Although the group felt satisfied that they had brought hope and new life to some, "at the same time we felt depressed at the thought that hundreds of thousands of others were to be left in these camps without any immediate hope of salvation." Upon his return, Shane worked to help arriving DPs integrate into the labour movement. He joined the Canadian Jewish Congress (CJC) as a representative of Montreal's Jewish workers, where he served on their executive and as chair of their human rights committee. He was also active in the Canadian Histradrut, the Workmen's Circle, the YM/YWHA, and the Canadian Labour Congress. In 1960, on his seventieth birthday, a group of DPs and their families celebrated Bernard Shane's life. They honoured him for his participation in the mission to get them out of the killing fields of Europe and for helping them to establish new lives in Canada.

JUDY COHEN

Most tailors in Europe were men and the title, The Tailor Project, suggests that only men, the traditional breadwinners of the family, were considered to be hired to work in Canada in the needle trade. However, like myself and my sister Eva, thousands of young, single women—all breadwinners in their own right—also came and we were classified as sewing machine operators and worked mainly in dress manufacturing.

I WAS BORN JUDIT WEISZENBERG in Debrecen, the second-largest city in Hungary, on September 17, 1928. Somewhere along the line my name was slightly altered, and I came to Canada as Judith, but I could never pronounce the "th" properly, so I switched my name to Judy. My father, Sandor Weiszenberg, owned a scrap-iron yard and—as in any family with seven children—my mother, Margit Klein, had the job of being a homemaker. And she was excellent at it. I was the youngest of the seven children, with three older brothers and three older sisters. Ours was, I guess, a typical middle-class Jewish family in a Jewish neighbourhood of Debrecen and we had a relatively happy and good home. My parents were moderate, religious, Orthodox Jews. I went to school and, for the most part, lived the life of an average Jewish schoolgirl.

When World War II broke out on September 1, 1939, I was eleven years old, attending middle school. I can't say that the war had an impact on my daily life right away. My family was quite political, as were most people in Europe in those days. There was a lot of anxiety about the war, what was happening, the rise of Hitler, and the German army invading Poland. Of course, all this filtered down to us children. What affected our family first was that my father's store couldn't operate as well when all kinds of restrictions and antisemitic laws were enacted by the Hungarian government. My father's yard sold everything conceivable that was made of steel and iron, along with the scrap iron. There were also very valuable metals, like copper and bronze. When

As Judy Cohen tells it, "This is me in my very first winter coat, bought with the help of a Canadian friend who took me to a wholesale place where it was cheaper. We bought it somewhere in the *schmatta* district. It was bottle-green with fur trimming done as a gift by a friend who also came to Canada with the Tailor Project. He came as a fur worker and he managed to create a really lovely trimming with bits and pieces of grey Persian lamb. I felt so elegant and warm in that coat. That memory is still vivid."

Hungary became a military ally of Nazi Germany, all of a sudden the government declared that everything my father sold was war material and took away his license to buy and sell because he was a Jew. At the same time, my father still had to pay taxes, which naturally put a great financial burden on us. Our family's economic situation got worse and worse as the war went on.

As young people, we were very aware of what was happening in the country right next door to Hungary—Austria was now occupied by Nazi Germany—but we were still teenagers. We did our best to pretend that everything was normal, that the war wasn't happening, but we knew it was. Although we all listened to transistor radios and wanted to know the news, we still wanted to go on outings and picnics. Our lives were not threatened—yet.

In Hungary, Orthodox Jews, including my parents, were generally anti-Zionist, but my oldest sister, Elizabeth, or Erszébet, and my second-oldest brother, Miklós, became Hashomer/Zionists along with a lot of other Jewish youth. In the 1930s, five years before the war, Elizabeth and Miklós went to Mandate Palestine to work, to help build a Jewish homeland. They worked hard there, gained a lot of experiences but for various reasons, they needed to return to Hungary in 1938, just one year before the war broke out and found heightened anti-Jewish sentiments all around them.

As the war went on, we looked for hopeful signs

that Hungary might escape Nazi occupation. We had the naïve notion that the Allied armies would defeat the Nazis before they got to Hungary. But the Nazis were faster than either the Soviets or the Allies. As the Allies were landing in Normandy, we were being deported to Auschwitz-Birkenau—on June 29, 1944—with lightning speed. It is ironic that three months after we were deported, my city was liberated by the Soviets. The man who had been my father's barber for thirty years offered to hide the whole family because he knew the Soviets would be coming very soon. But my father refused. Not many Jews from the provinces went into hiding. They just never believed that the Nazis would get to us before the Soviets would.

The Nazis came into Debrecen on March 20, 1944, the day after they had marched into Budapest. By early April, we had to start wearing a yellow star, but the Jewish schools had been closed right away. The next decree was for the Jews to hand in all their valuables. Since my father's store had been closed down, he had the space and ability to hide Jewish refugees from Czechoslovakia in the shallow attics of the sheds—where he used to store the precious metals. I remember once there were seventeen refugees hiding there for three days while there was a roundup of refugees. My father was a Righteous Jew.

We were deported from Debrecen on June 29 and arrived in Auschwitz-Birkenau on July 3, 1944. Men's

memoirs of the Holocaust sort of equate everybody's experience as the same —"We were all killed as Jews"— but in the concentration camps, women had a double burden: being Jewish and being women. When you read women's memoirs, they talk about the difficulties for the mothers, even in the ghettos—feeding children, being pregnant. All sorts of issues that are particular only to women.

I turned sixteen in Auschwitz-Birkenau. I was very lucky to have at least one sister still with me, Elizabeth who, at twenty-seven, was twelve years older than I. She gave me a birthday kiss and we were just happy to be alive. Six weeks after we arrived, in mid-August, there was a large selection to decide who would go to the gas chambers, who would be sent to another camp, who would be put to work. Two of my sisters, Eva and Klara, were selected out and likely sent to another camp. They were not in good condition, but not bad enough to go to the gas chamber. Elizabeth and I cried and cried as their group departed. I didn't know what happened to them until after the war. A while later, I got sick with aching joints in my hips and had to spend time in a so-called hospital. Elizabeth took good care of me, bringing an extra slice of bread every day that she earned by carrying the heavy food cauldron at mealtime so that I would not get emaciated. Lucky me, I was able to walk out of the hospital, cured after two weeks. Actually, it was Elizabeth who saved my life.

Judy Cohen's sister, Eva Weiszenberg, a skilled dressmaker who also came to Montreal sponsored by the Tailor Project.

When the next selection came in late September, however, I was very sick with a high fever and dysentery. I was selected to be gassed and was too sick to realize the danger I was facing or what was happening around me. We were all sitting there naked, the group of us marked for the gas chamber. They took away our shoes, the ones that I still had from home—the only thing I still had. All I remember is my sister looking at me from afar and crying. I didn't understand why she was crying. I was just sitting there, completely out of it. But the truck that was supposed to take us to the gas chamber never arrived. The rumour was that sometimes the Nazis ran out of Zyklon B gas and that was why we were lucky enough not to be gassed. Instead, a kapo—a prisoner put in charge of other prisoners—came and gave each of us a rag and some wooden clogs to wear. We were marched to another camp in the Auschwitz complex and, the next day, put into cattle cars and taken to the Bergen-Belsen concentration camp in western Germany.

On that train, sick and alone, separated from Elizabeth, I met two sisters I knew from my home city, Edith and Shari Feig, who took pity on me and invited me to stay with them as "camp sisters." That's what saved me, that I was never really alone. I had my own sisters first, and then the two Feig sisters who took care of me. Finally, I got well in Bergen-Belsen. Without those five women at different intervals, I wouldn't have survived. I would have given up. I know that. Especially on the death march, at the end. The very fact that I knew somebody cared if I woke up in the morning made all the difference. Compared to Auschwitz-Birkenau, life was much better in Bergen-Belsen. For one thing, there was no gas chamber. But as time went on, the living conditions got worse and worse.

One day, in January 1945, a civilian wearing a beige trench coat and fedora hat came to Bergen-Belsen and we had a big assembly. He told all of us that he needed five hundred strong, young women to work in his factory in Germany, which turned out to be the famous Junkers airplane parts factory. The three of us—Edith, Sara, and I—volunteered and I took on their name because we presented ourselves as three sisters. This was the first time that we could take our fate into our own hands and we hoped that we had made the right decision. We left almost immediately and arrived at a labour camp in Aschersleben, near Leipzig, in the industrial heart of Germany.

Aschersleben was a subcamp of Buchenwald, but we couldn't believe what we saw when we got there— this wasn't barracks designed for prisoners like us. There was hot water and we could shower every day. It was January and we had heated barracks with hot pipes running right through them, spreading blessed heat. We had individual bunkbeds with white sheets. The beds had straw mattresses with a few bedbugs, but in comparison with Auschwitz (which is not saying much)—even with

Bergen-Belsen—it was palatial. The food was much better than in the other camps, although there was never enough and we were always hungry. We were guarded by SS women, but we worked for a private firm. Private German industry was part and parcel of the Holocaust. We still had to be counted, coming and going, and follow all of that routine. In the factory we worked with a variety of forced labourers from Germany, Ukraine, and especially from France. My foreman, Argo, was a French prisoner of war.

To be able to shower and be clean every day at Aschersleben helped us to stay healthy and survive. Even though we worked twelve hours a day, survival was possible there—at least until the Allied aerial bombardments began. The Junkers factory was only damaged, but work stopped in the latter half of April 1945 and, since we had no longer had work, we had to leave the camp on orders from the SS staff from Buchenwald. They were merciless and we had to start our forced march to nowhere—the march that became a death march. That's where most of us died. Of the five hundred women who started out, maybe two hundred of us survived to be liberated. We were not given anything to sustain us: no food, no water, nothing. Just two old guards and no provisions. We had to run into the forests here and there to relieve ourselves. We seemed to have no destination; the Germans were just driving us away from the liberating forces. They didn't know who would arrive first, the Russians or the Americans; we just had to keep moving. We searched garbage cans, dug into the earth hoping to find vegetables and, when we found some, we ate them as is—muddy and dirty. It's a miracle that any one of us survived. On some days it was absolutely surreal. We went through neat little towns and, just a few metres away from us, we could see normal life. Normal life we too used to have. Well-cared-for gardens, cute curtains on the windows, children going to school, people going to work. We saw them, but they pretended not to see us. I don't how long, how many days, and how many kilometres we marched. Every day seemed like torturous and endless hopelessness.

One day, the *Bürgermeister*—the mayor—of one of the towns finally allowed us to sleep in an empty barn with some straw scattered on the earthen floor instead of outside. We were hungry and thirsty, but we just lay down on the floor and fell asleep. In the morning, we were woken by a loud knocking on the door and saw a man standing in the doorway. It was a beautiful, sunny day behind him so all we could see was his dark silhouette. In a nice strong voice, he said to us in German, "Fräulein!" ("Ladies!") The three of us looked at each other in a surprise at his civil language. We surmised the war was over. Indeed, in the next second he said, "Fräulein, ihr seid frei!" (You are free!) We went outside and saw that there were no more swastikas, just white flags everywhere. Imagine!

The *Bürgermeister* didn't offer us so much as a little water—he just wanted to get rid of us as quickly as he could. "There are two ways out of here," he told us. "Down this road in ten kilometres is the Soviet Army. Down that road in six kilometres are the Americans." We quickly calculated that six was less than ten. We would go to the Americans. That's how it happened, our liberation. It was May 5, 1945. A beautiful, sunny Saturday.

We walked on to Düben, the next town. The American military was in charge there and had difficulty figuring out how to take care of about two hundred women showing up so unexpectedly. They could give us sleeping accommodation right away because the SS officers' barracks were empty. We certainly appreciated the white sheets and bedlinen on the beds, the soap, the towels, and the showers. But feeding us was rather chaotic for three days. Then, on May 8, the war officially came to an end and some organized order was established to look after feeding us and attending to our important health requirements. We were with the Americans for three or four weeks and then the Soviet soldiers arrived. That area of Germany became the Russian Zone.

The Soviet soldiers were of a different ilk. When some of them got drunk, they wanted to rape us, but we jumped out the windows and managed to avoid them. It never happened again after we reported the incident to the military commanders. Actually, some of the friendly

Red Army soldiers came over occasionally during the day and sang beautiful songs, playing their little round *harmoshkes* (accordions). Most of them were also good looking. After a few weeks the whole lot of us were packed up and taken to Leipzig, to a big refugee centre, to sort out what we—the survivors—wanted to do next. Edith, Sarah, and I wanted to go back to Hungary. We hoped that if any other family members were alive, they too would be heading home. I was positive that if I—the youngest—survived, then surely my older siblings did too. It was traumatic to think that I would be the only one in my large family to survive.

American military trucks took our group to the Czech border, gave us some money, made sure we got on trains, and left. I remember very little of our difficult trip home. When I got to Debrecen, I found László—he later became Leslie—the youngest of my three brothers already there. From him I learned that my oldest brother, Jeno, had been murdered in Soviet Ukraine by the Hungarian officers in a special slave labour unit attached to the Hungarian army. Miklós, who was also in Ukraine as a slave labourer, had died in a big battle at Voronyez.

I went back to school to try to make up for the final year that I had lost, but I had a very tough time emotionally being back in Debrecen. It's complicated to explain this to the uninitiated, but the truth is, nobody in Debrecen knew about Auschwitz-Birkenau at that time. Everyone else who came back had been deported to Austria, where most people survived. They didn't know that a couple of transports went to Poland, to death camps such as Auschwitz. I had to tell some of my cousins who came back, "Your wife and your child were murdered in the gas chamber." And they thought I was crazy. It took the population years to learn the exact details of what happened to the people who were sent away in the various deportations.

After I'd been back a few months, a young woman knocked on our door and asked, "Who is alive from the Weiszenberg family?" She handed me and László a little piece of paper and said, "I am bringing you a message from your sister, Eva—she is alive, in the Bergen-Belsen DP camp." Oh, what joy! With the help of the Bricha—the Jewish underground organization formed to help survivors get to British Mandate Palestine—László immediately went to Bergen-Belsen to bring her home, but she didn't want to come. She said that she didn't ever want to go back to Hungary and already had a boyfriend in the camp. So, László came back to Debrecen and convinced me to leave Hungary behind for good, go to Bergen-Belsen to join Eva and wait there to emigrate somewhere outside of Europe.

We were so elated to see Eva again, but the news she had for us was devastating. After she and Klara had been selected out in Auschwitz-Birkenau, they were sent to the terrible Stutthof concentration camp, also in Poland. In November of the same year, a transport arrived in Stutthof and Elizabeth was among the arrivals. The three of them miraculously met again and Elizabeth told them that I had been gassed. At this point, Eva started to cry and finished by saying that, in March 1945, Klara and Elizabeth had both starved to death, practically in her arms, even though she tried everything she could to save them. I was also devastated by this news because I would never be able to thank Elizabeth for saving my life. And now we knew for sure that only the three of us had managed to survive.

I like to talk about the Bergen-Belsen DP camp, where I was for about two years. There were about twelve thousand Jews there—it was like a little village. The camp was in the British Zone of Germany, which meant that the British were the top authority in the sector, but the camp managers were Jews and had quite a bit of independence in running it. By the time László and I arrived in 1946, it was a fairly well organized place. There was a Yiddish newspaper called *Our Voice*, and a school for the kids, and everything was in Yiddish. There was even Yiddish theatre. As time went on, of course, the political debates started raging. As they say, as soon as you have three Jews, you have seven opinions. In particular, there was the whole argument about a Jewish homeland. It didn't exist yet, but the news reached us about what was happening at the United Nations. *Shlichim*, representatives came

from the *Yishuv*—the Jewish community in Mandate Palestine—to urge us all to join them there.

I found it interesting to observe people in the DP camp who had survived alone. There were mainly two kinds of people who were on their own—young women like me and my sister, and men who had been married but their wives and children had been murdered in the gas chambers. They mostly ranged in age from twenty-five to thirty and they craved companionship. Traumatized as we were, it was difficult to live alone. So they started dating and there were lots of marriages—marriages that under normal circumstances wouldn't have taken place. Mismatches. But people needed companionship and needed a sense of belonging. And once there were weddings, there were babies. Strollers and baby carriages started appearing on the streets. Life slowly came back and that was, I think, remarkable, for people who went through experiences that nobody ever could have imagined. In the DP camp, you always had a shoulder to cry on. And there was always somebody to debate with.

I was young, just going on seventeen. There was such a lively atmosphere in the DP camp—it was a place where we could go from being victims to getting ready for some kind of a normal life. I attended the ORT school, a Jewish skills-training organization, and took a course for dental technicians. I didn't know at the time that I would be going to Canada as a dressmaker, but being able to arrive with a diploma in my hand gave me some self-confidence. As it turned out, I wouldn't have been able to use my diploma in Quebec anyway. At that time, only a citizen could be a dental technician and it took five years to become a citizen.

László, Eva, and I knew that we didn't want to go to Israel—we weren't Zionists. I think it was the way my sister Elizabeth had talked about her five years in Mandate Palestine. She felt that being there had divided her socialism from her sense of nationalism. And the survivors could only live in Mandate Palestine as illegal aliens because the British didn't allow legal immigration. Some people from the camp who had tried to go illegally were taken to an internment camp in Cyprus and a group of them were sent back to Bergen-Belsen. Who needed that? We had papers to go to Brazil, but that didn't work out. We had cousins there who sponsored us, but the Brazilian government stopped immigration at one point.

While we were waiting to see what would happen, this scheme to come to Canada as a dressmaker, to work in the needle trade, came along. As far as I remember, it was advertised in the camp. I can't remember exactly how we heard about it, but we certainly knew that we wanted to be interviewed for the program and take the test. I think three men came to Bergen-Belsen and I don't even remember how we communicated. I think we spoke in broken Yiddish—as Hungarian Jews, our Yiddish wasn't that good. Theirs was better.

My sister Eva, who was three years older than I, was a skilled dressmaker and she passed the test with flying colours. "Sure," the commission members said. "You can come." Then, it was my turn. They had a sewing machine in the room and I just had to sew two pieces of material together. In those days, you worked the sewing machine with the pedal, with your foot. It wasn't electric. I just had to do a straight seam because later on, we learned, that that was all you had to do in some factories in Canada; it was called section work. At least that's all we knew. After I finished doing the straight seam the commissioners hesitated about my skill. Eva said to me in Hungarian, "If they don't let you go, I won't go either." So I gathered up my courage and asked the men, "Would you separate sisters like the Germans did?" They looked at each other, then nodded; I would be allowed go with Eva.

László flunked the test. For starters, he sat on the wrong side of the sewing machine, which immediately gave him away. But by that time he was working for the UNRRA, the United Nations Relief and Rehabilitation Administration, and they advised him, "Let them go without you and when they are in Canada, they can sponsor you later." That's what happened. We sponsored him and he came to Canada three months later, but not as a tailor.

In reality, matters unfolded for Eva and me

Judy Cohen's immigrant visa stamped by Immigration Canada in Halifax, Nova Scotia on June 11, 1948. The stamp "Domestic"—the most common category for single women immigrants—has been crossed out and replaced with "Garment Worker."

differently in Canada. Our very kind mentor—a Canadian woman who met us at Windsor Station when we arrived in Montreal and volunteered to guide us through the three resting days we had before starting to work—made a big mistake. Instead of taking us to the office of the Garment Commission that had hired us in Bergen-Belsen, she took us to the office of the International Ladies' Garment Workers' Union. An entirely different ball game. Eva and I ended up working in a union job, a dress factory where the work was different from what we were told when hired. There, we had to assemble a whole dress, not just sew a straight seam. I had managed to sew the seam for the test, but they saw right away that I wasn't very experienced. Still, it brought me to Canada.

It's interesting to look back and recall the details about applying to go as a dressmaker, about the sewing test, because to us, some things didn't feel important to observe. It was up to those three men to decide whether I stayed or went. I don't think we paid any attention to the details. There were three men and the sewing machine. I had to sit down—and I wasn't very relaxed—and sew a straight seam. I didn't think that it would become a historical event. For us the whole point was to get out of blood-soaked Europe and start a peaceful, new, normal life somewhere in the world. But otherwise, it was of no great significance other than in our own little lives. So, we came.

I still have a picture of the boat we sailed to Canada, the SS *Ernie Pyle* it was called, named after an American war correspondent who died during the war. I had a miserable time on the ship, but Eva fared very well. We arrived on June 10, 1948, at Pier 21 in Halifax. I remember that it was very humid when we arrived. We weren't used to that kind of climate. On the same day we were put on trains heading west. We disembarked in Montreal simply because Clara, our good friend from Bergen-Belsen, wanted to live in Montreal and her aunt was waiting for her at Windsor Station.

I'll never, ever forget that first day in the garment factory. The forelady brought me a big bundle of cloth pieces and I had no idea what they were. It turned out that they were, for example, all the parts for twelve dresses and my job was to assemble them into complete dresses. But the trouble was that I couldn't identify the pieces—that is, which was the back of the dress, which was front, which was the sleeve. I was clueless.

Eva got oriented within a couple of hours because she had learned dressmaking in a haute couture salon. But me? Oh, I died a thousand deaths! I knew I wouldn't qualify. I knew that one day, maybe my second day or third day there, they would realize that I didn't know what I was doing. I was so nervous. With these thoughts in mind I suddenly looked up and saw that something was dripping from above. Eva, sitting across from me, said, "Judy, watch out!"

"I don't know what's happening," I said. "Something is dripping here."

"Watch out!" Eva said. "It's your perspiration! Wipe it off before it leaves a stain on what you're sewing!" That's how nervous I was. Even though the forelady was kind with helping me, I learned very slowly. I just didn't have the necessary skills.

We had to walk back and forth from where we were living to the factory. We didn't have money for a streetcar. So, we were already hot when we got to work and then we had to walk up many stairs in that old building to where the factory was. Eating was an adventure as well. The first day was like fasting for Yom Kippur because by the time we ordered something in a restaurant, it was time to go back to work. And we never knew if we were going to get what we thought we'd ordered. It was both tragic and comic the first time. Finally, we learned enough English to know what we were going to get when we ordered something from the menu. But as soon as we became savvy, we started taking our own lunch to work.

Unfortunately, we had conflicts with the landlady from whom we were renting a furnished room. She verbally insulted us. But we were fighters, my sister and I; we didn't let her get away with it.

Eva and I were incredulous that the English-speaking Canadians in Montreal resisted learning French, while the French Canadians had to be bilingual.

I got along well with my French-Canadian coworkers because I always started off trying to speak French to them. (I had learned some French in my one year of high school.) As soon as they saw that I was trying, they would be happy to switch to English. At the same time, they did have some antisemitic notions. The only thing that the French Canadians in the dress factory knew about Jews was that all of their bosses (*les patrons*) were Jewish. So I told them, "Look at me! I'm Jewish. I'm sitting right beside you, trying to make a living, just like you. Look at the cutter at the cutting table. He's Jewish, working in the factory, like you. Not all Jews are bosses." Many of the French-Canadian workers came from small towns in Quebec and had probably never seen a Jew other than the boss in the dress factory. They didn't know that they were antisemites—they were falling back on stereotypes because that's what they knew.

My first winter in Montreal, in 1948, I didn't have a winter coat and needed something warm, so one of my Canadian friends took me to a wholesaler. We found a green coat I liked and a survivor friend who worked as a furrier added a fur collar of beautiful grey Persian lamb. The fur was free because it was made from scraps he had gathered in the factory where he worked, and his labour was a gift because he was a friend. I felt so elegant and grateful to him.

Until I came to Canada, I had never met so many "left-wing" capitalists. Our first employer, Dave, was such a person. He had been a cutter during the war years and made good money. So after the war, he decided to buy twelve sewing machines, hired twelve machine operators along with the other skilled people needed in a dress factory and, voilà! He was now a factory owner and a decent man. We didn't consider socialism to be such a terrible thing then. The Soviet Union was thought of as a liberator for people like us, especially for Jews in Europe. A lot of Jews in Canada and in the United States were what they called "pinkos." But soon enough, Dave wanted to make more money, so he hired more people and, as the factory owner, all of a sudden the bottom line mattered. How much he could produce mattered. Orders had to be delivered on time and if some of the workers were too slow, he would lay them off. In fact, he did lay us off after four weeks of working for him. However, he was very decent because he was very apologetic and wanted to make sure that we got other jobs right away. He arranged for his brother-in-law, a foreman in another dress factory with fifty machines to hire us immediately. There, he said, we would have a chance to learn the trade.

I can't remember the name of the second factory, but that was where I really learned the trade. A very kind forewoman with a Ukrainian background, Mrs. Wallace, taught both of us with immense patience. She taught Eva methods to work faster so she could make more money and, along with other tricks of the trade,

she taught me from scratch—how to quickly identify the pieces of a dress and how to successfully put in a zipper. I was never able to make as high a salary as Eva could. She became very good.

Then, for some reason, that factory closed its doors and we all lost our jobs. Eva was hired somewhere as a sample maker and she made good money, but I wasn't hired. By now it was the mid-1950s, and I took the opportunity of being unemployed to go on a car trip across Canada with some friends. I spent all my savings on that trip but it was worth every penny. It was a unique and unforgettable experience. I got a real appreciation for Canada's grandeur and natural beauty. When I came back, I found a job through the union and started to work at Kerner Dress.

Kerner Dress was quite a place. By that time, I was considered experienced, somewhat bilingual, and got on the price committee with two French-Canadian girls. In any union shop, there had to be a workers' price committee to assess the price of each garment and what we would get paid to work on it. The three of us did what we had to do—it became almost routine—until we came to assess one very fancy, complicated dress. The Kerners had brought it back from New York and wanted to copy it. When we looked at it, we said, "It's going to take a long time to make one of those dresses."

I can't remember how much we asked—maybe $1.75 or $1.80 to sew up each dress—and that was a lot of money. The boss, Mr. Kerner, wouldn't accept it. He wouldn't budge and we wouldn't compromise because we figured we had to make so much a day in order to make a living. After haggling back and forth, Mr. Kerner called on the union representative Jack, who was supposed to be defending *our* interests, said, "Girls, just start working and we'll settle it."

"No," we replied. "Once we start, we'll have no power to change it."

Jack left and, finally, Mr. Kerner came back on his own with another price. We were still far apart. We came back from his office and told the other forty girls on the floor, "Look, this is what Mr. Kerner wants to offer, and no more."

And all the girls said, "No!" So, we went back to Mr. Kerner and told him that his offer was unacceptable. He replied that it was his final offer. When we went back to the factory and told the girls, they again said, "No!" and our response this time was to turn off the power. We went on a wildcat strike. Well! That was really radical in that union! Jack came back and told us, "What are you doing? That's illegal!"

"We don't care!" we answered. "We have to make a living."

After a little while, Mr. Kerner came back into the factory and called me—only me—to come to his office. "Tell me, Judy," he said. "What is a nice Jewish girl like you doing on the price committee?"

"Mr. Kerner," I answered, "I'm on the committee because this nice Jewish girl has to make a living and with the price you're offering, we won't." I'm not sure what exactly happened after that—I think that Simpson's, a big department store, badly wanted the dresses and put pressure on Mr. Kerner—but finally, we settled for about fifteen cents less than we wanted. That was more or less okay with the girls and we started working again. That was the last factory I worked in.

Throughout my working years I had gone to school at night, taking McGill extension courses for English because the free Jewish Immigrant Aid Society (JIAS) classes were so uneven. I wanted to learn English faster. Once my English was good enough, I went to a business school and got my diploma in typing and bookkeeping. When I left Kerner Dress, I left the entire needle trade and started looking for an office job. By then, I was twenty-three years old, much older than the average person looking for a typist job. I only managed to get interviews with insurance companies. I was a very accurate typist, but I was too slow. Only speed typists had a chance to be hired into a steno pool.

After six weeks of looking for a job I was starting to get a bit desperate when I saw a little ad in a Jewish newspaper in Montreal called the *Keneder Adler* that said, "Textile wholesaler needs assistant bookkeeper," along with the address and phone number and the words, "Talk to Mr. Macklin." Finally! Not an insurance company! I went to the office the next morning, introduced myself to Mr. Macklin Junior, the son of the owner, and told him what skills I had. After a brief discussion I was hired to be an assistant bookkeeper. The business was a textile wholesaler and they taught me how to work all the machines that they used to calculate the yardages. I got along famously with Jack, the bookkeeper who was a very helpful, decent man. I learned a lot from him.

I'd been at the textile company for some years when three friends of mine went into the real estate business and needed somebody to manage their properties, small apartment buildings with up to eighteen apartments in each building. They offered me the job at twice the salary I was making working for Mr. Macklin. So, I gave in my notice. He was very sorry to see me go and offered to match the new salary, but my mind was made up. I was excited at the prospect of learning something new and getting more experience. So I became an assistant property manager. In addition to doing the books, I learned all kinds of new skills, such as how to deal with the tenants and service people. This job was many-faceted and interesting. That was my last place of employment in Montreal because while I was working there I met Sidney J. Cohen from Toronto, a born and bred Canadian. After sixteen months of long-distance courting we were married and I moved to Toronto in 1961. I didn't get married until I was thirty-three—marriage had been the furthest thing from my thoughts.

All I wanted to do was work and spend my money on travelling, seeing the world's wonders.

Since coming to Canada, my brother László, now Leslie, had been working as a silkscreen printer, but he also had further ambitions and took some accounting courses while he was working. Once he had his diploma, some of his friends in Toronto convinced him to move there as well. He got a very good job and eventually he became a controller in a company. This was the first time that the three of us, Eva, Leslie, and I, had separated since finding each other at the end of the war. Eva was the only one who wanted to stay in the garment trade and stay in Montreal. She took a design course and became an excellent sample maker. She made good money and was so accomplished that she was much sought-after. She never married and stayed in Montreal for the rest of her life. Tragically, she died when she was only sixty-three, two years after she retired. I still miss her.

It wasn't easy to make friends in Toronto. Everybody seemed to have their own little cliques, but I was able to find friends through my husband and functioned well enough. I only rarely mentioned the Holocaust. I think we had talked ourselves out about what had happened to all of us while we were in Bergen-Belsen. Everybody understood us there. We could cry and they understood. By the time we came to Canada and were confronted with the problems of everyday life, we stopped talking about it. Generally speaking, people in

Canada were not very interested. I think we brought the Holocaust too close to the doorstep; even people's relatives distanced themselves after a while. It was difficult for them to understand and I'm not sure they wanted to. So we hardly ever spoke about the Holocaust to people unless they were close personal friends.

In those days nobody in Toronto wanted to hire a woman in building management. They'd never heard of such a thing. Even with my bookkeeping knowledge, they wouldn't hire me, so I eventually had to find another a job as a bookkeeper. I worked for two different firms until my daughter, Michelle, was born in 1964 and I stopped working for twelve years. We adopted a son, Jonathan, in 1968, four years after Michelle was born. Michelle now works as the equity/education officer for CUPE, the Canadian Union of Public Employees, in Halifax. She likes doing labour negotiations and has a diploma in conflict resolution. She's a strong feminist and a staunch social democrat, a very astute, intelligent young woman. My son is in computers. He has a couple of degrees; one in commerce, one in law. But he's into computers. He's a technical writer and a promotional writer. He doesn't have anything to do with law now. So, they both are successful in their own way. They follow their own independent lives and, as far as I know, are healthy and well.

I was very careful about how much I spoke about the Holocaust at home. I know that when both parents are survivors, sometimes they can overdo how much they talk about it. But Sidney wasn't a survivor, so it wasn't an everyday topic in my home. I gave my children age-sensitive information little by little because some things are hard to understand, even for adults.

I went back to work again for eleven years at a public relations agency's accounting department. It was a wonderful new experience. Just before I retired in 1993, however, I had a life-altering experience in downtown Toronto. During a noon-hour stroll at Bay and Bloor, I had a confrontation with a neo-Nazi Holocaust-denier group who were demonstrating, yelling "White Power!" over and over again. That incident catapulted me into becoming a public speaker and teacher on the Holocaust and the dangers of advocating hate. I have been doing it ever since. However, for a long, long time now, I haven't presented myself as a victim. I prefer to call myself a witness. When I speak to students and adults, I don't want them to get the idea that I need pity. I say instead, "When you walk out of here, please don't cry. Think! Think of what I said about *how* the Holocaust developed and became lethal. That's what's important, not to be part of spreading the hatred that leads to genocide. I strongly emphasize personal responsibility. What we, each of us, do every day, what decisions we make, and what the consequences of those decisions are. Working on prevention is where we ought to put our efforts—civil societies can do it if the will is there. We can't count on the politicians.

ELLA BIRNBAUM AND MAX GREENHOLTZ

Based on interviews with their daughter, Fay Greenholtz.

My parents, Max Greenholtz and Ella Birnbaum, both came to Canada with the Tailor Project, although not together and not even at the same time. My father was a skilled tailor before the war and my mother was a trained seamstress. They met in Canada while working in the same garment factory in Winnipeg.

MY MOTHER, Ella Birnbaum, came to Canada from Hanover, Germany, with her brother, Abe Birnbaum, in January 1948 in the dead of winter. My father came later from Stuttgart, Germany, in September of the same year. They both worked in the Stall and Sons Ladieswear factory, where they worked on different aspects of ladies' coats. My mother's half-sister, Reshke Birnbaum—who had come to North America before the war and was living in New York—was so thrilled to learn that her sister and brother were alive. In the summer of that year, she came to visit and brought outfits for both of them from New York.

My father came later, as he had originally planned to settle in Israel. He started the journey and made it all the way down to Turin, in Italy, before coming down with malaria. He'd had it before, during the war, when he was in Central Asia. So, he decided that he'd better not to go to Israel and went back to Stuttgart. That's where he was recruited for the Tailor Project.

My mother and her older sister, Dora, grew up in an orphanage in Lodz, Poland, because their father, Efraim Birnbaum, died when my mother was only two or three years old. Her father had been fairly prosperous, but when he died there wasn't much money left. Her older brother, Abe, who was six or seven, was already in school and, according to the standards of the time, was able to take care of himself. So he was allowed to stay at home. Their mother, Ruhel (née Levine), supported the family by being a midwife. My mother and my aunt remained in the orphanage until my mother was eleven or twelve. There they were put to work taking care of

Ella and Max Greenholtz on their wedding day
in Winnipeg, December 3, 1948.

young babies and doing many chores including mending clothes. It was likely a Polish orphanage because my mother spoke Polish more than Yiddish. After leaving the orphanage, she went home and started to work as a seamstress to help out the family. She was very skilled in all the arts of sewing, knitting, and crocheting.

The war started when my mother was sixteen, so she didn't have much of a childhood. My uncle, Abe Birnbaum, left for Russia after being unable to persuade his mother (Ruhel Levine Birnbaum) and sisters (my mother and Dora Birnbaum) to join him. She and my aunt and grandmother were relocated to a section of Lodz that became the ghetto. My grandmother was sent to Auschwitz fairly soon after the ghetto was created. My mother and her sister made the straw boots that went over the German soldiers' leather boots. I didn't really understand what she meant by "straw boots" until many years later, when I visited the Imperial War Museum in London and saw an actual straw boot on display in a recreation of the Lodz ghetto. I finally saw what my mother had been talking about for all those years—it was a tall boot woven out of straw that was worn on top of the leather boot, to protect the German soldiers from frostbite in the frigid temperatures on the Eastern front. They were made by hand, and I remember my mother describing how the straw would cut into her fingers. But that's what they had to do.

My mother and her sister remained in the Lodz ghetto until it was liquidated. They were sent on the last transport to the concentration camps that left in September 1944. By the time they got to Auschwitz/Bergen-Belsen, they were no longer tattooing numbers on people. Nonetheless, they were still processing Jews and still marching them back and forth to Birkenau in the snow. Somehow, she survived with her older sister, who basically took care of her, until liberation in April 1945. One of my mother's half-sisters, Ruhel Rosenberg, was also there with her with her daughter, Alla, who was only around twelve years old. The Germans made Alla the kapo of the unit and she was able to give her mother and her sisters extra food.

Neither of my parents had fathers growing up. Max's father, Josl, was born in Kalushin, Poland in 1888 to Naha and Berish Greenholtz. Josl was a Torah scholar when he married Max's mother, Faigle Schotland. She was born in Bzrezhyn, Poland in 1887 to Sheindl and Avraham Schotland. Faigle supported the family by running a small store as well as taking care of their three children—Esther, Max, and Avraham.

Josl died in 1917 when Max was four, Esther was six, and Avraham was a baby. His mother, Naha Greenholtz, lived with the family and helped take care of the children. There was a big fire in Kalushin in 1920, when Max was eight. The family lost everything and decided to move to Bzrezhyn, where Faigle's family lived. Max went to work at twelve in a tiny little *shtiebel*, a little factory with around six machines, as a tailor apprentice. Tailoring was the specialty of Bzrezhyn. Faigle died at the age of forty-three in 1931, when Max was nineteen. Max's grandmother, Naha continued to live with Max and Avraham after Faigle's death and predicted that Max would live a long life, as he took good care of her, even carrying her to the outhouse when she could no longer walk.

At my father's bar mitzvah, when he turned thirteen, the rabbi said, "Bring the orphan up to the Torah." He was considered to be an orphan because he had no father. Since he had to go to work at such a young age, his schooling only went to Grade 5. Despite the lack of formal education and that he hadn't learned how to multiply or divide, he could calculate columns of figures faster than I could do it and would complete tax returns for all of us and many of his friends. At eighteen, he was recruited into the Polish army and managed to survive it despite the discrimination and poor treatment of Jews in the Polish army.

When the war began in the fall of 1939, my father decided to escape to the Soviet Union, but he was trapped for a while in the no-man's land between Poland and the USSR. Then, when the guards weren't looking, he made his way across the border. His brother, Avraham, and sister, Esther, were with him at the beginning, but then they went back to get their families—his sister and brother-in-law, Simcha Paicher, had three

children (two of them were named after Faigle and Josl) and his brother had a fiancée. Tragically, they couldn't get out of Poland again. On his own, my father just kept travelling down through Afghanistan and Uzbekistan to Tajikistan. He just kept moving. He always regretted that his brother and sister hadn't stayed with him because, in the end, they didn't survive. His brother and his fiancée had married during the war and had a child. My father's sister-in-law survived, but his brother and the child did not.

My father came back to his hometown from Russia after the war to find that there was nothing and no one left, so he continued on to a DP camp in Stuttgart, Germany. From there, he decided to go to Israel to make aliyah. He got as far as Italy and then he came down with malaria for the second time. It was at that point that he went back to the DP camp in Stuttgart. My mother and her sister went to Hanover and my aunt Dora met her husband, Benjamin Zolty, there. There were many marriages in the DP camps. My uncle Abraham, my mother's brother who had also gone to the Soviet Union, came back and found his sisters in Hanover. My mother was lucky to have some surviving family: her sister and brother, two half-sisters, and several nieces survived. Her half-sisters were much older because my mother was the daughter of my grandfather's second wife, who had three children with him, but who had been much younger than him. Only two of the first generation of eleven children—who were as old as my grandmother—survived, but my grandmother's three children survived and managed to find each other after the war.

My father had almost no family left. The whole family was wiped out except for one cousin who had immigrated to Israel before the war, and two other cousins. Nonetheless, he found some landsmen from Bzrezhyn in the Stuttgart DP camp and together they forged some kind of community there.

I knew that my father had come to Canada through the Tailor Project, but I didn't know that my mother had until I saw her name on the ship's manifest. My father told me that factory owners from Canada had come over to recruit people and knew that they were helping them out of the DP camps—that it was a way to get people into the country because Canada still wasn't very welcoming to European Jewish survivors.

I'm not sure how either of my parents heard about the project, but it makes sense that they were recruited. My father was a skilled tailor who could work the machines, and my mother was an experienced and talented hand-sewer. My father explained how the recruiters tested people to see if they could sew. They asked him to sew a seam—a straight seam—and soon as he'd done it, they said, "You're on." That's how he came to Canada.

My uncle Abe came over with the Tailor Project as well, but eventually he became a furrier instead.

When my mother and uncle came in January 1948, my aunt Dora and uncle Benjamin couldn't come as Aunt Dora had just given birth to my cousin Ruth. I think they must have been sponsored by my mother and her brother a year later. My uncle Ben was also a tailor, but he didn't come with the Tailor Project. He initially worked at a leather factory, but he left when he bought a little grocery store.

The single survivors who came through the Tailor Project went mainly to Winnipeg while the families generally stayed in Montreal and Toronto. As a result, many matches were made in Winnipeg. Max proposed to Ella shortly before his thirty-sixth birthday and they were married on December 3, 1948, on Max's birthday. Ella's sister and brother-in-law, Dora and Benjamin Zolty, made the wedding at the Ashkenazy Synagogue in Winnipeg.

Max and Ella had two children, myself—Fay—and my brother—Joe—both born on April 29, five years apart. We were named after Max and Ella's parents. Joe and I grew up in Winnipeg with these "survivor parents" in the North End of Winnipeg. It was a great community, a very vibrant Jewish community. All the *greene* (i.e., greeners, or newcomers), the Holocaust survivors who initially settled in the North End because it was a poorer part of the city, would get together regularly. There'd be parties to celebrate all sorts of events together, but it was a community apart. It wasn't part of the wider Winnipeg Jewish community until later; the *greene* and the *gayle*, or *gelbers* (i.e., the yellows—the established Jewish community), didn't always mix. Later, their children would meet other children and introduce the parents, but at the beginning they only interacted with other *greene*. They'd share their stories amongst themselves. The Winnipeg Jewish community certainly provided support for the survivors when they arrived. They provided room and board for them and had jobs waiting for them through the Tailor Project. They provided them with transportation to their factories on the first day to make sure that they got there. They welcomed them in that way. But nobody in Canada really understood what had gone on. At the end of the war, nobody wanted to talk about what had happened. So, it was kind of a strange situation. The survivors had survivors' guilt, and people in the established Jewish community probably felt guilty too, guilty that more hadn't been done for European Jews during the war. Nobody talked about what went on until much later.

We grew up without knowing many people in the generation older than my parents. My uncle Abe married a woman who was born in Winnipeg, Lily Smolensky—her parents were from Russia—and her mother became all the cousins' grandmother since none of us had any grandparents. Baba Etel, as we called her, took care of all of us—she was one of our only touchstones to an older generation. She was a lovely woman who made meals for all of us. The only other older person I knew growing up was a man from my father's hometown, Aron Badower, who had survived the war. He was about fifteen or twenty years older than my father and had no children of his own after the war.

My parents went to synagogue occasionally, but they didn't belong to any synagogue. My uncle who became a furrier and was president of the furriers' union was a fervent communist—he was very articulate, and he'd go to conferences all over. He wasn't such a strong communist later, but he continued to be anti-religion. My mother didn't have a Jewish upbringing at all since she spent most of her childhood in a Polish orphanage. My father did, so we had Yiddishkeit in our home and we celebrated the holidays. Joe went to a Hebrew day school until Grade 8—Joseph Wolinsky Collegiate in the North End. He was a choir boy, so we'd go to services at the little shul that was part of the school. My parents wanted him to have a Jewish education. I went, too, for a little bit, but when I was only six years old I told my parents that I wanted to go to public school and they agreed. Hebrew school was expensive. I didn't go to cheder, afternoon school. My parents always spoke Yiddish to us at home and I am grateful that I can understand and converse in Yiddish.

I can't say that I really experienced any antisemitism, but my brother was taunted by antisemitic bullies when he walked to high school. The public schools in the area were substantially Jewish. The neighbourhood in the North End was Ukrainian, Polish, German—it was mainly an immigrant area. My friends were not Holocaust-survivors' children, including gentiles. My brother and I belonged to the Young Men's Hebrew Association (YMHA) and B'nai Brith. I went to the B'nai Brith summer camp. My brother went to Camp Massad with the other kids from the day school. They did everything in Hebrew. I didn't learn any Hebrew at school, but I did learn at camp. We also did the *Birkat Hamazon*, Grace After Meals, and said other prayers and sang Hebrew songs. That was my Hebrew education.

It was a fine upbringing. We weren't wealthy, but we had a warm home. Both my brother and I were able to go to university on scholarship. I paid for the rest of tuition and books by working at Eaton's department store on the weekends, and Joe drove a cab a few evenings after school and on weekends. In those days, nobody went away to university. We had carpools from the North End to the university in the far south end of the city. It was about an hour's drive. When it was my turn to drive, I'd take my parents in the car with four other university students—seven people crowded into a Mercury Meteor. I'd drop my parents off at the factory and then we'd go on to the university. My father learned to drive, although my mother never did, and some of my most wonderful memories growing up took place on our summer driving vacations to places in Minnesota

and Iowa, and to Winnipeg Beach on Lake Winnipeg. We were very close to our aunts—Dora Zolty and Lily Birnbaum; our uncles—Ben Zolty and Abe Birnbaum; and our cousins—Ruth and Freda Zolty, and Zel and Rachel Birnbaum. We got together often, not just for holidays. We were always together.

My parents always talked about their experiences in the Holocaust. They weren't the type to keep it to themselves. When I was older, I was the one who typed everything up for their reparation applications. I always sat in when the groups of their friends got together and I listened to their stories. Every Sunday, Uncle Abe came to visit, and my mother would cook a gefilte fish in the morning. That horrible smell would waft into my room and wake me up. My brother had it worse as his bedroom was right next to the kitchen. Some of the other landsmen would come as well. All these men would get together at our house; they'd talk and I'd listen. They played cards and told stories. My father loved to tell jokes—always in Yiddish. Often, actually, men and women played cards together; my mother loved playing cards. There was a group of people that all lived in the neighbourhood in the North End and all got together to play cards at various houses, but it was mainly at my house. My friends also really liked coming over to play at our place. My parents fed them and nurtured them, too.

My father stayed with Stall and Son in Winnipeg

Two of the dolls that Ella Birnbaum made after she retired from working in the garment industry.

for his whole career. My mother, too. She stopped working for a few years when my brother and I were small children, but she went back to work when I was about eight and Joe started kindergarten. In the early days, when my parents first went to work at Stall's, there were many Jewish workers in the garment factories, and the foreman was Jewish. Much later on, toward the end of my father's working there, Filipino workers came in and many of the Jews—like my uncle—left the factories to buy small grocery stores. Some of them also bought properties and became fairly well off. My father didn't participate; he was proud of his tailoring skills and was satisfied with his life in Canada. Even after he retired from Stall's, in about 1980, at sixty-eight, he didn't stop working. He went to work for the Navy Surplus Store in Winnipeg as a part-time tailor. He enjoyed that and, with his gift of gab, he also enjoyed sometimes coming out to the sales floor to help.

My mother retired around the same time although she was a lot younger, only fifty-eight. But she didn't stop working either—she took care of children because she loved them so much. That's what she did in the orphanage when she was still only a child herself. After they moved to Toronto, she took care of the children of a rabbi up in Thornhill and she really enjoyed it. She also carried on with her needlework. I still have some needlepoint that my mother did, and doilies, and dolls that she bought and made clothes for. She was very talented and made clothes for dolls, combining her skills as a seamstress and needlework with her love of children. She knitted hats for children—she made them for my children—but she also made hats and sweaters to give to other children. And she made stuffed animals; she had them in her house even before my children were born. I think that she loved stuffed animals and dolls because she never really had a childhood. She created the things she never had as a child until her eyes started failing when she was in her eighties.

In 1984, my parents moved to Toronto because I had moved there in 1972 and married Michael Rotsztain in 1977. Michael was originally from Montreal and was also the son of Polish survivors, Sala (Teichner) and Cemach Rotsztain, who were in the garment industry as well. Uncle Abe and his second wife, Molly, moved from Winnipeg at the same time to be with his daughters and the other relatives who had survived. In 1984, they all pulled up stakes, sold their houses, and moved to the Steeles and Bathurst area of Toronto.

My parents were staunch Zionists, true believers in Israel until the end of their days. They went to Israel for the first time around 1998 on a seniors' tour. It wasn't a Jewish tour and they were the only Holocaust survivors on it. They got to visit relatives as well. Going to Israel was my father's dream and he finally did it.

Canada really was a magic land for my parents after all they had gone through. They were able to buy a house and a car. My brother and I went to university. When I was born, they took out an insurance policy so there would be enough funds for me to go to secretarial school when I finished high school. That was considered a fabulous job because it was not in a factory. The factory was hot—hot, hot, hot—in the summer and cold in the winter. I'd visit my parents at work there, and conditions were certainly not ideal. It was dusty and dingy and the light wasn't good. It was very important for them that my brother and I didn't work in a factory. For them, education opened the door to everything. My brother has a doctorate in education and I have two master's degrees. I am currently a consultant in finance systems at universities. Joe is an immigration consultant and translator. Joe and I both grew up with a strong work ethic; both of us started working when we were in our early teens. We had part-time jobs and summer jobs. I once asked my dad why I couldn't work in the factory for the summer and he just said, "No way!" As a result, we never worked in the factory.

My parents were so proud to be grandparents. My daughter, Elise, was born in 1982; my son Jonathan in 1985; and my younger son, Daniel, was born in 1989. My brother was married in 1982 to Hiroko Mizui and has three children: Emi, born in 1983; Naha, born in 1985; and Adam, born in 1988. The grandchildren are all educated with interesting and diverse careers in the arts and environmental advocacy. Two of the granddaughters are married. Max died on August 13, 2003, before the granddaughters had met their husbands, but Ella lived to meet both of their husbands, Kyle Knox, Naha's husband, and Ian Klesmer, Elise's husband. She really enjoyed spending time with them before she died on February 27, 2010. I now have a granddaughter, Simone Klesmer, who was born in March 2018. Her Hebrew name includes Esther for my mother. My mother, who loved children so much, would have just been so delighted.

THE SELECTION TEAM

ALTHOUGH ORDER IN COUNCIL 2180, which permitted the admission of 2,136 tailors, was not formally approved until October 1947, the May go-ahead by cabinet was enough to set the wheels in motion.[1] Hayes informed the American Jewish Joint Distribution Committee (JDC) and they conducted a survey that estimated there were 38,000 mostly Jewish garment workers among the 240,000 displaced persons under their supervision. With the JDC on board to help with recruitment, the industry needed a team in Europe ready to spring into action the moment Ottawa passed the order in council. Manufacturers and workers' associations were asked to choose representatives who were "men of expert understanding and knowledge, who are prepared to spend long hours in the displaced persons camp, examining and screening applicants." They were warned that this would "be no holiday job."[2]

By early September, five men were in place. The team included Max Enkin, president of the National Council of Clothing Manufacturers; Samuel Herbst, business manager of the International Ladies' Garment Workers' Union (ILGWU) in Winnipeg; Samuel

Posluns of the Cloak Manufacturers' Association of Toronto; and Bernard Shane, treasurer of the Jewish Labour Committee (JLC), and David Solomon, executive director of the Manufacturers' Council of the Ladies' Coat and Suit Industry, both from Montreal. While these Canadian Jews were joined in a common humanitarian cause that would deeply affect each of them, they were also representing their own corners of the management-labour divide. It was perhaps inevitable that some interpersonal conflicts and disagreements would erupt during their challenging mission. Max Enkin had been the unanimous choice to lead the team. David Solomon would later note that Enkin "proved to be a level-headed and dynamic personality who knew what was wanted and how to do it. If it were not for him, the different factions of the commission would have been split even on minor issues."[3]

An almost fatal blow to the project was sprung on the members just before they left for Europe. Jewish relief agencies had begun looking for Jewish tailors in the DP camps and word got back to C.D. Howe, who was in Britain for meetings before going to inspect the

The five members of the Tailor Project selection team in Germany, 1947. Left to right: Bernard Shane, Max Enkin, Sam Posluns, David Solomon, and Sam Herbst.

camps. Howe grew concerned that a preponderance of Jews chosen for the scheme would cause political repercussions at home, particularly in Quebec. He had not been present when the cabinet made its decision and was seemingly aware that the majority of garment workers would be Jews. But the bulk labour program was Howe's personal project and he feared that the whole enterprise could be damaged if publicity about an influx of Jewish DPs to Canada caused a storm of protest.[4] On August 1, 1947, he cabled the minister of labour that "selection teams be instructed that not more than 50% of workers should be of one racial group. Sending you this for reason that I am advised that one racial group is already busy selecting immigrants."[5]

Who was going to break the news to the commission? A few days later, an apologetic Arthur MacNamara, the deputy minister of labour, telephoned J.J. Spector, one of the lawyers for the commission. MacNamara claimed that the "Palestine situation" with the British and the DPs was causing concern, and he inquired what percentage of the tailors chosen by the commission might be Jews. When Spector told him, "over 50 percent, he said, 'Can you hold it down to 50?'" Spector immediately put out calls to the team. Solomon advised suspending the trip; Enkin, who was already in New York and about to leave for Britain, counselled pressing the government. Shane urged him to make it an "issue now, because the situation would get worse later."

Within hours Spector was back on the phone with MacNamara and "told him that we were disturbed and a little alarmed. I said that if every ripple on the international surface with respect to Palestine was going to set this project back, we wanted a discussion with the Minister." The deputy minister responded that he thought the project was advancing too quickly and he needed more time to put his team together. Sensing that there was some flexibility, the commission members decided to send Enkin and Posluns on to Europe where they would be in a better position to push for a resolution.[6] Perhaps it really was just about timing. A delay of the project to early September could be managed.

A week later, Spector and Norman Genser, the two commission lawyers, travelled from Montreal to meet with MacNamara in person. This time they were told that he had conclusively decided to choose garment workers on "a racial basis." They were told that "there was a large number of people in Canada who were opposed to any people of the Jewish faith coming into Canada." He knew that "it would cause us great difficulty and embarrassment," but he was not going to "coat the pill." The lawyers were shocked to hear such a clear articulation of antisemitic government policy. They told him that this was "too important a decision to come from a Deputy Minister" and they would go directly to cabinet. MacNamara responded that they could try, but then "the whole damn project would be

ADDRESS =NLT= NORMAN GENSER
276 St JAMES West
MONTREAL.

After seeing Howe and talking to Canadian Hias agent Sam and I believe Governmental ~~prop~~ proposal should be accepted stop Jewish DPS number fifteen to twenty percent in camps and general attitude is hostile to undue Jewish emphasis stop if ~~prop~~ proposal not accepted by our group believe whole project would be dropped suggest you now ask dress and allied trades to file applications with you thereby increasing overall number to be admitted stop As it takes almost two weeks to get passports for

Cable from Commission lawyer Norman Genser to Max Enkin, informing him that the government was insisting on a 50 per cent quota for Jews in the bulk labour scheme for tailors, August 15, 1947.

off!" If they agreed to the restriction, he would proceed to recommend the 50 per cent quota and, if it was accepted, the delegation could commence work after September 1, 1947.[7]

Saul Hayes also rushed to Ottawa to try to save the project. The Canadian Jewish Congress (CJC) had been fighting antisemitic quotas in Canada's workplaces, universities, hospitals, and private clubs for over a decade. This was, sadly, nothing new. Hayes argued with MacNamara until his "throat was parched," that the quota "was akin to *numerus clausus*, which bothered the Jewish community so much and which would be hard for history to justify." Hayes recalled that the minister was "not interested in history…. He was interested in the fact that he would not be able to get through this project if it was realized that 100% were Jewish refugees."[8]

In the meantime, Max Enkin had arrived in London and was invited to Canada House for a personal visit with Howe, whom he knew from his time on Howe's Wartime Prices and Trade Board. Enkin soon realized that this would not be a social call and Howe got right to the point: "Under no circumstances could they proceed with this scheme if there were more than 50% Jews selected." As Enkin later explained, "The federal Liberal government…knew that in order for them to stay in power Quebec was central…Mackenzie King was a very astute politician, and he never did anything

that wasn't approved by the Quebec powers." Despite his forewarning, Enkin was still taken aback.

I was shocked. I confess I was shocked…I am too pragmatic a person to not recognize what are the realities of the moment or of the day. I knew that C.D. Howe wielded such power that if I tried to make a big issue we could just be kept in London ad infinitum and there wasn't anything we could do about it…. If Howe didn't say yes, we'd be stuck in England and we'd have to come back empty handed… and the government would find a way of covering it up.[9]

Back in Montreal an urgent meeting was held to discuss possible plans of action. Commission members contemplated a public outcry to gain support but resigned themselves to the conclusion that "half a loaf is better than none." CJC representatives also met to try to "reconcile the humanitarian desire for the need to save some Jews against the principle of protesting racial discrimination." Although their principles might win them an "empty victory," agreeing to the quota would give them a "practical result." They were also concerned about "what kind of people these Gentiles would be." How could they be certain they weren't accepting fascists and antisemites? And who was going to pay for their settlement? They decided to approach non-Jewish agencies to assist with the costs, which they calculated would be about one hundred dollars per person. Contemplating the new restrictions, Genser wrote to Enkin "that much greater responsibility is now imposed upon you and your delegation, because the future of Jewish life in this country may to a large extent depend on the type of people you screen."[10]

And so, after a few procedural bumps due to government inertia, the selection team accepted their new instructions and made their way to Germany. Before he left London, Enkin wrote to Genser about the lack of coordination between Canadian government agencies and their daily frustrations working with them. "Fortunately I kept my temper," Enkin admitted. "We still manage to smile in spite of the feeling of frustration and, when it is all over, we probably will have some cause for satisfaction." Nor was Genser having much success in pushing for action in Ottawa where he was "literally living amongst these people hoping to get them to do something." As he noted, "Government does not pay anything extra for special energy." "I am not sure," Genser wryly wrote to his friend Max Enkin, "that I did the right thing getting you into this."[11]

What Enkin and Genser did not yet know was that the quota was just one of many obstacles the government had decided to place in the way of the garment workers project. Labour and immigration branch officials had interpreted Howe's quota to mean that the project should not be given any priority. Neither screening nor shipping would be easily available.[12] "I can see it will be a fight every inch of the way," wrote Enkin.[13] The fight to squeeze open Canada's doors to even a trickle of Jewish tailors and their families was off to a slow start.

DAVID SOLOMON (1890–1967)

UPON HIS RETURN from the DP camps, David Solomon wrote to his fellow commission member Max Enkin reflecting on how "the European *blitzkrieg* which we underwent must surely have left its scars on all of us."[1] Executive director of the Manufacturers' Council of the Ladies' Cloak and Suit Industry of Quebec, Solomon's assignment was to "sit at a table and register the DPs who applied for emigration. As each prospective emigrant appeared before me, I examined his papers.... I also checked medical certificates attached to each application and examined the miniature lung X-ray plate which had to prove the carrier was free from infection in order to be eligible for emigration."[2] The team had laboured for more than three months, he later recalled, "sometimes working from 7 one morning til 5 the following day, without sleep. I had by now lost 22 pounds."[3] No wonder the fifty-seven-year-old Solomon had written to his wife, Belle, "Oh! For a piece of your Roasted Brisket with nice browned potatoes and sour pickles." Solomon was not complaining about the team's "personal hardships"—he had been deeply moved by the plight of the survivors. He explained to his family the "freezing, waterless and lightless trains and hotels, the low vitamins content diet, the sickness we suffered are nothing compared to the suffering of the DPs."[4]

David Solomon understood poverty and deprivation. His tailor father, Hyman Solomovitch, had fled persecution and pogroms in Moldavia (Romania), settling in a mill town called Pendleton, near Manchester, England. David was born there, the youngest of eight children who survived to adulthood. His earliest memories were

of the click, clack of the iron sole rims on the pavement at 6 a.m. as the mill hands in their wooden shoes or clogs rattled on their way to work. Women with heads covered with shawls and collarless men wearing mufflers. Then there were the wakers-up, who traversed the district with elongated bamboo poles, tapping on the bedroom windows at five am rousing mill hands from sleep. In the evening, lamplighters with long poles further elongated with

David Solomon

wax tapers open the valves atop lamp posts and touch off the gas jets.[5]

Hyman found his place in this hardscrabble town, working as a raincoat-maker when waterproof fabrics and garments were a new innovation.

The Solomon family immigrated to Montreal in 1904, when David was fourteen. Although his first language was English and he wanted to continue his schooling, David went to work in a garment factory with his older brothers to help support his struggling family. He pursued his interests in music and painting, which were nurtured at the local Young Men's Hebrew Association (YMHA). Although he could never afford to attend university, Solomon was always keenly interested in the world around him. While he spent his entire working life in the clothing industry, he maintained an active intellectual and creative life and was extremely well-read.

Solomon married Belle Rosenthal, who became a pioneering businesswoman in Montreal with her high-end women's dress store, Belle's, located on the ground floor of an old mansion on fashionable Sherbrooke Street West. Before World War I, most women had worn homemade garments—only the wealthy could afford dressmakers. But in the 1920s, ready-to-wear clothing became all the rage. David helped support his wife's store while managing the Manufacturers'

Council, where he had to navigate a complex set of relationships and competing interests. One of his roles was to represent the owners in labour negotiations and the administration of pension funds. Solomon proved to be a natural diplomat and excellent communicator. His working-class roots and sympathies helped him maintain good relations with the unions over the decades before he was selected to join the commission.

Once the news spread that he had been selected for the team, Solomon, along with his fellow commission members, was bombarded with requests to include specific DPs on their lists. He always responded with great empathy. In July 1947, he wrote to his teenage daughter Nancy about an appeal he had received from a survivor in Linz, Austria. Commenting on the archaic dictionary English of the letter, he told her that the man had outlined the tragedy of his lost family and hoped that Solomon could find him a Canadian girl to marry and sponsor his immigration. "Between the humour in between the lines," David added, "there was a tear behind each smile." Visiting the camps only deepened his understanding and desire to help. The group was taken to see the memorials at Bergen-Belsen, which was now a DP camp. Solomon was given the honour of opening the ark in one of the camp synagogues on the Jewish high holiday of Yom Kippur. He described to his family how a six-month-old baby was passed among the 150 men during the service and how she melted their hearts—and his. "These are the things Belsen has done to me," he wrote, "I am converted to Zionism. I can't keep my eyes dry. The lump in my throat chokes me when I remember the simple monument erected over 30,000 Jews."

David Solomon returned to his position in Montreal and presented detailed reports on the mission to the Jewish community. He spent his entire career with the council and did not retire until he was sixty-nine. He became an active fundraiser for the United Jewish Appeal and in his later years he focused on painting. David Solomon died in Montreal in 1967.

SAMUEL HERBST (1892–1960)

SAM HERBST, or as he was wont to pronounce it in his thick Yiddish accent, "Oiybst,"[1] was born in Lithuania and arrived in the United States as a young man. In 1935, following a disastrous strike that had decimated labour relations in Winnipeg, the American International Ladies' Garment Workers' Union (ILGWU) sent Herbst to Winnipeg to organize the city's garment workers. Herbst went on to become the most powerful—and controversial—labour leader in Winnipeg.

The 1920s saw Winnipeg become the third-largest clothing manufacturing centre in Canada after Montreal and Toronto. As the opening of the Panama Canal to shipping in 1914 severely curtailed the city's value as a transport hub for goods destined for the West, the early-twentieth-century influx of Jewish immigrants with tailoring skills were soon hired to fill the cheap abandoned warehouses that had been snapped up by clothing manufacturers—many of them former immigrants who were building their own companies. By 1941 a third of the garment workers in Winnipeg were Jews.

Herbst arrived to find management exploitation of labour and low wages. It was the depths of the Depression and he had trouble convincing people who feared loss of their limited income to unionize. He worked day and night promoting the ILGWU. At a meeting at the Talmud Torah school, where he spoke in Polish, Ukrainian, and Yiddish, he found himself pelted with eggs and rocks by immigrant workers. Herbst eventually changed his focus to the employers. Through careful negotiation, he convinced one of the largest manufacturers that allowing unions would dispel unrest and increase their profit margins. Other companies soon joined them and implemented salary increases and a limited work week. While there were no strikes under the ILGWU for the following twenty-five years, there were drawbacks to Herbst's approach. Factories were closed to non-members and many felt the deal favoured the employers. His obituary in the *Winnipeg Tribune* noted that "testimonial dinners have been held by manufacturers in his honour, a rather unusual accolade for a union chief."

Herbst definitely had both supporters and detractors. One of his most positive initiatives was a "welfare and sick fund" launched in 1947 that became a model

Sam Herbst (left) with Sam Posluns, supervising a tailoring test.

for industry-union relations. The funding for it came from both payroll and employees. On the twenty-fifth anniversary of the fund, the medical group it supported joined with the ILGWU and factory owners in building a $200,000 youth centre in Rehovot, Israel that was named for Herbst. At the same time, however, he soon developed a reputation for being an iron-fisted dictator. Nonetheless, his tight control over Winnipeg's garment worker unions did bring him in contact with government officials. One of them—Manitoba labour minister Arthur MacNamara, who was brought into a cap makers' dispute over minimum-wage violations—developed a congenial relationship with Herbst, that later bore fruit when MacNamara was federal deputy minister of labour and assigned to negotiate the DP labour scheme with Herbst and his colleagues.

As the sole representative on the selection team from Western Canada, Herbst felt a great responsibility to bring qualified workers to Winnipeg and Vancouver. Like the other members, every one of them with deep roots in the world lost to the Holocaust, Herbst was driven to help those he could. Upon his return to Winnipeg, Herbst learned of the obstacles the government had placed in the way of the Jewish DPs they had selected and sent an urgent telegram to Max Enkin. "Am worried about the situation," he wrote. "I think it is dangerous and want to assure you if we have to go again and get our people I am ready to do so."[2]

From June 1946 until September 1947 I worked as a secretary at the Winnipeg Citizen, an organization attempting to start a new newspaper. My office was located in the Donalda Building. It was also the location of the International [Ladies'] Garment Workers' Union, led by Sam Herbst. He told me that he was going to Europe to bring tailors to Winnipeg and asked if I would type a list of Winnipegers who had relatives there, to "rescue Jews," in Yiddish. I did so and he offered to pay me, but I refused and asked instead that he bring over my relatives. Next to their names I put a red star. He did so. They were Bella and Mischa Swick and a young son.
—JEANETTE BLOCK

A protest by Jewish refugees in the Bergen-Belsen DP camp against restrictions on immigration for Holocaust survivors, c. 1947/48.

NEEDLES AND THREAD

The minute we started working we realized the heavy responsibility which this mission placed upon us. Before us appeared helpless, dispirited human beings who saw in our mission a spark of hope for their liberation from their present misery. They looked upon their present situation as a death-sentence and at us as saviours in whose power it was to liberate them and give them a new lease on life.[1]

—BERNARD SHANE

UPON LEAVING LONDON'S rubble and food shortages, Bernard Shane recalled that they felt "depressed, but unaware of the still more depressing sights awaiting us on the Continent." Their first billeting was in Hanover and they were stunned by the destruction they witnessed. Allied bombing during the war had destroyed 90 per cent of the city. It was the Jewish New Year, so the five men ventured through the ruins to pray at Hanover's makeshift synagogue. This was their introduction to survivors who had left the DP camps in hopes of starting new lives in the cities. Discussing their experience with a Canadian International Refugee Organization (IRO) official later that day, the team was warned that the atmosphere for Jews in Germany was dire. "Get these people out," he told them. "Get them out as soon as possible. Because when the occupation forces ever leave you will have a much greater blood-bath in this place than you have ever known." When he returned home in November, Max Enkin publicized what they had learned those first days in Hanover. As he told the *Vochenblatt* newspaper, not only had they found the surviving remnant in a "frightening situation in which a million people are literally in a mental jail," but emphasized that in postwar Europe Jews—"surrounded by people who don't want them"[2]—were in a precarious state.

The Jewish high holy days prevented the commission from commencing their screening so they proceeded to visit their first DP camp, Bergen-Belsen. They were accompanied by Morris Kraicer, the Canadian Jewish Immigrant Aid Society (JIAS) representative who was working to bring 1,116 orphans to Canada. The group was introduced to Josef Rosensaft, the thirty-six-year-old leader of the Central Committee of Liberated Jews.[3] He impressed Shane as "one of the legendary figures of Jewish resistance in Europe…a visible exhibit of Hitlerian brutality. Bodily maimed, he nevertheless retains that enormous energy which probably saved him from the fate of his six million co-religionists."[4] On a "night never to be forgotten," Rosensaft took the team to the "two mounds, the two hills, to which all visitors to Bergen-Belsen are taken." Shane described the mass graves, where tens of thousands were buried, as "indestructible monuments to man's inhumanity to man." Sam Posluns "was overcome with numbness and was very much affected." Struggling to contain his emotions, he began to walk off when he felt Rosensaft's hand on his shoulder and heard "a consoling voice telling me that he could appreciate the way I felt because his wife and family lie buried there." Rosensaft told Posluns, "Do not feel too badly. We must not live in the past; we must live in the future; if we were to dwell in the past, we could not go on living, so we must forget and we are trying to rebuild our lives for the future." It was this spirit that pushed the team to get on with their task and made them "proud of the kinship with those that survived."[5]

The DP camp that was established nearby was the largest predominantly Jewish camp in Germany.

(Another ten thousand Polish former prisoners maintained a separate camp.) Almost eleven thousand survivors lived in a well-organized community that was self-governed and carefully maintained. Although the overcrowded barracks had been designed for only 2,500 residents, the commission later recognized that conditions in Belsen were more tolerable than in many of the other camps they visited. Belsen was also deeply politicized. In most of the DP camps in the British Zone there were ongoing protests against Britain's refusal to open Palestine to survivors and for the creation of a Jewish state.

The political situation was exacerbated by tensions between leaders like Rosensaft, who felt all the survivors should be holding out for entry to Palestine, and those who supported other countries' recruitment programs. The leaders were concerned that if DPs appeared keen to immigrate to other countries, it would undermine their argument for a Jewish home in their own nation. Discussions with camp officials led Shane to believe that survivors wanted "to get out of there and it makes no difference to them where they go and that is in contradiction to the statements made by the Jewish administration of the camp which is completely in the hands of the Zionists."[6] To avoid conflict, the Canadians were advised that it would be wise to undertake their screening of Belsen applicants elsewhere. However, their time in Belsen proved to be an introduction both to the horrors of the Holocaust and to the realities of survival. They returned to Hanover "emotionally upset and ill from the experiences encountered there" and determined to set to work immediately.

By the time the five members of the selection team arrived in Germany in late September 1947, the IRO and the American Jewish Joint Distribution Committee (JDC) had been hard at work finding eligible applicants. They had been told that 2,114 refugees would be permitted into Canada and the team requested that groups of DPs be brought to several examination depots in the British, American, and French Zones of Germany and Austria. Visiting more than a few dozen of the hundreds of DP Camps would take many months and they planned to complete their task by the end of the year. All five had volunteered for this mission. They had jobs and companies to get back to and their travel funding was limited. The team's responsibilities were restricted to testing and selecting candidates based on the government's guidelines. The quotas could easily have been filled in one or two camps, however the Jewish agencies on the ground felt that the presence of the Canadian team would boost morale among the survivors. If even a few DPs from each camp were selected, that would instil some hope in those left behind. If only half of the DPs could be Jews, their odds of escaping the interminable powerlessness of life in the camps were still exponentially better than with Canada's other labour

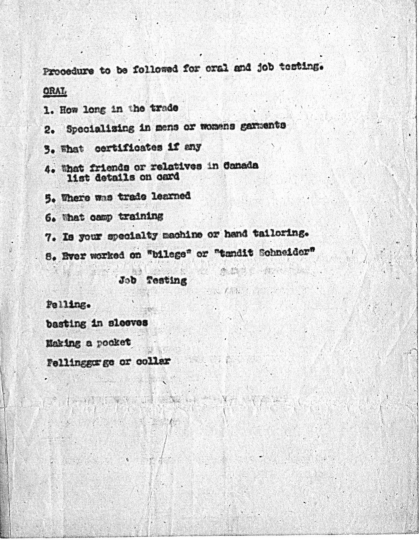

Garment Workers Commission sewing test instructions.

schemes. And so began in earnest what became known in the DP camps as Operation Tailors, Canada.

The first few days of screening took place during the holiday of Sukkot, and several hundred non-Jewish workers were assessed. Jewish applicants from Belsen comprised the next group. All the applicants had to be approved by the military and JDC authorities in the camps. At this early stage, the team set up a testing facility in the nearby Bucholtz camp. Through the JDC, they had access to sewing machines, shears, needles, thimbles, thread, and cloth—all of which were in short supply in war-torn Europe. The five men split their duties between Solomon and Shane, who conducted oral examinations and filled out the necessary forms, and Herbst and Posluns, who conducted the practical tests. Enkin was kept busy arranging the schedules. The test was comprised of the "operations a tailor is called upon to perform daily in the making of a garment; the fitting of a sleeve into the garment-body, the placing of a lapel and collar, the making of buttonholes and the operation on the sewing machine."

The team soon discovered that every applicant either believed they were expert technicians or were certain they could easily learn to be. They found it increasingly hard to deny anyone as the "almost endless tragic procession unfolded" but they also felt that "rules were rules" and they did their best to abide by them. Solomon explained that they also had to check the "medical certificates attached to each application and examine the miniature lung X-ray plate which had to prove the carrier was free from infection in order to be eligible for emigration." Families with more than two children, and married women whose husbands were not qualified, had to be turned away. The commission complained about this to the Canadian immigration representative on the ground and were told that they could pass the larger families on to be considered, but there were no guarantees.

The team's encounters with the Belsen applicants further initiated them into the horrors that the survivors had endured and their unique perspectives on the meaning of life. Solomon recalled meeting a custom tailor who had his own sewing machine and was making a good living outside of the camp. Since the economics of the time had devalued local currencies, he had accumulated a cache of precious jewels through bartering. When Solomon asked him

why in the hell he wants to come to Canada, when he is getting so rich in Germany. He gave me two reasons, goodness. He said he is rich right now, but one can never tell when he will lose his riches together with his life. The other reason is his wife saw her father and mother and five other members of the family murdered. She herself was forced to dig the grave and bury them. She can't cry any more, her tear ducts are dried up.

The first screenings also introduced the team to the challenges of identification. The desire to escape Europe was intense and it was perhaps not surprising to discover DPs attempting various deceits to get on the tailor lists. X-rays would be swapped. Experienced tailors would return to take the tests for their friends. Once the government agents working with the team became aware of these subterfuges, the examiners were forced to "watch their step." They obtained "huge resettlement forms" with photo identification. Anyone caught participating in these impersonations risked rejection. It took half an hour just to fill out the paperwork for each applicant. For this first group, they had eight secretaries working from six in the morning to midnight filling out the forms. Within a week, they managed to approve two hundred non-Jews and three hundred Jews.

The commission realized it would be more efficient to split into two teams to visit as many camps as possible. Deciding how the group would be divided became problematic because they also had a second— even more complicated—agenda to deal with. And it required a level of cooperation between the men that had already begun to unravel. Each was representing a specific group and each came with a list of survivors whom they were expected to include in the project.

In total, these lists held 1,100 names of DPs scattered across the camps. Most were relatives and friends of union members, employees, and members of the associations they represented including the Canadian Jewish Congress (CJC), JIAS, the International Ladies' Garment Workers' Union (ILGWU), and the Jewish Labour Committee (JLC). If just 2,114 people could be selected, then it was clear that only a small percentage on these lists could be included. Every team member was under pressure to locate and screen as many people on their list as they could. Enkin was told that "the finding of these people with special names is almost mandatory. These names represent the hopes and the prayers of a great number of people." He responded that "We of course are going to try and fit the names in somehow." To expedite matters, all the members agreed to consolidate their lists— all, that is, except Bernard Shane.

Shane, a prominent union leader representing the JLC, was more proactive. He attempted to ensure that his list would get priority by sending it to the IRO, reassuring his JLC colleagues that "it is understood they are to get preference."[7] Shane advised his teammates that "his mission to Europe was for greater importance than the Industry's plan, because he was ordered by Dubinsky [the powerful New York leader of the ILGWU] to go overseas on behalf to the JLC—whose special list of names must be given first consideration."

The other union leader on the team, Sam Herbst from Winnipeg, also presented them with challenges. He had been temperamental since his arrival and Enkin had been warned that Herbst had "a fixation that no one is capable of choosing prospective tailors except himself."

Herbst seemed to be holding some kind of grudge against the JLC and the CJC director of Western Canada was unsure if it was ideological or personal, but it played out in his dealings with Shane.[8] The two union representatives quarrelled constantly. Solomon recalled that they "had to be separated. In fact, Shane quarrelled with everyone and became known as the S.O.B." No one wanted to travel with Shane, who had "already fought with every other member of the team and who displayed arrogance, non-cooperation and a sole interest in procuring names on his preferred list. Enkin, therefore, reasoned that the only way to prevent Shane from disrupting the work of the Commission was to have Shane near him, so he could watch him." They decided on a quota system so that every group would get a fair share of applicants from their lists. Solomon made a deal with Shane that as long as he was willing to work with their consolidated list, he could also look out for his people.

Enkin, Herbst, and Shane set out on their own to visit several camps. When they reunited with Solomon and Posluns, they discovered that Shane had completely neglected their list and replaced their numbers with his. In one camp, where they could accept only sixty-five survivors out of 17,500, he had convinced the IRO commandant to squeeze in a further twenty of his group, excluding everyone on the larger list. Shane had his own explanation for this:

> As a trade union leader I had an added responsibility. Members of our union were willing to accept hundreds of DP tailors into the trade provided the relatives of members be given preference. They did not mind sharing their work with their own. But we had to guard against an influx of skilled craftsmen who… would compete for jobs with Canadians. It was a matter of guarding the jobs of our union members and prevent, if possible, threatening to saturate the industry with new help.

This was clearly not the humanitarian approach that the other members of the team espoused. They held a meeting and Solomon recalled that

> there arose harsh words against Shane from the lips of Enkin and Posluns…. The blow-up came. I levelled charges at Shane, accusing him of dishonesty and subversion. Enkin and the others backed me up. Enkin told Shane that

if he did not stop these tactics, a full report would be sent to the Canadian government and the entire project stood a chance of being kicked out. Shane then agreed under pressure to desist from further actions of this kind.

Solomon determined to keep an eye on Shane, Herbst was assigned to travel with Enkin and Posluns, and the two new teams set off on their gruelling mission.

They travelled in small Volkswagens that could barely hold the men, let alone their paperwork and luggage. Sewing machines became too cumbersome, so the tests were simplified. Enkin explained that "we would have them show that they could handle a needle and thread in sewing a buttonhole. It became sort of a joke. The grapevine would pass along—all you gotta do is learn to have a needle and thread and you would get a permit." The examiners became expert at assessing the applicants' abilities within a few minutes. They visited twenty-one cities in twenty-seven days and were screening twelve to fifteen DPs at a time—as many as two hundred on some days. "We tried to be meticulous to our sense of obligation to the government," Enkin recalled. "We didn't want to just make a joke out of it."

Dealing with the quota was emotionally draining. Fifteen to 20 per cent of a camp might come to be tested, but out of four or five hundred DPs, they could only choose fifteen or twenty. "You found yourself like the gods," Enkin explained, noting that the commissioners would have to say, "that you can go but they have to stay, and it was a very soul-searching process of decisions." The team argued with the Canadian officials that excluding widows with children, sixteen- and seventeen-year-old boys, and skilled craftspeople over the age of fifty-five was depriving the industry of capable workers. And they had trouble finding skilled non-Jews—those people could more easily qualify for the other Canadian bulk labour schemes. To compensate, they chose as many married Jewish men with families as possible.[9] Their children, however, could not be older than eighteen. One day a tailor whose son was nineteen confronted Enkin, who advised him that he would be able to sponsor his child once he settled in Canada. "He just looked at me and said: what do you want me to do with my son? We had two daughters—both of them were violated and killed by Germans, and I had to wash and bury them. Do you want me to now wash and bury my son? Are we doomed to stay here?" A young man who passed the test asked if he could bring his brother, who had lost both his legs. There was nothing Enkin could do. "Here were men," he reported, "who would not leave their kinsfolk, even after being offered the opportunity of going. We here in the North American continent callously stand aside and just admit a [trickle] of the most skilled and healthy individuals."

On one of his few days off, Shane visited the

JOSEPH KLINGHOFFER AND MAX ENKIN

Commission members tried to be conscientious about following the restrictions laid down by the department of labour during their selection of garment workers. They were hesitant to bend the rules, even for the most heart-wrenching cases. As Max Enkin explained, "We tried to be meticulous to our sense of obligation to the government. We didn't want to just make a joke out of it." Then one day he was introduced to Dr. Joseph Klinghoffer.

Forty-four-year-old Klinghoffer was raised in Lvov, Poland and educated in Vienna, Heidelberg, and London. Before the war, he had been in charge of the modern language curriculum for the province of Lublin. He was also an officer in the Polish army. In 1941 Joseph and his piano teacher wife, Gisella, fled to Warsaw and acquired false identities. Klinghoffer worked in underground schools organized by the Polish resistance and translated nightly BBC radio transmissions for the underground press. Joseph and Gisella survived many close calls during the war and, after liberation, they discovered that their entire families had perished.

Seeing no future for Jews in Poland, the Klinghoffers made their way to Austria, where Joseph eventually found a position with the Jewish Immigrant Aid Society (JIAS). From there, his language skills led him to a job with the Canadian consul in Salzburg around the time that the Garment Workers Commission was interviewing prospective immigrants. One day, Joseph approached one of the Canadian officials, asking, "Does Canada need only tailors and furriers, they don't need one intellectual maybe?" He was told that he should seek out Enkin and, if he agreed, the consul would "close his eyes and give me a visa." Joseph met with Max the next day. "I was very honest with him," he said. "I asked him 'couldn't you do something for me and select me as a tailor'…. Mr. Enkin got mad at me for that. He says, 'What do you suggest, Dr. Klinghoffer, that I cheat my own government for…your sake?'" Joseph responded that he had been very honest with him. "I told you I am no tailor. The only thing that I know is for sewing on a button…If you can't do anything, I'm sorry." Much later Max told Joseph that he had had a very sleepless night. Enkin recalled, "I thought for a little while. Here is a man whose only penalty for not being a tailor was that he was a qualified English professor. And I took his name and I spoke to the official," explaining that "we need in industry people of executive material as well as just pure industrial workers. I will personally take responsibility to see that he's placed."

The next morning Enkin called Klinghoffer and said, "Didn't you mention to me that you can sew buttons on? I say, 'I think I can.' He says, 'You know we need in our tailor's profession people who sew buttons on. Would you like to pass an exam?'" Joseph went to the examination centre and when Max saw him he said, "'Oh, you, Klinghoffer, you already had your examination!' I didn't deny it. I didn't say yes, I didn't say no.... The next day I find myself on the list of tailors to Canada."

The Klinghoffers arrived in 1948. Joseph was immediately hired by the CJC to run the reception centre for child survivors who had been settled in Toronto. He then served as director of education and culture for the CJC for twenty-three years. Joseph never worked one day as a tailor.

He died at the age of ninety-seven. On his tombstone is the following inscription: "A Cultured Man of Integrity, Modesty and Charm, He Lived a Life of Achievement and Tragedy." As Max Enkin remarked, the Jewish community was "better off for having Professor Klinghoffer in Canada."[1]

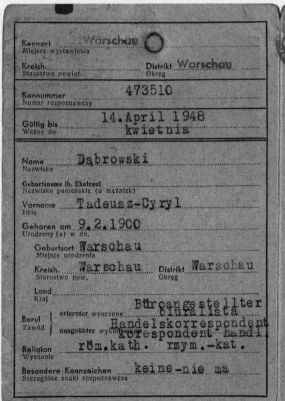  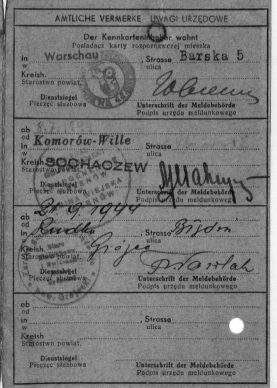

Dr. Joseph Klinghoffer's fake identification as Tadeusz Cyryl Dabrowski, April 14, 1943. Joseph used this pseudonym while he was living in Warsaw (Poland) working for the Polish resistance.

synagogue in Emberg, near Stuttgart. The rabbi seized the opportunity to ask questions about the test and plead the case of survivors who were not living in the camps. Shane explained that the commission believed that the need to emigrate was more urgent for the Jews in the camps. That night the synagogue was transformed into a tailors' workshop where the congregation's experienced tailors became "professors." The next day the entire Jewish community of Emberg appeared at the examination site demanding to be tested. "It was unbelievable," Shane recalled, "but there they were. The very same butchers, carpenters, painters, peddlers, grocerymen, all of them and their wives, suddenly as though visited at night by some gentle fairy tale who taught them the trade while asleep."[10] This placed the team in a very difficult position. They knew that "the rabbi's intentions were honorable and humane" but doubted that "even a benign angel could teach tailoring in the space of a couple of hours." Although the team could not accept any of this group, the episode convinced them that "the Jews now living in Germany find every moment in that country an eternity." As they left, the rabbi made this last plea: "Get us out of here before we perish."

The selection teams worked long hours, some days going without sleep, commenting privately in letters home about their poor rations and discomforts. While Solomon wrote that he'd lost twenty-two pounds,

Shane quipped his "only complaint is that I can't reduce on such a diet because of the amount of potatoes." They knew they had it easy compared to the DPs. Enkin thought that some of the camps in Austria would not have passed the Geneva Convention with regard to the treatment of prisoners of war. With fifteen to twenty people in one barely heated room, surrounded by mud and slush, he wrote,

we who had adequate warm clothes and certainly had much better resistance than a DP could barely stand a day working in these unheated buildings, but at least at night we had a hotel room that was partly heated. How these people will stand this day after day, week after week, is beyond our perception. It is no wonder that the TB rate is rising, and if the people are not moved from these camps many will be buried there.

They were deeply disturbed by the 1,500-calorie-a-day rations in the camps. Children were served their meals first to ensure that they were not starving. "The sight of these children eating their soup," wrote Shane, "the intensity with which they licked every drop left in the bowl and the disappointment at not being able to get a second helping is the most pitiful sight we had to witness during our journey." At the ORT vocational training school in a camp near Salzburg, "the bitter cold in the rooms made the job of examining unbearable. Candidates were unable to thread needles; frozen fingers and blue hands were unable to operate the machines. But despite all these handicaps a number were chosen and we anxiously awaited the moment to get a place with more heat."

In other camps where conditions were better, they witnessed the remarkable ingenuity and industriousness of the survivors. In Feldafing, for example, Shane was "particularly touched" by their tailor shop, which was "unlike any tailor shop I have ever seen. No clothes are manufactured here. But hundreds of garments are being 'renovated' by being turned inside out; worn-out clothes of older persons are being re-cut for children…. A piece of new material and the garments made of it are allocated to those whose clothes have been worn to shreds." In the mechanic shop, DPs were using derelict military vehicles to build cars "of a Thousand Different Parts." Every camp visit brought new meaning to the word survivor.

By the time they were finished, the team had examined more than five thousand applicants and, in the end, they selected about three thousand to allow for the inevitable rejections by immigration and medical authorities—they estimated that as many as perhaps one-third of those chosen would not be accepted.[11] With the addition of dependants, some six thousand refugees eventually came to Canada as part of the Tailor Project. As far as they knew at this point, only half of them would be Jews.

Upon his return to Toronto, Sam Posluns gave several speeches about his experiences. He wanted his audiences to understand that the Jews of Europe did not fit the common stereotype of "the poor remnants of a decimated people." Posluns had expected to find people who had been so damaged by "suffering and torment that they would become bitter and ruthless rebels against civilization." But he told Canadians that the DPs he met "were kind and considerate…keen in mind…who know what they want. They want the right to rebuild their lives and their families and to live as you and I." He believed that the survivors comprised the "foundation of a people that will rise again, and if given the opportunity will make their full contribution to the world." All the commission team members were anxious to impress this message upon their communities. Once they arrived in Canada, the tailors and their families would need the full support of the Jewish community to ease their settlement and integrate them into their new country. This turned out to be a much more challenging task than anyone expected.

Mendel Good (centre) with other survivors
on the USS *General M.B. Stewart*, heading to
Canada in 1948.

MENDEL GOOD

When I registered as a tailor in the Bad Gastein DP camp, the gentleman who interviewed me asked me in German, "Are you a tailor?" He was wondering because I was so young. I said yes, so he opened my file and read through it. Then he said, "Are you sure you're a tailor?" And again, I answered yes. By that time I wanted to get out of Europe so badly. Trying to trip me up, he asked, "Could you"—in German they don't say sewing, they say stitching—"Could you stitch a suit out of sand?" Once more I said yes. "How are you going to do it?" he asked and I answered, "If you cut it for me, I'll stitch it." He immediately got up from his chair and stamped my papers. "Young man," he said, "you're going to Canada. We need guys like you. It doesn't matter if you're a tailor, yes or no, but we need you in Canada."

I WAS BORN MENDEL AFTERGUT on March 26, 1925 in Nowy Sącz, Poland—in Jewish (Yiddish), we called it Tsantz. It was a beautiful city between Kraków and Tarnow and about a third of the population was Jewish. My father ended up working as both a baker and a cobbler—when my mother's father died, my father added his father-in-law's cobbling business to his baking. It was a happy environment to grow up in. The strong sense of Jewish identity that my parents gave all of us kept me going through everything I went through in the war.

I was fourteen when the Germans arrived in our town and forced all the Jews to live in a ghetto there. I was in two different ghettos—the one in my hometown and then one in Tarnow. After that I was in one forced labour camp after another.

I escaped from the first labour camp—it was not far from Tarnow, in a place called Rożnów. It was really terrible there. We lived in what had been a pigsty and we had to work exceedingly hard. They were erecting the first electrical transformer in Poland and we had to move all the building materials. It was so bad and there was no ceiling. The pigs should have slept in that place. After about three weeks there, I managed to loosen the boards beside my bed by banging my head against them. I slipped outside, into the forest, and just kept going, intending to go home. All of a sudden, through the darkness, I saw two lit candles glowing in a window and I realized what they were: it was Friday evening, Shabbat! And I knew that Jewish women, as the heads of the home, lit two candles to usher in Shabbat.

I made my way through the woods to get to that house. It still makes me laugh to remember that there were four animals, running past me on my way. They stopped and looked at me, and then kept going. I found out later that they weren't wild animals, they belonged to somebody and were heading back to where they lived. I knocked on the door of the house and heard the husband get up and take a few steps. But it was the wife who opened the door just a couple of inches. She must have recognized me because she opened the door a little wider and she called out, "Mendeleh!" Then the husband came jumping down the few steps from the bedroom and when he saw me, he hugged me so hard that he almost broke my neck. "Mendeleh!" he said, just like his wife, and started to cry. "I was there at your circumcision," he sobbed. "I was at your bar mitzvah!" And who was the man? He was a milkman who used to deliver milk two or three times a week to my house, to my family's bakery. The couple fed me and let me stay

there overnight. From there, I made my way home.

As I said, I was in a lot of different camps from 1943 to 1945—Płaszów, Mauthausen, Melk, Ebensee. That's where I was liberated in 1945, in Ebensee.

After the war, I stayed in Austria because I had tuberculosis. Austria was the right place for me because there were the mountains and fresh air. That's actually the reason I didn't go to Israel; people talked me out of it because the weather in Israel would have been terrible for me after all I had gone through in the camps. I did go later…but not to live.

I spent almost three years in hospitals right after the war. I'll tell you, we were very, very lucky to have had the man we did as Commander in Chief of US Forces of Occupation in Austria. I even remember his name, Mark Clark. In one of the most beautiful places in Austria, Bad Gastein, he confiscated five hotels and he put us—the survivors—into those hotels. That helped a lot. I wouldn't be here today if I hadn't been in Bad Gastein, with the fresh air and the waterfalls. The people with me there were young, like I was; no old people had survived. There were also a lot of Russian Jews.

The hotels were used as kind of DP camps, since we were all displaced persons. But it was no comparison to the kind of camps I'd been in before. We were living in hotels, being served by other people. And they made sure that we had good food because we had to get better. Somebody asked me one day how much I weighed right after the war. Well, nobody ever weighed me, but all I know is that when I was in the hospital, the nurse would come and put her two hands under me, put me on a table, make the bed, put her hands under me again, and move me back to the bed. I couldn't have weighed very much.

I was in the hospital until almost the end of 1947 and then into regular quarters in Bad Gastein. A commission from Canada came to the camp looking for tradespeople, so I registered with them as a tailor. When I'd first gone back to Nowy Sącz after escaping from Rożnów, my father asked a tailor friend of his to take me on as his apprentice and I learned a little bit from him. Later, I was in a concentration camp in Płaszów—with huge barracks that were called in German a *Großschneiderei*, a tailoring place—and I did some work there.

After I was interviewed by the commission people and approved to go to Canada, there were medical tests. I remember having many, many X-rays. And I even remember the name of the professor who looked after me for at least two years, when I had TB—his name was Weidinger. The important thing was that I passed the medical tests.

I travelled from Austria through Germany to the port of Bremen where I boarded a ship called the USS *General M.B. Stewart* with other refugees. The first couple of days of the voyage from Europe to Halifax were pretty miserable. I was sick for the first two days but, after that, I settled. We arrived in Halifax on September 8, 1948, and were met by a man from the immigration department, a Mr. Hochgemein. Fortunately, he spoke many languages, so we could communicate with him, and he gave each of us a number for the very long train that was waiting to take us to other parts of Canada. While I was waiting beside the train, a Ukrainian fellow came over and asked me if I would mind changing numbers with him, which would mean that I would have to move to another part of the train. What in the world did I care which part of the train I was in? I was twenty-three years old and had no idea about Canada. The only thing I knew about Canada was what I learned in Grade 11 or 12: that there were igloos and "Eskimos." That's all I knew about Canada! I didn't know the name of any cities or anything. So I changed numbers with him. What did I care?

The train arrived in the outskirts of Montreal and we were taken to army barracks where we slept overnight. When we got up in the morning, we had breakfast, and then we all went outside. There was maybe six or eight people from the Canadian Jewish Congress. I didn't speak a word of English or a word of French. Mr. Hochgemein, who'd travelled with us, called out people's numbers to board different trains until I was the only one left. Little did I know that during the train from Halifax to Montreal, they had disconnected quite a few of the train cars. He yelled at me, "Did you pull a shtick on me?" I asked him what he meant and he said, "Is this the number I gave you?" When I said no, he said, "Do you have any idea who you exchanged that number with?" I answered that I didn't, that some guy had just come over to me and asked if I wanted to exchange tickets. Well, he was furious and jabbed his finger at me, yelling, "No wonder you befriended me and ate my food!" I protested that I wasn't trying to put anything over on anyone. It turned out that the guy who had asked me to change numbers with him was a Ukrainian poet. He'd wanted to go to Vancouver because there were a lot of Ukrainians there. But little did he know that the whole train station in Montreal was decorated with flowers for him, and that a dinner had been planned for him. I couldn't convince Mr. Hochgemein that I hadn't pulled a shtick on him. I didn't; I couldn't care less where I went.

The barracks were closed by then, so, when Mr. Hochgemein left, I laid down with my little suitcase, my head resting against this gigantic boulder in front of the building. All I had with me in that suitcase was some underwear and a couple of shirts. People passing by spoke to me in French and English, but I didn't understand any of it. I just stayed there—I didn't know where else to go. The following afternoon, a taxi pulled up and Mr. Hochgemein got out. Pointing his finger at me again, he said in Yiddish, "You pulled a shtick on me, eh?" I repeated that I hadn't. He then told me that he lived in Ottawa and worked in the immigration department. I didn't know what Ottawa meant but he continued, "I'm going to take you with me to Ottawa. I phoned a friend of mine, Mr. Ben Fleisher and asked him to give you a job."

So that's how I ended up working as a tailor in Ottawa. Mr. Fleisher was a tailor who was well into his eighties and I managed to bluff my way into the job. To be honest, I told him in Yiddish, "Mr. Fleisher, I come from the Old Country. And the way we worked in the Old Country I'm sure is not the same way you work in Canada. The only thing I ask is that you show me once what to do and you'll be satisfied." I did everything he showed me and he was very happy. There had been a fellow working there six months before, a tailor much older than I was, who'd had problems with the old man because Mr. Fleisher only wanted to work the way he worked at home. He was happier showing me what to do.

The old man had two sons and two daughters; one son was named Ben and the other son was Gordie. They practically adopted me. As soon as I arrived, Ben said, "It's okay. I'll give him a job." They were running a made-to-measure in their living room, mostly for the military. I've never met an individual with such heart and feelings as Ben; we became very close. I worked on the made-to-measure clothing, mostly doing alterations and adjustments. Flesher's son did a lot of military work, but he didn't do the sewing. He just took the measurements and had the work done in Montreal and Toronto. In Toronto, he dealt with Levine, and in Montreal, with two or three different places.

The old man spoke Yiddish, but not the two boys—they only spoke English. I used to have fun with them, saying, "I speak Polish, I speak Yiddish, I speak Hebrew, I speak German, and I'm going to learn English." During lunch, I used to run to the library and look at picture books so I could compare the pictures with the text to work on my English.

I was with Ben Fleisher for a year and a half, earning eighteen dollars a week, and I paid the Philipsons fifteen dollars for room and board. I also found two tailors who between them gave me three extra hours a week in the evenings. So at night I went to the two other tailors, working for Ben Fleisher from nine o'clock in the morning to one o'clock—or noon on Sunday. At the place where I worked at night for three hours, I worked with the man's son, Norman. After a while, Norman went out on his own and offered me a job. Can you imagine? I went from earning eighteen dollars a week to fifty dollars a week. I quit the other jobs to work with Norman's father, Sam.

About this same time, I saw that the Ottawa High School of Commerce was advertising English classes in the evening. The very first night that I went to the

Mendel Good and his son Bernie in front of his store near Ottawa's Byward Market.

school, I saw a girl who made my knees go weak. Shy, I'm not, so I walked over to this young lady, took her hand, and introduced myself. She had a friend with her, and they were both Hungarian. Her friend told her not to bother with me because I was a *piszkos* Polack (meaning in Hungarian, that I was dirty Polack). I guess she thought that I was Polish because I had blond hair. But I knew a bit of Hungarian and answered, "Nem vagyok koszos Polak, én vagyok a piszkos zsidó." (I'm not a dirty Polack, I am a dirty Jew.) That beautiful girl—I found out that her name was Valerie Blau—laughed and allowed me to take her home on the bus that night. Valerie and I were married two and a half years later, in 1951, and, believe it or not, we were married for sixty-seven years. My wife was also a Holocaust survivor, born in 1929 in Tarpa, Hungary. She was such a wonderful person, and so beautiful. She died in August 2016. I loved her so much. I don't think there's been a night in sixty-seven years that I haven't thought about her.

Three and a half years after Valerie and I got married, I went into business for myself. At the beginning, I did made-to-measure but I was having a hard time making a living because making a suit or a coat took four or five weeks by the time it was all sewn up. So I decided to add alterations and picked up thirty-two accounts—stores that needed me to do alterations. I was a block away from the market—at 343 Dalhousie Street. That was a key area in Ottawa. I ended up employing nine people and was very, very successful. I had that business for forty-eight years.

After I'd been in Canada for five years, I got a letter telling me to come and pick up my citizenship papers. When I did, I got a surprise. My original last name was Aftergut, so I should have been one of the first people called since my name started with A and it was done alphabetically. I waited and waited, but the judge didn't call me. Finally, at the end I walked over and showed her my letter, asking why I hadn't been called. That was when the judge told me that my name wasn't Aftergut anymore, it was Good. I really felt bad when I heard that because I was still hoping that somebody from my family would be searching for me. The judge could see that I was upset, but she said that changing my name back would take three or four years. So the Canadian government just circumcised my name; they cut it in half.

Valerie and I had three children, Bernie, Beverly, and Gloria, and I wanted my children to have what I didn't have. I was a Hebraist—I studied Hebrew. I regretted the education I lost during the war and read and studied as much as I could throughout my life in Ottawa. All my children went to Hebrew school. My son went to Montreal to finish Hebrew high school, Gloria went to Toronto, and my oldest daughter, Beverly, went to New York, to Stern College. After my son finished the Hebrew high school, he went to Jerusalem to study.

I chaired a group of twenty Holocaust survivors in Ottawa for twelve years. I also organized a gathering of Holocaust survivors on Parliament Hill in 1985. On that occasion I spoke for half an hour—even though I'd just come out of hospital—and I spoke the whole time about Canada. I thanked Canada for opening the door at least a little and giving us the opportunity— for the first times in our lives—to start a normal life, to find beautiful wives, to have children and educate them, children who have gotten married and given us grandchildren. Many of them have become professors and doctors and engineers. For my last words, I turned to the Peace Tower, raised my right arm, and thanked the Peace Tower for giving us peace for the first time in our lives. There were five thousand people there. It was something.

I ended up meeting two very important people through my work in Holocaust education. The first was Bora Laskin, chief justice of the Supreme Court of Canada—he was Jewish and spoke Yiddish better than I do—and the other one was the governor of the Bank of Canada, Louis Rasminsky. They both called me by my first name and asked me to call them by their first names. I'm very honoured by that.

I was in business for forty-eight years and I had no problem whatsoever with anybody. My best friend was a fellow named Johnny, who was Irish. I had another friend, Gordie Johnson, who was half French and half English. But I was invited one night to an event at the Catholic University of Ottawa—now Saint Paul University—to debate the question: Could the Holocaust happen again? The answer is, it could. I have never personally bumped into any antisemitism in Canada, but where do you have no antisemitism?

Eventually, my age and my background caught up with me and I had to sell my business. It got to the point that every time I bent down to take a measurement, I'd end up on the floor. My knees just went under me. At the age of seventy-eight, I had already sold my business, so I moved to Toronto to be closer to my children and grandchildren.

I have to say, my life turned out better than I could have imagined. I have been able to raise my family in the most beautiful country in the world. I am proud of what I have been able to accomplish and proud of every single member of my family. We remember the past but live with hope in the present and a sense of optimism about the future.

FAYE KIEFFER

It wasn't easy when we arrived. We came without money, without being able to speak the language, without family. It wasn't easy, but we were free. We weren't persecuted. We had rights, like anybody else. We were very happy. I remember when we got our citizenship, we made a big party. Oh! To belong somewhere! Do you know what it means that you are a citizen, that you have papers, that you can travel somewhere? It was completely different. I was thankful for it every minute, and I'm thankful for it today.

I WAS BORN FANIA WOLPIANSKA on April 3, 1928, in Bieniakonie—a small town in what was then northeastern Poland. The closest big city was Vilna, about fifty-five kilometres away. My father, Nachum, worked at the large mill owned by his family and my mother, Sarah, owned a delicatessen. My mother was a very independent woman and always made sure she could support herself. She read to me and my brother and sister constantly, and the house was always full of books. My sister, Rachel, was born in 1931 and my brother, Israel, was born in 1935.

There were both Poles and Jews living in Bieniakonie; the population was divided about half and half. Most of the people in the town were artisans, bakers, tailors, and grocery store owners. Once a week, the farmers came to sell their goods in the marketplace, and people from Vilna would bring readymade clothes to sell.

Our family wasn't religious, but we did attend Hebrew school three times a week after school. I don't remember experiencing any antisemitism until we started school—that's where we were definitely made to feel unequal and different, bullied and picked on. What was even worse, there was nobody to complain to, nobody willing to defend us.

In 1939, when the Germans invaded Poland, our part of the country came under Russian rule. We were so happy to see the Russians because we knew what we could expect from the Nazis—we had read all about

Faye Kieffer, age eighteen, in 1946

what was happening in Germany. The main difference for us is that my father's family mill was taken over by the state, although my father continued to work there. And I learned Russian, in addition to the Yiddish and Polish that we spoke at home.

We really thought that everything would be fine, and it was—until June 21, 1941, when the Germans attacked the Soviet Union. Two days later, they were in Bieniakonie. Right away, we weren't allowed to go to school, and a month later we had to start wearing yellow armbands. They put big yellow Stars of David on our houses. Non-Jewish people stopped coming to visit. Everyone was afraid.

On May 11, 1942, the Germans made an announcement over the loudspeakers for all the Jews to assemble in the marketplace to have their documents checked. But when we got there, more Germans and Lithuanians came with machine guns. They started dividing everyone up. My family, for some reason, was sent over to the left, but my grandparents, friends, and everyone else we knew were sent straight ahead. As soon as they were out of sight, we started hearing shots. I could hear the shots and the screams. The remaining people were split up again, going straight ahead or to the right. Again, we heard shooting. All the people who walked straight ahead were shot immediately. During the night, the Germans had ordered the firemen from around the area to dig ditches, so they were ready. It didn't take long

to kill twelve hundred people. My whole family—except my father, my mother, my sister, and my brother—and all our friends, everybody was gone.

Our family, again for an unknown reason, was pushed to the right. That night, my father said that we had to leave—there was no telling when the Germans would decide to finish us off. So, the five of us left town. We walked at night and hid in the daytime. My father knew many of the farmers in the area and some were willing to hide us—in one place, they hid us where they had hidden their pig from the Germans; it was full of water and frogs. But the farmer couldn't feed us, so my mother and father had to sneak out at night to look for food. We stayed there for a while, until it got too dangerous. So, we started walking again.

By this time, it was the summer of 1942. We found shelter in various places before ending up in a small labour camp. When that camp was dissolved, we were taken by truck to the large ghetto in Vilna. They just dumped us out of the truck and left us on the street. We managed to find a cousin of my mother who was a violinist in the Vilna orchestra. We couldn't live in her home, though, because there were so many people there.

Every day in Vilna I was expected to work—I was tall for my age, even though I was only fourteen. The good thing about being able to work is that, every day that I worked, I was given a piece of bread. First, I was put to work digging ditches for the Germans to hide their artillery. Our guard must have been from a mental institution because he screamed at us from morning to sundown. He had a special whip made out of leather with knots tied at the ends. Seeing blood seemed to give him great satisfaction—it would calm him down. Every day, somebody was beaten bloody. And one day it was my turn. According to him, my shovel wasn't full enough, so he gave me one strike with his whip that was so hard it broke the bone behind my ear, and then he beat my back and legs until I they bled. I had to walk six kilometres back to the ghetto, all beaten up. But the next day, I had to go back to work to get my piece of bread. That's just the way it was.

My brother, Israel, was seven when we arrived in Vilna. He was a born genius. When we were in the ghetto, plenty of teachers used to come and listen to him. They gave him hard mathematical problems and he'd solve them in a second. Israel said to me many times, "I won't survive, but you will. Remember, as long as you live, to tell the story of what one human being can do to the other. Don't forget to tell. People should know what's going on."

One day, my mother didn't return from work. She was just gone. My father was so shocked that I couldn't talk to him anymore. Then, not long after, I came back from work to find that the rest of my family was gone. There was nobody left. I didn't know where they were,

or what had happened to them. So I decided that when I went to work the next day, I would run away. I knew that it was dangerous, but I told myself, "Whatever will be, will be." I made sure I had my lunch—bread and watery soup—and then after lunch, I took off. I just started walking. I had no idea where I was. A truck with two young Polish boys stopped and offered me a lift, saying, "We can see you don't know where you're going. You're heading to the killing place. Come with us and we'll take you out of the city."

I gave them money that my cousin had given me, bribing them to not turn me in, but I didn't trust them. When they let me out of the truck I went in the opposite direction from where they told me to go. I managed to hide myself from the police, but I knew that I couldn't stay there. I started walking again, but only at night. I still had no idea where I was. I had nobody to talk to. Nobody to ask a question. I hid wherever I could—in a hole, under trees. Mostly under fir trees because their branches hung down. The rattlesnakes and the field mice were my company. I spoke to them. And I was jealous of them, because they were free. At night, if I was lucky, I would find a barn with a cow in it so I could get a little bit of milk. I begged for food, and sometimes people gave me something.

That whole winter, in 1943—when I was fifteen years old—I lived in the forest, scrounging for food and hiding. One day, I must have fallen asleep under a fir tree with my legs sticking out because I was woken up to the sound of two men in Polish saying, "We've got one!" They pulled me out from under the tree and brutally raped me. I didn't know anything about sex. I think I must have fainted. When I came to, I was alone again and bleeding. I got up and ran under another tree, making sure that my feet were well hidden. And I carried on, walking at night and hiding during the day.

I continued walking until I saw a little house with a little light in it. I was so tired and hungry that I was willing to take a chance. I knocked on the door and, can you believe it, the young man who opened the door— his name was Michael—recognized my family name. His mother, who had passed away six months ago, had told him that if anybody from my family showed up at their door, he should take them in and hide them. Apparently, my grandparents had helped them during the Depression, given them food and clothes, and they had never forgotten. In the barn, Michael created a little hole in the hay where I could lie down and hide. I stayed there for a while until one day, while Michael and I were talking in the barn, somebody started banging loudly on the door. I ran back up to my little hiding place in the hay loft and Michael opened the door. A man standing there, a neighbour, demanded to know whether Michael and his family were hiding Jews. He denied it but the man didn't believe him and argued for a while before leaving. When he'd gone, Michael told

me that I'd have to run because he knew that man well and knew that he wouldn't waste any time in bringing the police. He told me to keep heading west until I came to a swamp. On the other side of the swamp were partisans who would take me in. I didn't even know what a swamp was, but there was no time to ask.

I ran as fast as I could until I came to a little shed, and I hid there until dark. When it got dark, I kept going in the direction that Michael had told me to go. I couldn't see a thing and had no idea where I was. Suddenly, boom! I fell into some water. Even though I was soaking wet and freezing—it was the late in the fall of 1943—I forced myself to keep going farther and farther through the water. By this time, I was so tired, and the sound of the coyotes and the wolves howling all night almost drove me crazy. Eventually I found myself on dry ground and fell asleep.

When I opened my eyes in the morning, I could see that I was lying on a little patch of earth covered with a few very thin trees. I could see more dry land across the water, but I was stuck. So I went back to sleep and was roused in the morning by a tall man who told me not to be afraid, that he was a spy for the partisans and knew how to get across the swamp. He said that his house was in the forest and he would take me there before taking me to the partisans in the Rudnicki forest. I had no choice but to trust this man. When I tried to get to my feet, I found that my boots were full of water that had frozen during the night. The movement pulled the skin off my legs with the ice. The man had to carry me to his house on his back because I couldn't walk. I'll never forget what it was like when we got there. His wife was making pancakes. Oh! the smell of the pancakes in that cozy house. The man's wife got my boots off and did her best to bandage my skin. There were no medications in the house, nothing, but she got some clean linen cloths and put a flour mixture on my legs that burned like fire. I didn't have any other shoes, but she got some rags and cut up a sweater to make a pair of shoes for me.

After I'd eaten, the man took me to the partisans. We went to the Russian compound first, but they wouldn't take me because, according to them, I looked like a German spy. So he told me about a Jewish partisan compound with people who had run away from the ghettos. When we got there, what do you think? I found somebody from my hometown! These partisans took me in.

I went through a lot of pain until my feet and legs healed. It was very, very painful. We slept in a hole in the ground lined with straw—six of us in one hole. There were quite a few people in the Jewish partisan group. They'd leave the camp at night to get food and do their military work. Many of them got killed. Many of them were injured from fighting with the Germans, with the Ukrainians, with the Lithuanians. The Ukrainians and the Lithuanians were all working with the Germans. It

was very, very hard. That was the life in the forest. There were very few young women with the partisans.

When we were liberated by the Red Army near the end of April 1944, I couldn't stop laughing—I remember kissing a soldier, my first time, when I saw that we were free. On the second or third day, when we were still in the woods, I got such terrible pains in my stomach that I was screaming my head off. We were fifty kilometres from Vilna and two guys took turns carrying me there on their backs. A doctor examined me and said that I had appendicitis, that they had to operate right away. But they didn't have any anesthetic. They'd have to operate without it. But I didn't care—that's how much pain I was in. But they did it.

On my second day in Vilna, the Germans started bombing the city. We heard an announcement over the hospital loudspeakers that anyone who could run to the basement should. I got out of bed—the day after my surgery—and ran down. I don't know where I got the strength. I guess it was just the willpower to live. When I got back to my room, my whole bed was covered in glass from the shattered windows. I stayed in the hospital for a while until they could take out the stitches. When I decided to go home, I realized that I had no place to go. I didn't know anybody in that big city.

In 1944, the trains weren't running yet. So, I walked out to the edge of the city. A truck came by full of Russian soldiers and I stopped them and asked in Russian whether they were heading in the direction of my town. They said yes and invited me to climb in. They let me out in Bieniakonie and kept going. It was about six o'clock in the evening and already dusk. It was awful. There was nobody there. The Jewish homes had been broken into, with no windows or doors. Nobody was there. I was alone again and thought to myself, why did I fight so hard to live? Then I remembered a neighbour of ours, a Polish woman who was a very fine person. When I got to her house, she took me in like a child, like her own. She didn't have any children of her own. She said that I could stay with her.

Of the maybe six hundred Jewish people who had lived in our town, fourteen had survived. They were all older than I was and living together in one house. I decided to stay where I was, with our Polish neighbour. I wanted to go to school. I wanted to be a dentist. Stalin was letting Poles leave what was now Soviet territory and go west, but I didn't want to go. The older Jewish survivors convinced me that I should, saying, "You don't know what Stalin could decide to do tomorrow. It's a dictatorship. He could close the borders and you'd never be able to leave." I thought about it and realized that I didn't have anyone left in Bieniakonie. We all left together to go to Poland. We were free to go. But when we got to the city of Lodz, everybody went their own way and I was left alone again.

Jewish organizations in Canada and the United States had started helping survivors in Europe and they funded a Jewish Committee in Lodz to do what they could for people. It wasn't a DP camp; it was just a place where a lot of survivors had congregated after liberation. I remember going once a day to the soup kitchen there. I met a lady there who knew my family, and she took me in. She didn't have anything and I didn't have anything, so we used to go together to the soup kitchen for a meal.

Another thing that the Jewish Committee helped with, through the Red Cross, was posting a list of the names that other survivors—especially people in the DP camps—had sent out looking for family members. Every day, I went just to look at the list of names. Maybe somebody was looking for me. And then, one day, I was reading down the list of names and found that my mother was looking for me! I was so shocked that I fainted. Imagine! Being alone, having nobody and, all of a sudden, finding that my mother had survived! A young woman who was there asked, "Are you Sarah's daughter? I was with her in the concentration camp, and we were liberated together. I'll give you the address where your mother is."

This is something that would be so hard for other people to understand. To be alone and go through such a hell, and then to find your mother. My mother was alive, and she was in Germany! She was in Bergen-Belsen. It had been one of the really terrible concentration camps, a forced labour camp, but now it was a DP camp. My mother had been in Auschwitz. I'm not sure how, but somebody in one of the Jewish organizations was able to arrange to get me Greek identity papers. They told us that they would get a group of us to the Czech border. And, since I was supposedly Greek now, with Greek papers, I was told that I shouldn't say one word in Polish or Russian. Nothing. The less I said, the better. Because we were still in Poland, and Poland was now occupied by the Russians. They took us to a train and when we got on, I showed them the Greek papers, indicating that we were going back home to Greece.

All of the Jewish organizations were doing this. They wanted to help get Jews out of Poland because the Communists were pretty bad, too.

So now I had my mother's address. The Jewish organization took us to Bratislava, in Czechoslovakia, where we stayed in a terrible hotel. Then one day, a man came to take us to the Austrian border. We would have to cross the border to go into Germany. It was all completely illegal, but we had to try. I remember that it was such a foggy day you couldn't see the person next to you. It was also very slippery and I fell—I actually fell onto the Austrian side! There was an American soldier standing there and I knew that he turned people back across the border to Czechoslovakia. I was so scared that's what he'd do to me. "You have to go back," he said. "You have to go back." He was speaking English

and I had no idea what he was talking about. He tried to show me by gesturing that he wanted me to go back across the border. I looked at him and thought, he looks a little Jewish. So I decided to try speaking Jewish to him. If he understood, okay. If he didn't, he didn't.

I asked him if he spoke any Yiddish and he replied, "A little." So, I explained to him what was happening— that I thought I had lost everybody but I'd found my mother. He said, "Okay, come with me." He took me to the station on the American side. First, though, he gave me a piece of chocolate. I had forgotten what it tasted like! Then, he took me to their camp, where they gave me white bread. We didn't have white bread in Europe, but I ate it. I couldn't make out what it was—it wasn't sweet enough to be cake and it wasn't like any bread I'd ever seen. But whatever it was, it was good. When I told him that I didn't have any shoes, they found a pair for me. And he gave me a note from the American military government saying that I could travel on the train without paying. It was all official, with a seal.

Finally, I got to where my mother was. I had the address, but I didn't want to give her a shock, so I sent somebody in to find her. There were maybe six women in one small room. They were living in what had been the German officers' quarters. What had been individual rooms were now doubled up, with two women per room. As I've said, my mother was a very smart lady. As soon as the man asked for her by name, she immediately said, "Do you know something about Faye?" When he said yes, she asked, "Is she alive?" Just like that. He said, "Yes, she is and I'll take you to her."

In a nearby building, we just sat across from each other, staring at each other. We couldn't say a word. It took a long time until we could speak. My mother later told me that she had forgotten what I looked like. "When I was liberated," she said, "I used to sit in the window and look for you. I knew you had blond hair. I knew that you had blue eyes. So, whenever I saw a girl approximately your age, I was always thinking, is it you?"

She told me what had happened to her. The Germans had come into the ghetto in Vilna to get people for work. They took them away to a concentration camp in Estonia where they had to cut huge trees and send them by water to Germany. Later, they brought the families to Estonia, too. They brought the children to my mother. My father was in the men's camp. He would come to look at her through the fence. When a German guard saw what my father was doing, he beat him up and shot him right there. Right in front of my mother. It was a terrible camp. One day, a German guard was hitting my mother and my brother said, "Quit hitting my mother. You won't win the war." This German was so angry that he gave my brother a push right in the stomach with his heavy boots. Then the guard beat up my mother.

After a year, they took them from Estonia to Auschwitz. When they got to Auschwitz, the orchestra was playing. They took them off the train, the cattle cars, separated the children from my mother, and gave them chocolate milk to drink. My brother could see that it was a trick. They gave them the chocolate milk and then took them to the showers. My mother never saw him again. My sister and my brother, that was the day they killed them. They gassed them. My mother was in Auschwitz until January 1945, when the Germans forced the remaining survivors on a death march from Poland to Germany, to Bergen-Belsen. Mother said that thousands had died on the road. Nobody had the strength to walk many miles. She said getting to Bergen-Belsen was the worst because they weren't taking you there to work. People were just left there to starve to death.

After liberation, the survivors were put in DP camps. No other countries would take us in. A lot of countries took in collaborators, but we sat in this DP camp for three years until some people in Canada came up with an idea. In 1948, the owner of Tip Top Tailors, Mr. David Dunkelman, came to Bergen-Belsen with some dignitaries to register tailors who would be allowed to come to Canada. This Canadian Jewish committee had come up with a brilliant idea to get Jews into Canada by advertising that Canada needs tailors. I was encouraged to pretend I was a tailor and in September 1948 I was issued a visa to come to Canada.

Actually, I almost didn't get the visa. When I was applying to come to Canada, I was completely bent over. I couldn't walk straight because of the damage in my body from the beatings in the work camps. They never healed properly. When the time came to stamp my visa, the Canadian consul said, "We need healthy people in Canada."

I told them, "I'm healthy, but my back was damaged. It wasn't my fault. I was born normal, but people without a heart made me like this. And I'll be a good citizen." I remember saying to him, "I'll be a good citizen."

The consul said, "It's against the law. I'm only allowed to let in healthy people." I started to cry and told him if I could find a good doctor, I could get better. I guess he felt sorry for me. He said, "I'm putting my job on the line for you, but I have an idea. Get somebody who is healthy, approximately your age, and bring me the healthy X-ray." So that's what I did. I found somebody and paid her to get an X-ray with my name on it. I brought it to him, and he stamped my visa. He told me if I went to Toronto, he could recommend a very good orthopedic surgeon, one of the best, Dr. H. Campbell.

We boarded the ship in Bremen in 1948 and spent eleven days at sea. The conditions can only be described as horrible. Finally, we arrived in Halifax and spent four more days being transported from the port city to Toronto. I was amazed at how unpopulated Canada was, how few towns there were. When we got to Toronto, we were told not to ask for anything from the government. If we were sick, we were told to only go to Mount Sinai, not to any other hospital. I met a Jewish doctor who told me, "You aren't well and we'll have to look after you." I told him that I didn't have money, but he said, "I'm not asking you for any money. I am asking you to come to my office." He explained to me that Jewish doctors were only allowed to work at Mount Sinai Hospital. And Mount Sinai, at the time, was only two houses. They didn't open the new building until 1954.

To tell you the truth, I didn't have time to see a doctor when I arrived in Canada. I had to work. Unfortunately, working as a tailor was out. My first day, I was put to work on this machine and I knew that there was no way I could work there. So I got another job, folding sweaters. All day folding sweaters and putting them in a box. One person I worked with spoke Ukrainian and the other one was Italian. I'll never learn English from this, I thought to myself, never. So, I worked, but I went to school at night. That's where I met my husband, in the English class, a loving, compassionate, and understanding man who had also come to Canada as a tailor. We were married within the year and had two sons.

A year after we arrived, we were able to bring my mother to Canada. She had cousins here, so they actually sponsored her because with my income, I couldn't. I was so lucky to have her with me for twenty years.

Life continued. We worked hard, bought a house, and rented out every room to pay the mortgage. But I wasn't well. I suffered constant headaches and backaches. One day, I suddenly couldn't walk. My husband had to work two jobs to pay the bills and my mother was busy working in her grocery store. I finally decided that it was time to take the advice given to me when I boarded the ship to Canada—to see Dr. Campbell, the orthopedic surgeon. I told him the story of what had happened to me and, when he examined me, he cried like a baby to see—after so many years—that I still had the whip marks on my skin. Dr. Campbell said that he would make me walk properly again. It would take a long time, but he would make me walk. He didn't want to do surgery—he wanted to pull the muscles, to use traction. It took five years and the pain was terrible. I remember bringing him five dollars. To me, five dollars was a lot—I worked for thirty cents an hour. He took the five dollars, put it back in my hand, and said, "Don't you ever do that again. I have enough money. Take these five dollars and buy good food. You have to eat well, to build your muscles. As long as it takes, I'll look after you. Don't you ever pay me again!"

Today I can walk straight. Life is not easy, but I remember my brother saying that life is precious. And it is. I am thankful for every minute I live. I am free. I have a nice home. I have everything I need. I had a wonderful husband for over fifty years, and I live with his memories.

People who are born here, they don't appreciate the freedom that they have. When I talk to children, I speak about the hate that brings all the trouble. Only hate. How can you hate a person when you don't even know them? Just because that person is different—with a different religion, a different skin, a different whatever. And you hate that person. But you don't know who that person is. Maybe he or she is the most wonderful person in the world. That's what I try to tell the children in school, that hate brings all the problems. Hate brings the killings. And they should appreciate the land they live in.

What else can I want? I thank God for every minute. That's the way I understand life. Complaining won't help. I think this is a wonderful country and the people are wonderful. But it's hard. After all this, it's hard because I do still live with these memories. When we were young, we worked. You come from work, you're tired. You sleep. Now, we have too much time on our hands. And all the memories keep coming. It's hard, but you have to go on. You have to be strong enough to go on. That's what my brother used to tell me. "Remember, remember. Fight for your life! Fight for your life!"

I wrote something about my hands, that it's true that the hands can do a lot—and I did—but your hands can't mend a broken heart, my dear. This, my hands can't do, so I wrote about it, that a broken heart is very, very hard to mend.

YUDEL NAJMAN

Based on interviews with his son, Sol Nayman.

People in the Wetzlar DP camp were talking about the call for tailors in Canada. "What do you know?" people asked. "What can you tell me?" "What have you heard?"
—SOL NAYMAN

IN 2004, when my wife, Queenie, and I were at the Holocaust Museum in Washington, the person in the library looked up my name and said, "You're not registered with us as a survivor." When I replied that I didn't consider myself to be a survivor and told him my family's story, he said, "You are a survivor." He read me the definition of survivor, which, according to the US Holocaust Memorial Museum, is "any persons, Jewish or non-Jewish, who were displaced, persecuted, or discriminated against due to the racial, religious, ethnic, social, and political policies of the Nazis and their collaborators between 1933 and 1945. In addition to former inmates of concentration camps, ghettos, and prisons, this definition includes, among others, people who were refugees or were in hiding." So, I became a survivor.

I was born in Stoczek-Węgrowski, or Stok, as most Jews referred to it, in Poland, on November 5, 1935. I was the second child of Yudel Najman and Sore Roize Rosenberg. My sister, Mania, was born November 13, 1928. Stoczek-Węgrowski is forty-five kilometres from Warsaw and, more particularly, twenty-five kilometres from Treblinka, my neighbourhood death camp. Everyone who stayed in our town perished there.

We fled from Stoczek after it was destroyed by the German army on September 9, 1939. All of us—my father, Yudel Najman; my mother, Sore; my sister, Mania; and my maternal grandmother, Esther Dobe—hid in the nearby woods. There was nothing in our town that was of any strategic value, it just happened to be in the way of the Wehrmacht, the German army. My grandmother, the only grandparent I had by that time, heard that our little hospital was on fire and insisted on going back to see if she could help. We waited and waited and waited, but we never saw her again. Others who had

Yudel Najman working on the press at the back of
the photo in the Schiff garment factory in Montreal.

fled with us said that if we stayed any longer, we would be found out. So, we kept going and somehow ended up in Białystok, on the border between Poland and the Soviet Union, one hundred kilometres from Stoczek.

Without my grandmother, it was now just the four of us, but in Białystok we reconnected with *land-sleute*, other people who were from all over Poland. From Białystok, we were deported to Syktyvkar, in the Komi Autonomous Soviet Republic, to build housing barracks. Syktyvkar was just on the edge of permafrost, close to the Arctic Circle, just west of the Ural Mountains and Siberia. There was a lot of lumber there. My father had no trade; he was a ferocious reader, but he had no trade, no particular skills. In Syktyvkar, he became a glazer—someone who cut glass. Those barracks we built and lived in were horrendous places. We were crammed into a small room with another couple, with just a sheet hanging between us for privacy. There was no electricity, no heat, no sanitation. We had to use outhouses and to use an outhouse when it's about -40 Celsius is not very pleasant. There was a long corridor in the barracks, where anyone who did not have a room had to sit. One day my father struck up a conversation with one of them, asking, "Amcha?" (in Yiddish, Are you a Jew?). He turned out to be none other than his nephew Moishe, the only son of my father's brother, Dovid Leib. So, Moishe joined us in our palatial suite and we became five. We were five from Syktyvkar,

through the Ukraine, through West Germany, and—through a fake marriage certificate—to Canada. Moishe did all the negotiations. He was sort of our mediator and our doer—the person who got things done.

The only things of value we had managed to take out of Stok were the duvet I was wrapped up in when we fled, several Fraget silverware pieces that my parents had received as wedding gifts—Fraget was well known around Europe, and we were able to sell some of the pieces on the black market in exchange for necessities—and a twenty-two-carat gold coin from the Czarist era. A five-ruble coin was sewn into my jacket for emergency use. The Soviet authorities rarely bothered children, but my father or Moishe would have been jailed, or worse, if they'd been caught. We somehow survived Syktyvkar for more than four years. We still have two of the Fraget spoons, the only tangible items remaining from my parents' wedding.

In the spring of 1944, we were shipped from Syktyvkar to a village in the Haivoron area of Ukraine to work on rebuilding a burned-out sugar factory. It was brutal—Ukraine had been absolutely destroyed by Stalin's scorched-earth policy. Ukraine had been the breadbasket of Europe, but all the crops had been destroyed. All the infrastructure had been destroyed.

In summer 1945, after the war was over, we were finally allowed to leave the Soviet Union and were sent to our next destination, in Lower Silesia, part of the

Soviet Zone of Germany, where we were reunited with my mother's cousin, Isser Rosenberg. From there, we were shipped to a DP camp in the American Zone of West Germany. It was a tent city near a town called Kam, which I think was near Bad Kissingen. There, we found my mother's aunt Rifke and uncle Avrom, and their daughters, who subsequently immigrated to Palestine and lived in Netanya.

In 1946, we were sent to another DP camp, where this time we were housed in a massive former SS camp, just outside the city of Wetzlar. Life sort of began again for us in Wetzlar. There were 4,200 of us there. People set up political parties—Hashomer Hatzair, Beitar, Hapoel, and so on. There was a soccer team and there were chess tournaments; we watched films and Yiddish plays; there were schools; people got married; and children were born. We were in the camp for almost three years, so a lot of life events occurred. We were looked after by the United Nations Relief and Rehabilitation Administration (UNRRA). Since we were in the American Zone, we were treated far, far better than we had been in Lower Silesia, which was under Soviet control. I went to Hebrew school and became fluent in Hebrew. My father did nothing, though. Nobody worked because there were no jobs. There was really nothing to do other than watch a soccer match or a chess tournament.

We were in the Wetzlar DP camp from 1946 to 1948, when I was age ten to age twelve. We were cared for very well in the camp, and we were reunited with more family—my father's other nephew, Shulem, got married in Wetzlar and had a son there, and then ended up in Israel. We also reconnected with a number of *landsleute* from our town. Unfortunately, however, my mother was ill while we were there. Her health was so bad that everywhere we went, she had to be hospitalized.

When we arrived in Wetzlar, that's when we learned about the Holocaust. That's when we met the emaciated survivors and saw the numbers tattooed on their forearms. Nonetheless, as I said, life restarted for refugees and survivors in Wetzlar. The big question was, however, where do we go next?

Everyone was looking for ways to get out of the DP camp. Again, it was primarily Moishe's thing to have his ear to the ground, so to speak. To find out how people ended up going, say, to Sweden. We had some relatives who went to Sweden and we later reconnected with them in Montreal. We had *landsleute* who ended up in Cuba and we reconnected with them again in Montreal, too. So the important thing was to find out what might be happening. Some people said if you got married, you'll have a better chance of getting accepted to another country. If you were skilled, you might be able to do this or that. Maybe someone needed a doctor or whatever. And that's how we found out that a tailor could get to Canada.

We knew that it would be difficult and dangerous to go to Palestine—especially because of my mother's ill health. We tried to get into the US, but that proved futile despite our uncle Sam's help, so the next target became Canada. But the stories of interviews by immigration officials were horrifying. A person who walked into a room with an official behind a desk might be told to sit even though there were no chairs. If the person sat down on the floor—which was a logical response—they'd then be told that they were unsuitable to come to Canada because people there didn't sit on the floor. At one interview with my family, we were told that my sister and I could go, but not my parents because of my mother's ill health. A family friend suggested that Mania and Moishe get "married" to see if that might improve our chances of getting into Canada as a family group. Mania was about twenty at the time and Moishe in his mid- to late-twenties. They somehow managed to get a local "marriage certificate" and reapplied. Incidentally, they did get married officially in Montreal and raised two wonderful children.

When we reapplied to the Canadian officials, we learned that Canada was accepting a limited quota of tailors who would be sent to Winnipeg to work in the growing garment industry there. Several prominent Canadian Jewish manufacturers—Horace Cohen, Max Enkin, and the Posluns family—had petitioned the Canadian government to allow tailors to come in—undoubtedly with adequate financial guarantees, or "blood money," so that they would not be a burden on the state. My father didn't know one end of a needle from another, but our cousin's husband, who was a master tailor, agreed to pose as my father to take the tailoring test. He filled out the form saying that his name was Yudel Najman. He did whatever sewing task he was asked to do—basted a hem, or whatever. Then, boom. My father, Yudel Najman, was a tailor. Maybe a week or two, or days later, that same cousin's husband—his last name was Eisler—came back and did his own test. He also ended up coming to Canada as a tailor and ended up in Montreal the same way we did.

Armed with my father's "tailored" credentials and the fake marriage certificate, Moishe again appealed to a Canadian official. With the added "gift" of our only Russian gold coin, this official was finally persuaded to grant our family a visa. I don't remember anyone taking a medical test. My mother certainly wouldn't have been able to come to Canada if she had because she'd been sick all her life with severe stomach problems. My father was emaciated, but reasonably healthy, reasonably strong. Ultimately, of course, before we qualified for a trip to Canada, we were deloused and disinfected and checked for any communicable diseases. I guess we passed those tests. My mother was, just simply, a very, very sick woman. She passed away six years after we came to Canada, at the age of fifty-two.

The extended Najman family at the Wetzlar train station on their way to the port of Bremerhaven in Germany, October 7, 1948. Yudel Najman on the far left, facing back; third from left is his wife, Sore Roize; in the centre is his daughter, Mania; and Sol, age twelve, is on the right.

When we were told that we were approved for Canada, we all thought, Wow! I knew nothing about Canada. But in 1948, just before Rosh Hashanah, we were shipped to Bremerhaven and sailed across the Atlantic on the USS *General S.D. Sturgis*. My mother was separated from us on the ship because she was in the infirmary most of the trip. I was on the deck most of the time, throwing up. It was a US army boat—a transport ship—with hammock-like bunks. Yom Kippur occurred during our trip, so there was a facility set up for prayer. The American officers supplied us with food. It was a horrible nine-day crossing because once we got through the English Channel and into the Atlantic, well, sailing across it in mid-October is pretty rough. The USS *General S.D. Sturgis* is not exactly the *Queen Mary* either. It was hardly a cruise ship where everything is nice and smooth. It was as if we were being tossed around in a tin can, but other than sea sickness, which everyone suffered from, it was okay. We managed. When we were on route, I tried to find out what I could about Canada and I knew a few words in English. The American officers on board were courteous, kind, and helpful. I tried to say a few words to them in English and they did their best to respond.

Although the whole trip was organized under the auspices of either the International Refugee Organization (IRO), or the UNRRA, again, I believe that the Enkins, and the Cohens, and the Posluns, paid for us, for the tailors.

We arrived at Pier 21 in Halifax on Shabbat, October 16, 1948. When we landed and saw the lighthouse on Georges Island, well, for me it was like the Statue of Liberty. After various official checks at immigration, we were issued temporary passports, deloused again, and sent to the train station. No one greeted us in Halifax other than the immigration officers. We had no one to welcome us until we contacted my mother's uncle, Sam Zelenetz, who flew in from New York on Colonial Airlines and met us at Central Station in Montreal. Our joy at seeing him knew no bounds.

Uncle Sam was an incredible man. He had moved to New York in, I think, 1927. Many Jews left Europe in the 1920s and early 1930s—they knew that when the Earth began to rumble, they'd better be ready to move. My uncle in New York was by this time fairly well established—he was a furniture manufacturer in Brooklyn, so our first kitchen set came from him. Our first refrigerator was also sent by him. My first *tallis* and *tefillin* came from him. He was very kind and we were very close. He had five nieces, my mother being one of them, and he maintained contact with his nieces until he passed away. On occasion, he sent us a US dollar or two, which we'd get if they weren't seized by the people who checked mail.

Jews are a wandering people. Wonderful people and wandering people. We always have to be aware what might the next step or stop be. Many of our *landsleute* ended up in Mexico, including two of my mother's cousins—Uncle Sam's nieces—one of whom went to Israel; many also went to Argentina and to Uruguay. When we got to Canada—or maybe even before—I think my mother and father, or my sister, communicated with the Argentine *landsleute* and with the family in Mexico. In Buenos Aires, in particular, there was a very large and very dedicated Jewish community. In 1974, they published a memorial book with input from people from around the world who were from Stok. It's an incredible memorial book.

My father didn't get to choose whether to go to Toronto, Montreal, or Winnipeg—the destination he was given was Winnipeg. Fortunately, however, our uncle was able to get us off the train in Montreal by arranging for two families, the Petrushkas and the Krantzes, to sponsor us. They put us up in their homes for a while. Mr. Petrushka taught me how to put on *tefillin* because my father was not observant. He also suggested that I enrol in the Talmud Torah school in Montreal. He was a very prominent Yiddishist whose brother had translated the Chumash, the printed book of the Torah, into Yiddish. They put us up on Saint Urbain Street, where most Jews congregated at that time, until we were able to find our first lodging.

We would all get together at the Petrushkas' for a meal, but I slept at the Krantzes' house. Mrs. Petrushka and Mrs. Krantz were sisters. I stayed with the Krantz family and my parents and sister stayed with the Petrushka family. I had to share a bed with Abe Krantz and on the first night I ended up accidentally kicking him out of bed because I hadn't slept in a bed for a long time. The second night I kicked him out of bed again; on the third night, I slept on the sofa. Our first dwelling, a rental, was on Waverly Street. I enrolled in Talmud Torah, where I began my first week in Grade 4, my second week in Grade 5, and then, ultimately, was put in Grade 6. Our life in Canada had begun.

At first my father worked as a shipper—I think with Syndor Radio—and then he somehow got a job in the garment industry, at the Schiff Company, as an under-presser. A presser is one who presses the whole garment, but on a coat or jacket, for example, an under-presser presses the shoulder pads. There was a tag with the value of that particular press, that particular job. So, a shoulder pad might have been, say, fifteen cents. A pair of pants might have been a dollar. At the end of the day, my father would come home with an envelope full of those tags and he'd have to list them. So many shoulder pads, or so many whatever. At fifteen cents per piece, he might have three dollars to his payroll credit. He worked as a presser at the Schiff factory for the rest of his life.

Talmud Torah only went to Grade 7, and in the fall of 1950, I went to Herzliah, a junior high school, for Grades 8, and 9. My greatest influence there was the famous Canadian poet Irving Layton. Herzliah graduated some of the most brilliant people—for example, Leonard Cohen; Irwin Cotler, the former minister of state; and Moses Znaimer, the founder of Citytv. It was a parochial school under the jurisdiction of the Protestant School Board, essentially a parochial school with the full Protestant school curriculum plus Hebrew and some religious curriculum. From Herzliah, I went to Baron Byng for Grades 10 and 11. Baron Byng was 99 per cent Jewish students.

In Grade 10, I became school president of Baron Byng, which led to my being invited to join the Eaton's Junior Council. We were paid two dollars for the meeting, which was good, and given a summer job. So, my first retail summer job was with Eaton's. After I graduated from high school, I went to work at Simpson's, the competitor department store.

I attended McGill engineering, but unfortunately the major exams occurred during shiva when my mother had passed away. I decided to go to evening school at Sir George Williams (now Concordia) and continue taking chemical engineering there. I did that for one school year, but it was just too much. Working during the day, going to evening school. I decided to quit school and stay on with Simpson's. That lasted from 1955 to 1985—thirty years. I started as a salesperson in the hardware department, but I worked my way up and ultimately became vice president of the whole organization until 1985. After that, I was part of the founding team of Club Monaco and executive vice president until 2000. Queenie and I got married on August 27, 1961.

My family was very fortunate. We were able to get to this country under a tailor ruse, if you will. I don't know if I'll be deported now for admitting that, but that's our tailor connection. I have no qualms about sharing the fact that my father wasn't actually a tailor. I think, if anything, that it's another incredible story of Jewish survival chutzpah. We had to survive. We had to find the next step. The other sort of creative thing we did was my sister obtaining a marriage certificate with my cousin Moishe—our cousin, our father's nephew—whom we found in the Soviet forced labour camp—because they were told that a marriage certificate might be helpful. So, they got a marriage certificate in Wetzlar and my father got a tailor certificate, but, as it turned out, even that wasn't good enough. In addition to all that, it was the gold coin that proved to be our key to Canada.

When the war ended, we'd been shipped from Ukraine, across the Soviet-controlled zone of Lower Silesia, to a tent city in West Germany, and ultimately to Wetzlar. Three years. Three long years of not knowing where we would end up. "Tell Me Where Shall I Go" was a very well-known song at that time. Some young people braved the blockade and ended up in Palestine. Others ended up in different countries. We know survivors that ended up in Tangiers, Morocco, or in Cuba; some got into the United States. We don't know where we would've ended up had we not had the opportunity to come to Canada as part of the Tailor Project.

I really don't know what happened after 1948 because suddenly the borders, the doors, did open up. Could we have come in under other auspices? Our uncle in New York tried to get us a visa to the US, but it didn't work because, again, there was a limit, a quota. The US didn't suddenly say, "Welcome, survivors" to the roughly million and a half Jewish refugees after the war. The only country that opened its arms unconditionally was Israel, when it became a state. And many went to Palestine, then to the State of Israel, to fight with the Palmach, with the Haganah. According to my understanding, every aspect of survivors coming to Canada was paid for and sponsored by Jewish communities. What did we come in with? Threadbare clothes. I was put up with one family, my parents and sister with another family, until we could find our own rental accommodation in Montreal. Despite having little or no help from the government, becoming citizens of Canada was certainly one of the greatest moments of our lives.

For years and years and years, I didn't talk about our experience. I wasn't hiding anything. I started talking about it after Queenie and I were in Washington at the Holocaust museum. And it's now more than seventy years since Israel's independence. In my Tarbut school in the Wetzlar DP camp, we were told on Friday, May 14, 1948, that we would hear a special announcement. Over the radio, we heard David Ben-Gurion proclaim the State of Israel. Seventy years later, on the March of the Living, I was in in Jerusalem, speaking to the entire Canadian contingent from Vancouver, Calgary, Ottawa, Montreal, and Toronto, telling them how I was standing there seventy years later after that announcement, celebrating Yom Ha'atzmaut. It was one of the most powerful moments of my life.

Finally, seventy years after the declaration of the State of Israel, seventy years after we came to this incredible country of Canada, in 2018, I celebrated my bar mitzvah. For the first time, I recited my Haftorah. I've been very fortunate. I've been successful in business, and Queenie and I have raised a wonderful family. Seeing my grandchildren grow up has more than rewarded me for having lost my childhood in the Holocaust. We need to learn about what happened. We need to remember. And, at the same time, we need to keep on moving forward. *Kadima*, moving forward but never forgetting where we came from. So, that's our story.

WELCOME TO CANADA

BY MID-OCTOBER 1947, the commission had interviewed more than a thousand displaced persons (DPs) and the team expected that the first groups would be leaving for Canada by mid-November. Matthew Ram, a young Canadian social worker who had worked with the team, would be left behind in Europe to keep the project on track. Ram was soon advised by the American Jewish Joint Distribution Committee (JDC) that not only were Canadian officials "very rigid" in their interpretation of the screening guidelines, they were giving precedence to the other bulk labour schemes. The JDC informed Ram that instead of the one hundred Jewish DPs expected to sail on the first ship, there would be only thirteen.[1] When the USS *General S.D. Sturgis* left for Canada on the first day of December, there were indeed some tailors on board. Not one was Jewish. Ram immediately telephoned Hayes, telling him that he had been told that Canadian officials suspended approvals when they uncovered Jewish DPs submitting false medical records. Ram "made it clear that these fraudulent practices, the extent of which he is unable to indicate, not only affect the Jewish DPs but also non-Jewish DPs and moreover

took place in [other bulk labour] schemes." Ram also told Hayes that medical rejections were running at 65 per cent and, despite labour department assurances to the contrary, shipping for the garment workers was "not high on the order of priority."[2]

Toronto MP Joe Salsberg, in Germany to observe the progress of the Tailor Project, advised Saul Hayes that the absence of Jews was "no accident. To make things worse," Salsberg reported, the Canadian vice-consul who went to examine the next group of tailors "baldly stated [to Ram] that he had instructions to examine the non-Jews first." After Ram contacted the Canadian Mission in Germany to complain, the vice-consul was given instructions to proceed without discrimination.[3] Not surprisingly, this new turn of events caused considerable consternation among the Canadian Jewish leadership. When Hayes approached the immigration branch, they came up with another explanation altogether. They claimed that

the reason there were no Jewish garment workers on the present sailing of the SS [General

The Greek ocean liner, the SS *Nea Hellas*, was one of the ships that carried many Jewish refugees who were part of the Tailor Project from Europe to Pier 21 in Halifax. Not all the vessels bringing the DPs to Canada were comfortable passenger ships—many were unconverted troopships pushed into service.

S.D.] Sturgis is because 27 of this race from Amberg Camp which were earmarked for this vessel were being held for a recheck of X-ray and blood check which had not been completed prior to the ship's sailing. It was necessary to replace this group by others at short notice whether they were Jewish or otherwise.[4]

Despite all their efforts, and government assurances, the Garment Workers Commission was clearly being given the runaround. Off to Ottawa went Enkin and Genser to meet with the labour and immigration departments. They were assured that officials would do "all within their power to determine the cause of the irregularities as alleged and that once this difficulty has been solved there will in fact be no suspension of processing the persons chosen by the industrial delegation."[5] Enkin was skeptical. He continued to monitor the situation, observing, "I guess we still seem to rate last on the priority list, and it looks as if we will holler a little louder."[6]

Ottawa had promised workers to the garment industry and, despite the anti-Jewish discrimination of their officials on the ground, they were prepared to follow through with the commitment on numbers. Canada's Jewish community, less than 2 per cent of the population, held little leverage. Admission of any more than that low percentage of Jewish immigrants had to

be considered a win. As the DPs moved through the next levels of screening, even the 30 to 40 per cent of surplus tailors who had been chosen to "allow for wastage" proved insufficient. Many of the non-Jews were not passing the medical screenings. The government agreed to relax the quota slightly, raising the proportion of Jews to "not more than sixty percent of any one persuasion." The news was to be kept confidential lest it appear that there was some softening of policy in favour of the Jewish lobby.[7]

Conditions in Europe remained challenging for the implementation of the project. In a report published by the Canadian Jewish Congress (CJC), Matthew Ram described his frustrations working through details when making a local telephone call could take over an hour to arrange; calling another city could take most of a day. The typewriters and stenographers needed to complete the copious paperwork for the immigrants were in short supply. Transportation was overcrowded and difficult to arrange. Ram was also faced with the increasing frustrations of the survivors who were waiting for passage.

Ram shared his reflections on the challenges he faced, as a Canadian-born Jew, comprehending the experiences that Holocaust survivors had endured and the impact it had on them. The corridors where he worked were always crowded with "people desperate to get out of the camps and to a normal economy once more." He soon developed "a great deal of admiration and respect for their resourcefulness and vitality" and was "was amazed at the comeback that these people had made."

Imagine, a people who for ten years had lived a hand-to-mouth existence, in daily fear of their lives and who still retained their sense of humour, fundamental human values and who were deliberately rebuilding their shattered family lives as is indicated by the phenomenally high birth rate among them.

Ram began to understand that, although survivors were now properly fed and clothed, "the problems existed on a deeper and much more fundamental level." He heard their "tales of horror" and realized that each one of them "carried locked within his heart the despair and agony rising out of the loss of friends and family. I have heard hundreds of stories that unnerved me, and I have often wondered what gives these people the courage to carry on."[8]

MATTHEW RAM (1919–1986)

THE FIVE MEMBERS of the commission completed their selections and headed back to Canada in early November 1947. They had good reasons to be concerned that without continued pressure on officials in Europe, their DPs might never make it to Canada. Assuring that transport was assigned to the garment workers was a challenge, as was the more than 50 per cent rejection rate by Canadian immigration examiners. They needed to leave someone in charge who they could trust to follow through. They hired Matthew Ram, a young social worker from Montreal who had been sent to Europe by the Canadian Jewish Congress (CJC) to work with the American Jewish Joint Distribution Committee (JDC).

In early October 1947, Ram met with Allan Bronfman, the youngest son of the Bronfman family and a community leader in Montreal. Bronfman was visiting Germany to survey postwar conditions for a report on "Overseas Jewry." He wrote to Saul Hayes at the CJC that Ram "struck me as a most intelligent young man, keen and alert." Ram was assigned to the selection team and was soon shuttling them between DP camps in a rusty Volkswagen. Once they returned to Canada, Ram acted as liaison between them and the various organizations in Europe on logistical matters, ensuring that the project stayed on track. Introducing Ram to officials in the immigration department, Max Enkin assured them, "You will find that he holds the same sympathetic interest of the problems involved and since he has worked with us for some weeks he is fully acquainted with all of the details and procedures."[1] Ram was also tasked with recruiting more eligible DPs if immigration screenings depleted the numbers below the quota that had been agreed to.

Ram was profoundly moved by what he heard in the camps. "Each individual had his own tale of horror to tell," Ram later wrote, "and each carried locked within his heart the despair and agony rising out of the loss of friends and family. I have heard hundreds of stories that unnerved me and I have often wondered what gives these people the courage to carry on."[2] Ram was soon reporting back about the challenges he faced. He wrote to Enkin that "the hardest part of the whole scheme is over for you, but it is just beginning with me."[3] His dealings with those rejected by immigration

Matthew Ram

screening could be heartbreaking. Ram recorded some of his experiences in the Canadian Jewish press:

"If you don't arrange for me to leave on this transport, I'll commit suicide," the woman said to me when I entered the transit camp. "My husband says he'll take our child and leave without me unless you do something. I won't remain in Germany alone." She was in a terrible state, with disordered hair and her eyes a little wild. Her husband stayed in the background, a little sullen, embittered by years of harrowing experiences. Eventually I got the full story. The family was proceeding to Canada on the tailor's scheme and had arrived at the transit camp, ready to sail. In a routine medical it was discovered that the woman was pregnant. The ship's regulations stipulated that no woman past five months pregnancy could sail. Another ruling had it that children under six months were not permitted to sail. This family was to be sent back to their camp of origin to await until the child was six months old. No wonder there was consternation and concern. After a round of conferences with the IRO [International Refugee Organization] directors and doctors, we were eventually able to arrange for their shipment.[4]

Perhaps because of his social work training, Ram developed a "great deal of admiration and respect for the resourcefulness and vitality of the survivors. Imagine a people who for ten years had lived a hand-to-mouth existence, in daily fear of their lives and still retained their sense of humour, fundamental human values and who were deliberately rebuilding their shattered family lives."[5] He worked hard to enable all the tailors to find shipping. Ram was then appointed by the CJC as its chief liaison officer in charge of all the subsequent immigration schemes sponsored by Canadian Jewry.

After he returned to Montreal with his young family, Ram's experiences in Europe led him to the position of director of community services for the CJC. He also worked as a fundraiser and director of several communal organizations, including the Zionist Organization of Canada, Maimonides Hospital, and the Miriam Home. Matthew Ram died in Montreal in 1986.

SETTLING IN

THE JEWISH GARMENT workers and their families were the first large group of Holocaust survivors to gain entry to Canada. They were soon followed by DPs who joined other labour programs initiated by the Jewish community, notably by the furrier and hat-making industries. Jewish survivors comprised about 10 per cent of the 165,000 DPs who were admitted to Canada between 1947 and 1953, most of whom arrived as part of bulk labour schemes. They lived under threat of deportation to Europe if they did not complete their contracts. Jewish DPs realized that they had more reason than others to be concerned about their status when, in February 1948, seven survivors who had entered on forged passports were tried as illegal aliens and deported. It seemed that the flexibility shown to Estonians and Polish war veterans who arrived suffering from tuberculosis but were not removed—in these cases, on medical grounds—did not apply to Jews. As the Cold War developed, security screenings by Canadian officials focused less on Nazi war criminals and collaborators from Central and Eastern Europe and more on barring immigrants with communist sympathies.

In 1948, just as the tailors began boarding ships to Canada, Comte Jacques de Bernonville and five other collaborators who had been convicted of war crimes in France were discovered living in Quebec. They had been sentenced to death in France for their crimes and had entered Canada on false passports. Quebec clerics, government officials—including the mayor of Montreal—and, eventually, the federal government, protected them from extradition. This enraged Canadian Jewry. The outspoken rabbi of Holy Blossom Temple in Toronto, Abraham Feinberg, noted that the Jewish DPs had been deported "to a living death in Germany" for entering with forged documents, while these convicted murderers had been welcomed and permitted to live freely in Quebec. Feinberg called it a "revolting" case.[1] With their protests falling on deaf ears, the Canadian Jewish Congress (CJC) refocused their energy on the issues of survivor settlement and integration.[2]

The original plan was to have all the tailors transported to Canada by the summer of 1948, yet some were still arriving in Canada a year later. The government subversion of the program through overzealous medical and security screenings of Jewish survivors and the shipping priority given to other groups was not the only obstacle to its implementation. Canadian cities were experiencing severe housing shortages in the immediate postwar years. Industrialization during the war had brought an influx of workers into urban areas and a huge surge in industrial building had monopolized resources. An estimated 400,000 families and returning veterans struggled to find proper accommodations.[3] While the Jewish community was looking to fulfil its promise to government to house the DP workers, it was also struggling to find homes for 1,123 young survivors who were due to arrive through the orphan scheme in 1948. The director of the CJC office in Winnipeg pointed out that settling the garment workers would "be incomparably more difficult than the problem of placing the orphans. Emotionally the community will respond more readily to come to the aid of the orphans."[4] Adding to the shortage was the challenge that many Canadian Jews were in the process of sponsoring relatives who would be sharing their homes.

Housing was the first priority for the CJC and Jewish Immigrant Aid Society (JIAS). Saul Hayes was anxious that if there were "insuperable difficulties and insoluble problems" the labour department would "terminate" the project. During a telephone conversation with Saul Hayes prior to his return to Canada in November 1948, Enkin urged Hayes to quickly resolve

any problems, that it was "a priority to rescue these people irrespective of all the difficulties and despite obstacles."[5]

The CJC and JIAS leadership undertook a massive publicity campaign to convince Canadian Jews to find housing for the DPs. Upon their return, commission members wrote articles and spoke publicly about their experiences in the DP camps, urging their community to do their part in this last stage of the rescue of European Jews. Max Enkin spoke in Toronto about the DP camps and concluded that he hoped "it has awakened within your hearts a spark of that feeling of the religion and faith we profess and that we accept the view that we are our brother's keeper." He explained that immigration would be held up unless "you now extend the hospitality of your homes and your good will to that trickle of people from these camps."[6] From Halifax to Vancouver, Canadian Jews were urged to open their hearts and their homes, while Jewish organizations and unions organized their meagre resources to welcome and integrate the survivors.

Matthew Ram worked with the American Jewish Joint Distribution Committee (JDC) in Europe to prepare the tailors for their voyages. The precise number of tailors onboard were relayed to the CJC in Montreal before each ship sailed. The lists outlined the number of their dependents and whether they were Jews or non-Jews. Plans were prepared to determine the ultimate destinations of each tailor and then organizations in those cities were notified to arrange housing and employment. It was much easier to assign tailors who had been specifically requested by the unions or who had family who could accommodate them; the needs of employers dictated decisions about the destinations of the rest. Beginning in January 1948, groups of Jewish DP tailors arrived at Halifax's Pier 21 and in Quebec City.

In the spring of 1948, Canada's premier newsmagazine, *Maclean's*, assigned a journalist to meet 431 DPs arriving on the SS *Marine Falcon* and accompany them on their way to new lives in Canada. Among the Poles, Ukrainians, and Estonians destined for mines, forests, and factories were Jewish survivors arriving on the orphan, domestic, and tailor programs. "To Canada," she wrote, "DPs are so many strong backs. To DPs, our Canada is a distant dream of freedom and plenty miraculously come true." The journalist described their reception that foggy morning at Pier 21 as follows:

Sheltered from the thin grey rain in the gaping immigration shed doorway stood a small group of harbor police, immigration officials, representatives of the CNR, the mines and other interested employers, men from the local ships' agency and a couple of reporters. It was early and it was a dreary morning. The bleak reserved line of faces looked down on them.

The absolute stillness of the crowd was almost a shock. There was silence. "It's a pity there is no way to say welcome," someone on the dock said. "Even a band—" "They don't need a band," someone else said. "The fact they're allowed to come here is good enough. They should be grateful."

A.G. Christie, inspector-in-chief of immigration in Halifax, a quick-moving slight man, took a couple of swift steps forward. He lifted his hand and the smile that breaks up his whole thin face came out. "Welcome," he shouted and waved. The two solid lines of brightened faces, the sudden wave of motion as though the still people had been brought to life, was literally like light bursting out of a thick cloud bank. With almost hurting eagerness the people on the ship answered him in a universal smile. Christie spoke softly to his neighbor on the dock. "Treat others as you'd like them to treat you. Especially people coming in to become our fellow citizens. First impressions stay with you a long time."

After an onboard medical inspection, the DPs entered Canada. Twelve tables with twelve immigration officials checked the passengers off the ship's manifest

A polyglot crowd of Central European refugees from PCIRO camps in Germany and Austria is just about to file up the gangway of the SS *Nea Hellas*, bound for Winnipeg, Canada, from Genoa, where the DPs were brought by a special PCIRO train. They were joined on the same day (March 10, 1948) by a group of eighty-two Jewish war orphans and seventy-five other refugees from PCIRO camps in Italy. This was the first large-scale movement of DPs from Italy to Canada under PCIRO sponsorship.

and issued entry stamps. Imperial Tobacco handed out free packs of cigarettes.[7]

Multilingual representatives of JIAS welcomed the newcomers to Canada. One was known as the "Flying Dutchman."

Henry Hochgemein, formerly a successful Warsaw attorney and now official JIAS receptionist at ports of debarkation, has earned the moniker the "Flying Dutchman" because of his frequent air trips to Halifax where he is sent to meet the DPs who come here under the Tailor Project. White-haired, glib-tongued, ever-smiling Hochgemein, himself a refugee from the first Nazi onslaught on Poland who came to Canada via Japan only ten years ago, is well suited for his job. An expert linguist, he is the first person to greet the newcomers in their native tongues on their arrival in Canada. His charm and attitude dispel their anxieties and make them feel that they are among friends… His usual mission involved clearance of several hundred Jewish and non-Jewish immigrants and their families through customs and immigration. He arranges for their transportation, seats them on the special trains and then regroups them according to the cities to which they are destined.[8]

There were also members of the Halifax Jewish community at the wharf to assist the newcomers. Among them was Meta Echt, a Jewish refugee from a small town near Danzig whose family had escaped Germany in February 1939. Although her husband was a pharmacist, they had arrived as farmers and were so appreciative of their welcome into the Jewish community that they settled on a farm in Nova Scotia. Remembering the warm reception she had received, Meta volunteered to become the mayor's representative and official JIAS greeter at Pier 21. With the help of her daughter, Marianne Ferguson, Meta assisted the survivors with the immigration process, distributed funds and kosher food, and guided them onto their trains.[9] When survivors arrived in Halifax during Rosh Hashanah, the Jewish New Year, the local community offered shelter for the tailors, furriers, and orphans. They hosted them in their homes, and they prayed and celebrated with them before the new arrivals moved on to their destinations. In Quebec City, the local JIAS committee worked with the Jewish Council of Women to "welcome them in the true traditional Jewish spirit of hospitality." They helped process the arrivals through immigration, provided food parcels and milk for the children, and arranged their rail transportation.[10]

Survivors with relatives in Canada were sent to join them. JIAS representatives accompanied some of the groups as they travelled on the train—known as the

"DP Special"—to Saint-Paul-l'Ermite, thirty-five kilometres outside Montreal. This wartime government hostel became the way station for the new immigrants. Walter Friedman, the coordinator of the Garment Commission, was struck by the "moving dramas of Canadians being reunited with their European kin after years of separation."[11] After several days the new immigrants were taken to Montreal and placed on the trains that would take them to their designated destinations. The tailors remaining in Quebec were taken to the JIAS office where they were assigned temporary housing and given some cash and household essentials.

Most of the tailors arrived with little more than the clothes on their backs. The International Refugee Organization (IRO) had funded the processing and passage for the DPs while employers, through the Overseas Garment Commission, fronted the costs for transportation from the ports to their Canadian destinations. These outlays were to be reimbursed over time by payroll deductions, beginning four to five months after arrival. The newcomers were assured prevailing rates of pay. The commission was responsible for ensuring that both the employers and the tailors fulfilled their one-year government contracts. If they changed jobs the new immigrants were required to notify the commission. Department of labour officials could make unannounced visits to check job sites and if tailors had not notified the commission of new jobs and could not

be located, they would be reported to the RCMP, the Royal Canadian Mounted Police. Any breaches of contracts could result in relative sponsorships being denied and could ultimately cause problems in the tailors' citizenship applications. The estimated 10 per cent of DPs who came to Canada with the Tailor Project but had no actual tailoring skills, as well as people who lost their jobs during industry downturns, were granted some leeway—as long as they found work in other trades and fulfilled their contracts.[12]

Although several agencies and offices were involved in the settlement of the tailors, the CJC was ultimately responsible for funding assistance. Other ethnic organizations were brought into the process to take care of the needs of the non-Jewish DPs.[13] In Toronto, a representative of the Canadian Polish Congress worked in the commission offices.[14] The proposed geographic division of the estimated 2,279 DP tailors was to be 55 per cent to Montreal (946 for men's clothing and 315 for ladies' wear), 36 per cent to Toronto (436 for men's clothing and 387 for ladies' wear), with the remaining tailors to go to Winnipeg (7 per cent) and Vancouver (2 per cent).[15] By the completion of the program in 1949, the tailors were settled across Canada in roughly these proportions, although some individuals and families had been sent to smaller communities.

MONTREAL

THE MOST COMPREHENSIVE settlement program was developed in Montreal, where the national headquarters for the Canadian Jewish Congress (CJC) and Jewish Immigrant Aid Society (JIAS) were located. As shelter was the most urgent need, JIAS hired staff to locate and maintain a housing registry, with most of the initial accommodation for the survivor tailors in rooming houses and hotels. Finding landlords who would allow small children was a challenge in every city, so some families were placed in rented suburban homes. As soon as they arrived, the former DPs were given financial assistance to pay rent and purchase furniture and other household goods. They could apply for both grants and interest-free, long-term loans through the Hebrew Free Loan society to help them purchase their own homes.

JIAS' social service department was entrusted with providing welfare aid for the tailors and their original mandate was soon extended from six months to a year. When JIAS received applications from the survivors for welfare, childcare assistance, and long-term care, as well as help with other urgent issues, they referred them to the appropriate agencies.[1] Across Canada, Jewish women's groups also devoted their resources to helping the new arrivals. In Montreal, the National Council of Jewish Women ran the JIAS clothing centre stocked with donated items three times a week. One chapter, the Dina Lily Caplan Social Service group, "adopted" some of the DP families.[2]

Representatives of the International Ladies' Garment Workers' Union (ILGWU) and the Amalgamated Clothing Workers of America (Amalgamated) interviewed the tailors for placement at the offices of the Garment Commission. These interviews were designed to determine the workers' familiarity with Canadian procedures and machinery and assess their tailoring skills. The tailors were then taken to their designated job sites and introduced to their employers; the commission remained available to the immigrants to help smooth out any difficulties that might arise.[3]

Of course, not all the DPs who arrived as part of the Tailor Project were actually tailors. While the commission might be wary of acknowledging this due to their contract with the government, community workers were sometimes able to help move individuals into more suitable employment. Days after his arrival, for example, twenty-five-year-old Polish survivor Shmul G. approached JIAS for assistance in acquiring a suit. He revealed that he had explained to Walter Friedman during his interview with the commission that, although he had some knowledge of sewing, he was an auto mechanic by trade. Friedman permitted him to break his contract and seek other work. JIAS worked with Shmul and the Jewish Vocational Service (JVS) to find him employment while he mastered enough English to pass his certification as a mechanic. They accompanied him to meetings and job interviews and granted him loans to help supplement his rent.

On one occasion, Shmul froze and was unable to complete an exam. He explained to his aid worker that before the war he had been employed at his brother's auto repair shop. As he was writing the test, buried memories of his lost brother and family rose to the surface and he blanked out. "The worker mentioned that probably Mr. G. had not thought about his past very much since his arrival in Canada because there were so many new things to adjust to here." Shmul admitted that "he had not thought about his past during the few years since the war period." The worker suggested that "it would be difficult for him to forget and that it was perhaps better that he had had a chance to tell his story. Mr. G. sighed again and agreed."[4]

Shmul continued to have difficulty passing the technical tests and his JVS worker tried to persuade him to find another vocation. But he persevered. A sympathetic employer provided him with the books he needed and helped him translate technical terms. Four months after Shmul came in for assistance, he called to report his happiness at passing his exams.[5] Montreal's agencies helped the tailors find housing, provided necessities and, in cases like Shmul's, were able to smooth the road to successful settlement. Not every survivor needed or wanted assistance. Others were frustrated with their interactions with the organized Canadian Jewish community.

ERNEST GROSS

We had a choice about where to go in Canada, but it was a bit like asking someone if they prefer grey or red when they've never seen colours before. You could choose either because you don't know what the colours are. Do you want to go to Montreal or Toronto? I didn't have any idea what Montreal was. Or what Toronto was. Those were the two choices that most people were given. There were some people who had relatives in, let's say, Winnipeg. Or Vancouver. But otherwise it was all unknown. People didn't research where we were going. I chose Montreal. I didn't have anybody in Montreal or Toronto. But we had no way to make a distinction. So, I said, "Montreal. Let it be Montreal."

I WAS BORN ERNOE GROSZ on August 12, 1925, in Miskolc—a city of eighty thousand, with about nine thousand Jews.

My dad, Jozsef Grosz, was a teacher—actually he was the vice principal of a school in Miskolc, Hungary. The interesting part about that is that the school had never had either a Jewish teacher or Jewish student before. However, my father was highly respected by all. He was married three times. He lost his first wife to sickness and the second was my birth mother. Then, after my mother died in Auschwitz, he married a pharmacist who lived in Miskolc.

My mother, Terez, had to take care of five children—two from my father's first marriage, Ilona and Elza (Elizabeth), and her own three children, Aranka, Magda, and me.

My mother stayed at home looking after the household. I remember that she was also very involved in charitable work. She kept a strictly kosher household, so it was a more difficult life. If she bought, say, a goose at the market, then she would have to take it to the slaughterhouse to be prepared in the kosher manner.

Ernest Gross and his sister Magda before they left for Canada under the auspices of the Tailor Project.

We had a place where we cooked the meals. It's not like here where you put the food in the oven.

My mother and two of my sisters, Ilona and Aranka, were murdered during the war. But my father, his new wife, and my other two sisters, Elza and Magda, all survived Auschwitz. Even though Elza started showing signs of odd behaviour even before the war, you can imagine the effect that being in Auschwitz had on her; I found her in a mental institution in Budapest after the war and brought her home to Miskolc. Magda, who is a year and a half older than me, came with me to Austria in 1945 and then immigrated with me to Canada in 1948. She now lives in Oakville, Ontario. She's married and has two children—one lives with her family in Israel, and the other one is a podiatrist in the United States. Both Elza and Magda were teachers until 1994.

I was exceptional. Why? Because I was the only son in a Jewish family. After four years of elementary school, I completed eight years of *gymnasium* (high school) in Miskolc, but during the war years, I had to move to another *gymnasium* that was Catholic. There was a quota by then—a limit to how many Jews could be registered in a particular school or grade—and the Catholic school only allowed about six or eight Jewish students to attend. Still, we were very lucky because there was relatively little antisemitism in the school. The most senior teacher, although he was very Catholic, was definitely what I would call a philosemite. He came in many times to talk to the Jewish students, telling us not to worry. "This will pass," he would say. "Just don't give up." Another time, a priest from the Minorita, or Franciscan, order gleefully told us, "The Russians pushed back the Germans in Rostock."

After I had finished at the *gymnasium*, the school principal—I still remember his name, Zelenka Arpad—asked the few Jewish students a question about Roman Catholicism. Not one of us knew the answer and his displeasure showed up later on our last report card. I had always been in the top quarter of my class, but Arpad put in the worst possible grades, which prevented any of us from even applying to university. I ended up learning a bit of the jewellery trade after I left school. By this time, the Hungarian authorities had started sending Jewish boys to do manual labour, and I remember being sent to neighbouring city to work in the forest. To avoid being sent for more manual work or away from my hometown, I registered in the only Jewish teachers' seminary, in Budapest, where I stayed for a year, until 1944.

On March 19, 1944, the Germans swept into Hungary and most of the Jewish students went off in different directions. Some went home and others went into hiding, but four or five of us stayed at the school in Budapest. We had to start wearing yellow armbands with a Star of David. The school and the adjacent rabbinical seminary became a kind of internment camp.

The richest and most influential Jews were picked up and brought in there and four or five of us had to do some maintenance jobs. Having the relative freedom of going in or out of the camp with the yellow armband, despite being interned, I was able to connect with family. This clandestine operation had its consequences later on when I was caught bringing in a newspaper. Eventually, when we were all to be taken to a larger staging camp in Kistarcsa—on the outskirts of Budapest—I said to myself, "Don't count on me." Jews from other Hungarian cities were also taken there before being deported out of Hungary, and I knew only too well what it meant to be taken to Kistarcsa—punishment.

One day in June, posters went up all over Budapest, saying, MESSAGE TO THE JEWISH PEOPLE. By then, most of the Hungarian Jews had congregated in Budapest. The message was that all Jewish men had to go to a certain town at their own expense and register by a certain time. Instead of going where I was supposed to go, I went home to Miskolc to say goodbye to my mother. That was the last time I saw her alive.

Things were difficult when I got to Miskolc because by then they had set up a ghetto. I managed to slip in and out of it with the help of a former gentile student of my father. My mother told me that all Jewish men there had to go from Miskolc to Jolsva, Hungary (now Jelšava, Slovakia), so I went there instead. On the day that I arrived in Jolsva, I found my father amongst thousands of people. From that fateful moment, we shared our pain, our bread, and our instinct to survive. From Jolsva, we were marched through Miskolc to Budapest—the way I saw it, the aim of our captors was to eventually move us from Budapest to the Austrian border, and from there to Auschwitz. When one person in our large group tried to escape, he was immediately shot and left to die on the roadside. In the meantime, all Jewish women were being deported to their final destinations. For the next week or so, we marched through all kinds of places. When we reached Budapest, a rumour started flying around that there was a Swiss attaché who was giving out *Schutzbriefe*, Swiss "protective letters."

My father registered both of us. A relative of ours declined; to our knowledge, he died in Majdanek. The Germans still respected Swiss citizenship, and it was somehow useful because we came under the direction of a well-intentioned Hungarian officer and a Jewish former officer. We marched west again. By the time we'd made it through the Lake Balaton area, the Soviets were very close. The German army began to retreat, leaving behind the ineffective Hungarian militia.

We thought that the war had ended, but it hadn't. We were still marched back to Budapest and into the ghetto—but not out of Hungary, as the men who did not sign onto the Swiss list were. There was almost no food in the ghetto, but there was a Jewish centre that distributed soup. I went there a couple of times—under

fire from the Soviet artillery. Whenever I heard the *pop! pop! pop! pop! pop!* of the guns I'd have to run inside to find cover. We lived in a basement near the famous Dohány Temple—it was impossible to live above ground for safety reasons When I did go up for food, Hungarian soldiers grabbed me, along with some other people, and took us to work in a large military warehouse, Gresham Palota. While we worked there, we were still allowed to go back to the ghetto at night.

When one of our group was caught stealing a tiny piece of food, he was shot on the spot. A soldier—I can't remember if he was German or Hungarian—ordered us to take off the man's boots before throwing his corpse into the Danube. We didn't obey him; we weren't willing to rob the dead. We stayed in that ghetto until the Red Army came in and took over the whole of Hungary in the spring of 1945. They had already liberated Budapest—and the ghetto—in February.

I remember the day we heard that the Soviets had arrived—we all came out of the basement and greeted them, hugging them. They told us that we needed to get a *propuska*, an official document that would allow us to go home. We were directed to a collection place in front of the largest railway station plaza, Keleti, where about thirty thousand people were gathered. We waited impatiently for the so-called *propuska*—we wanted to start the train journey home from Budapest. But nothing happened because it turned out that from that point on, we were considered prisoners of war (POWs) of the Soviet Union.

This time it was the Russians who led us on a thirty-kilometre march from Budapest to Gödöllő, another camp. Gradually, out of the original thirty thousand people, seven thousand of us were taken to yet another camp, in Cegléd, and from there out of Hungary; mostly to Ukraine. I chose to go with a small, selected group of only forty people, even though I'd been told to stay with the large group. Among this small group were some Germans who were being protected because of their support of Russia. Eventually, they gathered the Jewish POWs and told us that we could go home. We were relieved, but it was also taken as another opportunity to rob the Jewish prisoners of whatever small possessions we might have had. A Soviet officer brought in a doctor to check whether we were in good enough physical condition to make the long trip. My father was half-starved, so he was allowed to leave the camp almost at once. He was free and, as I found out a few weeks later, alive. They also called for whoever was underage and, although I was nineteen, I was able to pass for a sixteen- or seventeen-year-old. I gained my freedom and went home in March 1945. To my real home.

When I got back to Miskolc, my father, Magda, and Elizabeth were already there, along with the woman who became my father's third wife. I registered for medical school and was attending classes in the third semester when I heard that a lot of Jewish people were going to Israel or to DP camps in Austria. One Jewish organization wanted to take all the Jewish survivors to Israel, but some—like me—said no. I wanted to get out of Hungary, but to a DP camp in Austria with my sister.

A Soviet truck driver took a group of us to Austria illegally. In return for some money and gold, he just drove us through the gates. He took us Niederscheld, where we were finally completely free. From Niederscheld, Magda and I went to the Wegscheid camp near Linz, the Puch Oberalm camp near Salzburg, then finally to the Hallein camp south of Salzburg, on the Austrian border with Germany, not very far from Munich. We were there from 1946 to 1948. I have to admit that we had a good life in the DP camps. We had no obligations. We were fed. We had places to sleep. From time to time, we got about ten dollars from our US relatives, which was quite a lot at that time. Our friend also took us to some beautiful places, such as Zell am See and Bad Gastein, and took us skiing. But it had to come to an end at some point; somehow we had to find a way to regain a normal life.

While we were in the Hallein DP camp, we met an influential person who worked with one of the organizations looking after DPs and he took a liking to us. When we saw the notice with the Canadian call for tailors, he was the one who put me and Magda on the list. A lot of people signed up whether they were tailors or not. I'd never had a needle in my hand, but there was no sewing test. Almost everybody knew that we weren't tailors. But we had to find a way to leave the DP camps and move to someplace where we could have a normal life. If we were accepted into the project, we would go first to Germany and, from there, to Canada.

Hallein wasn't a very large camp, just a few hundred people. The people who didn't sign up as tailors mostly wanted to wait until they could move to a camp in Germany and perhaps from there go to the United States. A lot of people wanted to go to the United States, maybe because they had relatives there. We also had relatives in the US, but I didn't end up going there because some relatives told me that I would have to contact the consul in Prague and I didn't want to risk travelling through the Russian Zone. I didn't want to be grabbed by the Russians, so I stayed in the DP camp. But I knew that it wasn't a permanent solution. When the opportunity to go to Canada came up, we were happy to go.

Magda and I left for the German port of Cuxhaven on the Atlantic, where we boarded the SS *Samaria* to sail for Canada. I was really excited when I saw such a big ship for the first time in my life. I used to draw pictures of the *Queen Mary* and loved the idea of a sea voyage. But the reality was different and not quite as inspiring. The day we left was very grey and rainy. All I could see was the ocean—nothing but water, all over. Nothing but water and other ships anchored there. The *Samaria* had previously been used as a troopship—it certainly wasn't like today's luxury ships. We slept in bunk beds and everybody got seasick on the first or second day. I was okay on the first day but on the second day I was really sick. The trip across the Atlantic took about ten days. We weren't sick all the time, though. Only at the beginning. But we still didn't have much appetite. I remember that they served green pea soup. It was so thick that you could turn the plate upside down and the soup wouldn't fall out.

We landed near Halifax and most of us weren't in great shape because of the seasickness. Magda and I went to Montreal by train and the whole group of us were met by people from the Jewish Immigrant Aid Society (JIAS). We got off the train in a suburb somewhere north of Montreal East, Saint-Paul-l'Ermite, and stayed in what used to be a military camp. We had a good meal there, but we only stayed for one day. From there, JIAS gave us five dollars per person and made arrangements for places for us to stay. They also looked for employment for us. At that time, the needle trade reigned, especially in Jewish circles, and Montreal was the centre of the needle trade in Canada, mainly along Chabanel Street. It still is today, even though it's not as strong. The needle trade had many different aspects, like being tailor or a designer or a shipper, so there were many possibilities for employment then. It didn't take more than a day from our arrival to get a job for fifty or sixty cents an hour.

That first five dollars didn't go too far, but for eighty cents per person, you could get a full-course meal at the Mount Royal, a kosher restaurant. And apart from that income, we got a few dollars whenever any relatives from the US came to see us. We certainly didn't starve or anything. My sister was assigned to stay with a Jewish lady from a well-known family in Montreal, the Barza family. The mother came from Lithuania and only spoke Yiddish, along with a few English words, but there were lots of doctors and lawyers in her family. It was a beautiful family, and the lady—who lived on Waverly Street—was really kind to us. I was assigned to another place on Hutchison Street with another family, but this lady told us, "Why should you go to that place? If you don't mind sleeping on a stretcher underneath the stairway, then you can stay here with your sister. She can cook for you and for herself, and also a third person." I was extremely happy that I could stay with her. We didn't have to pay rent until two years later, when we rented our own apartment.

We got our first jobs a few days after arriving in Montreal. Magda was hired at Ideal Dress, which at that time was a very large needle trade company. I got a job at the Chenille Bedspread Company for fifty or sixty cents an hour, but I worked close to sixty hours a week, so my weekly pay was about thirty-three dollars. That was big because real tailors only got about twenty-five dollars. To make thirty-three dollars at my job required

speed. I had to stretch out a blank sheet and then, with indigo, transfer the design to the bedspread, putting on and taking off the bedspread as I went.

Being a single person, I was able to save money, but we also knew other young people who came from the DP camps and spent time with them. We had company and we had a social life—we went out to the same places in Montreal. We'd go up north and rent a boat for a few hours, or go to the same movie, the same sports events. We had lots of things in common. We started going out, boys and girls, to some places on the Décarie, and a few of them already had cars. The first question that I got from at least one of the girls I met was, "Do you have a car?" No, I didn't. How could I have a car when I'd just arrived a few months or a year ago. But then, finally, after a few years, I was able to buy my first car, a 1948 Ford. It was a hatchback, with no heating, so I couldn't drive it in the winter. I also worked for a photography shop, delivering pictures.

I never did learn to sew. I stayed at Chenille Bedspread until early December, when the owner told us that he would be closing the factory for a few weeks. "Just come in and find out when we'll be open," he said. But I knew that I couldn't afford to wait to see when he would re-open. I had to look for another job. So, I got a job in shipping. Actually, I wasn't even a shipper, but an assistant shipper. My income went from thirty-three dollars a week to twenty-five. That was still enough.

Then someone I knew said, "Why don't you call my brother and find out if he wants to change jobs?" I called and he told me where he was working and that he would be moving to another job, so I could take his job. I followed him that way on more than two occasions. That worked out for a couple of years.

After I'd been doing the shipping jobs for a while, I didn't see much future in it and was happy when the next job I was offered was bookkeeping. "I don't mind doing it," I said, "but I don't know a thing about bookkeeping." "Never mind," he answered. "I'll show you what to do and you'll learn it as you go." That was at London Felt. I was their so-called bookkeeper and it did actually turn out to be a self-teaching job. The three owners couldn't care less. One of them didn't know even how to spell his name. The other two were more intelligent.

I had several other jobs as a bookkeeper—in one place I was also a one-person office manager—until I decided to take night courses at the same time. The first course I took was biology and then I had to take English. I picked up credits year by year and finally received a bachelor of commerce degree from Sir George Williams College (now part of Concordia University). After that, I spent most of my working years as a bookkeeper, a one-person office manager, and as an accountant. In fact, I worked for a chartered accountant for two years.

With my acquired knowledge and luck, I was hired by a mid-size handbag manufacturer and importer. The company grew and I grew with it, becoming part of the executive as vice-president of administration, with a wide range of responsibilities as controller and administrator. The advantage of being with a medium-sized company was that I was able to oversee all areas from petty cash to executive functions. I retired in 1992 after twenty-nine years of service with Cabrelli Inc. (formerly Handbags Limited).

I met my wife, Daisy, nearly sixty years ago when she was staying with some of her relatives. She was working at a mental hospital and became an assistant nurse. She got her nursing diploma and worked there for a year or so. After she left nursing, she worked for a wholesale jeweller for quite a long time, selling to Montreal retail stores and visiting Toronto customers. We have two children. The older one, our daughter Olga, is a musician and has been a pianist with the Montreal Symphony Orchestra for about twenty-five years. She also plays with the National Arts Centre Orchestra in Ottawa. As an additional source of income, she is called upon by her agent to play her repertoire of harp music in other places. Our son, Alexander, works for Wood Gundy investment company—a financial arm of CIBC—and has done very well. He has his own financial group within Wood Gundy.

Whatever comes, you never know, but we are enjoying our grandchildren and our children, too…most of the time. What else can I say? I told you a lot.

TORONTO

THE TAILORS DID NOT have an auspicious start in Toronto. As Max Enkin politely recounted, "social agencies were not as well organized" as they were in Montreal. When the first group of 266 tailors and their families arrived at Union Station on January 18, 1948, there was no one there to greet them. Soon a fleet of taxis and volunteers with their own cars appeared at the station, sent by the panicking staff at the Canadian Jewish Congress (CJC). Not only had none of the Toronto agencies been informed of their arrival, very limited housing had been arranged. The disoriented immigrants were taken to the union-owned Labour Lyceum where, amidst the pandemonium of unleashed children, the tailors were given their job assignments. Some of the couples, single men, and single women were taken to rented rooms. The rest, including all the families with children, were placed in a hastily furnished hall at the Folks Farein (Hebrew National Association) on Cecil Street and the gym of the Community House on St. George. Meals were brought in from nearby restaurants on Spadina Avenue. The next day seventy-five people were moved to similar makeshift quarters in Beth Yehuda Synagogue on Dovercourt Avenue, but Max Enkin took one look at it and declared that it was "not fit for human habitation." This fiasco was not officially recorded in CJC records, for fear that the labour ministry would find out and suspend the program. Saul Hayes took immediate control of the situation. Toronto's Jewish Immigrant Aid Society (JIAS) was stripped of responsibility for settlement and a few days later the commission set up an office managed by Tom Aplin, with the CJC paying for an assistant. Max Enkin recalled that Aplin was a huge asset to the program. The tailors could come to him for help finding jobs and housing, and dealing with a multitude of problems. "He was always one of those who had a willing ear."[1]

Salary advances of twenty-five dollars to the men and twenty to the women were disbursed the first day to enable them to pay their rent and purchase household goods. As elsewhere, the Council of Jewish Women provided donated clothing and furniture for the rented apartments. Loans of up to $250 were provided for deposits on the purchase of appliances and furniture with flexible repayment schedules.[2] The tailors were

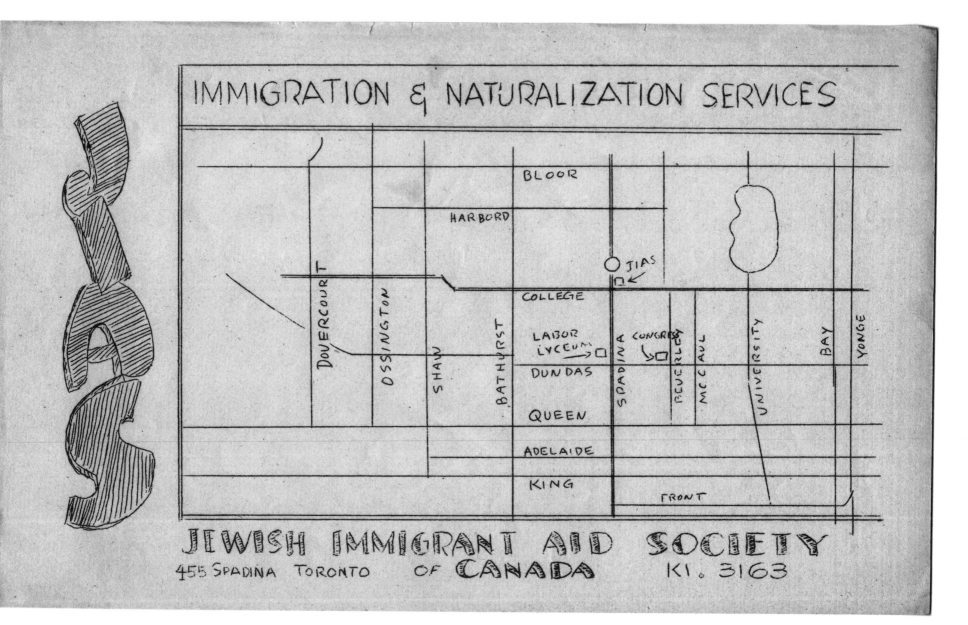

Hand-drawn map of downtown given to tailors arriving in Toronto by the Jewish Immigrant Aid Society of Canada (JIAS).

accompanied to their work sites and introduced to their employers. One of them, W. Roussell, the general manager of a Hamilton firm, wrote to thank the commission for the "friendly procedure followed in receiving and settling the 5 people from DP camps who recently joined our organization." Surprised to have only one day's notice of the arrival of the new workers, and "frankly more than a little concerned" that they would not be able to communicate with them, he was relieved to find them accompanied by two "most friendly, cooperative representatives." The commission workers remained with the five tailors until they were satisfied that they were completely settled into the workplace. "That gesture alone possibly did more to make the strangers feel at home than we can put into words."[3]

Max Enkin and a group of Jewish business leaders had founded Toronto's Jewish Vocational Services (JVS) in 1947 to provide employment and vocational services to Holocaust survivors and veterans of World War II. JVS workers monitored the tailors' placements and found other employment for those unable to adjust to Canadian methods and the approximately 10 per cent of the DPs who were not actually tailors. JIAS was brought back into the program to improve the family housing situation. They purchased a house at 147 Beverly Street that provided apartments for up to five families above their offices. With no other viable solutions in sight, the CJC decided to set up a holding corporation and by the end of 1948 they had purchased fourteen homes and rented two others. Seventy-five families, comprising three hundred people, were settled in the homes; their rents would serve to pay off the cost of the houses. Volunteers from the Council of Jewish Women and B'nai Brith set up English-language classes and provided forums for introducing survivors to Canadian life.[4] The Folks Farein remained a clearinghouse for the survivors, a place where Yiddish speakers could come for assistance with medical issues. Volunteers accompanied them to hospitals as translators. Despite the rocky start, the Garment Workers Commission and Toronto's Jewish agencies were soon able to cobble together a streamlined reception program for the immigrant tailors.

After the war, the Ladies' Union held a meeting at the Labour Lyceum on Spadina Avenue, inviting all the owners to attend. They let it be known that they were sending representatives to Europe to the displaced persons camps to see how many they could bring to Canada. Each owner pledged an amount of how many persons they could take into their shops. It was most successful, as quite a few came to Toronto and were housed on Cecil Street. The house on Cecil Street was furnished by people donating furniture, dishes, linens, and anything else needed to make this into a livable home. Money was also donated. My parents, Pearl and Dave Shadlesky, z'l, were actively involved in helping with this project. The neighbours on Oxford Street were most generous. I came home from school one day to find I was missing some of my clothing. My mother assured me that they would be replaced in due time. After getting the people settled and sent to the different factories, the few that ended up at Sunlight Cloak, where my father worked, didn't have a clue as to what to do. My father brought them home one at a time and taught them how to use a sewing machine and how to sew a garment. My mother taught some of the ladies to sew by hand, this was called "finishing." A few of these people became good friends of our family for many years.

—LAURA GREENBERG

CHARLES GOLDFINGER

Based on interviews with his sons Ralph, Lorie, and Howie Goldfinger.

It was a source of tranquility for him. Some people do garden work. Tata's way of gaining solace was to cut and to sew.

OUR FATHER, CHARLES GOLDFINGER—in Yiddish his name was Yechezkel or Chaskiel—was born on June 6, 1917, in town called Radomyśl Wielki, in southeastern Poland, about one hundred kilometres from Kraków. In 1939, when the war started, the population of the town was about three thousand, of which 1,422 were Jews.

His mother's name was Leiba and his father—our grandfather, Mordechai Goldfinger—was quite an entrepreneur. He owned a liquor license in their town in Poland. He had a retail store, a retail clothing store, where our father actually worked as a tailor. That's where he learned his trade. The family also ran a fruit and vegetable wholesale business in Kraków, and our father would tell us stories about how he went to Hamburg, Germany, to buy containers of fruit and vegetables that came in the port. They would then transport the produce back to their warehouse in Kraków.

Eventually, our grandfather also had our father working in the liquor store in Radomyśl Wielki, the Polish town that his family originally came from. The family also owned a building in Kraków. That's where our father must have gotten most of his work ethic, working in all the different types of family businesses. He must have worked seven days a week when he was younger—that was just the lifestyle he grew up in.

Our mother, Regina Schenker, was also born in Radomyśl Wielki in 1923; she and our father were second cousins. Our father was very spotty in talking about his background. He never sat down and said, "Here's my family tree. Here are the names." Whenever he felt good enough, he told us some of it. But he never did it in any kind of systematic way—he would just do it because he was able to talk about it in that moment. Tata, as we called him, had two sisters and an older brother. The older brother was the educated one. Our father went to a public school and never made it past Grade 7.

Charles and Regina Goldfinger at their
wedding in the Linz DP camp, Austria 1945.

Tata did tell us that he was in Kraków when the war was declared. He was supposed to enlist at a particular spot in Kraków, but when he got there, the war was already over for Poland; within a few weeks, the Germans came in and took over the country. He didn't know what to do, so he went back to Radomyśl. The Germans took over the town shortly thereafter in September 1939.

Neither of our parents ever wanted to talk about the past. My mother eventually did twenty or thirty years later, but when we were smaller, we barely knew about the Holocaust. They wanted their children to live a better life. They were very protective. My father was a bit more receptive, but as soon as he started talking, our mother would cry, "Shut up! Shut up already!" At home, at the dinner table, she didn't really want to talk about what happened.

Our mother was quite young when the war broke out, only fifteen or sixteen years old. She had a terrible time during the Holocaust. She and her family spent the first couple of years hiding in a bunker in the forest. Eventually she was caught and arrested as a spy, then jailed and tortured. When she was released, she was taken to the forced labour camp in Płaszów, just outside Kraków. From there she spent time in Auschwitz, Ravensbrück, Leipzig, and Radomyśl Wielki concentration camps. At the very end of the war, when the Germans were clearing the camps, she was sent on a death march. She must have had such a strong will to survive all of that.

Tata started out the war in a ghetto, but eventually he was transported to the Auschwitz subcamp Monowitz-Buna—also known as Auschwitz Three—where he worked for I.G. Farben. That was the company that manufactured the Zyklon B used in the gas chambers. There is one story that our father liked to tell about that time. He was valuable to the German officers because, as a tailor, he sewed uniforms for them. They would keep him hidden in the back room. That's how he survived. They would throw him some pieces of bread or an orange from time to time. So, he was well-fed, relative to others.

Then, when there were enough uniforms, they started killing the tailors. But they said that they needed people to build bunkers. "We're looking for bricklayers," they said. "Who here is a bricklayer?" My father raised his hand, even though he wasn't a bricklayer. When we asked him how he managed to fool the Germans, he replied, "Well, every bricklayer needs an assistant, so I became the assistant. The bricklayer teaches the assistant how to lay bricks, so I became a bricklayer."

He was in Auschwitz for two years, from 1942 to the end of 1944. Then, when the Germans were retreating and liquidating the camps, he was sent to Buchenwald, a notoriously brutal camp. The Allies had bombed some areas of Poland and, while he was at

Buchenwald, one of his jobs was to go to these bombed-out facilities and retrieve whatever was valuable. While he was doing that, he managed to find some fruit—bananas and oranges—and he stuffed them in his pockets. The first night, other prisoners in the barracks stole the fruit while he was asleep. After that, he'd eat as much as he could at the site and whatever was left over, he'd take to the barracks. The same thing happened when he was being a tailor. They let him into the barracks, to measure them and to sew, and so on. He said they used to tease him by putting out food, and seeing how much he would steal. They thought it was funny, but he didn't care because he ended up eating as much as he could. So, he survived that way. He survived through his wits, not missing an opportunity to be able to survive, by using those chances and opportunities.

After liberation, Tata did return to Radomyśl Wielki, but there was no one left from his family. Our mother's family and our father's family were all wiped out.

Our parents ended up meeting in Kraków after the war. The way our mother tells it, she arrived in the city in 1945 with nothing, just after being liberated from Malchow, where she ended up after the death march. She unexpectedly ran into a friend from Radomyśl Wielki who told her that her second cousin was still alive and living in his family's building in Kraków. When she eventually went to see him, he said to her,

"You know what? A first cousin you're not supposed to marry, but you are my second cousin. I think we should get married." Our mother answered, "You want to marry me? I just came out of the concentration camp. I can't think about marriage." But after they talked, they realized that life in Poland was still too dangerous for Jews. And this was after the war! They decided to flee to Austria, where, with help from Simon Wiesenthal, they found refuge in the Saalfelden DP camp near Linz. That's where they got married, by a rabbi, in 1945.

In Saalfelden, they shared an apartment with four other couples—five rooms for five couples. They cooked together and shared the food that came from the Red Cross. "It was like luxury," our mother said. They told people running the camp that our father was a tailor and they took us to the Canadian consul to make an application to come to Canada as a tailor. That's how they came to Canada on June 14, 1948. They sailed across to Halifax on the SS *Marine Falcon*. They brought with them our older brother, Marvin, who was born in 1946 while they were still living in Saalfelden.

Our parents had some relatives in New York who had immigrated before the war. They tried to get our parents into the States, but they weren't successful. Fortunately, the Tailor Project got them into Canada. Apparently there was some question of our parents staying in Halifax, but our mother wanted to go to Toronto.

Before Tata was able to start work, our parents

rented a place on Shannon Street. The apartment was on the second floor. The landlady didn't want to take them with a baby at first, but our mother begged them. The landlady agreed—only after she made it a condition of the rental was that our mother had to clean the steps. They also had to make a first and last month's payment of fifty dollars. They didn't have the money, so they went to the Canadian Jewish Congress (CJC), and the CJC gave them the fifty dollars. When our father got a job the week after—he made about a hundred dollars that week—our father immediately paid the CJC back the fifty dollars. That's all the help that he got from here, in the social system, as far as we know. Fortunately, their relatives in the US helped them out quite a bit as well.

Our father worked in a number of companies, but he wanted to stay with Gould and Son because he liked the business model of men's wear. He always talked about why men's wear was a good industry to go into because fashion didn't change as quickly as it did in women's wear. So, he worked for Gould and Son, which had more than five hundred sewing-machine operators at the time. And they were probably the premier outerwear maker in Toronto. There were many, many firms. At that time, around 1953, when our father was working as an operator, there were more than forty companies producing men's outerwear.

Later, we remember him having a cutting table and a cutter and a sewing machine and patterns in the basement of our house. He worked during the day, sometimes a second job, after he finished his first job. He would come home at night, and he would work. He would have dinner, and then he'd go downstairs, and then he'd work on making a couple of garments.

But Gould and Son eventually went bankrupt. So, our father said "Look. If they can go bankrupt, I can go bankrupt, too, meaning I would rather have my fate determined by my own hands. I'm going to go and start my own company." He had five hundred dollars to put toward it and he read an ad in the newspaper about a factory for sale. There was another guy looking to buy into that factory, a man named Irving Borenstein. After our father and Irving looked at the factory, they decided to form a partnership and buy the factory together. It cost about one thousand dollars to buy the factory with all of the equipment and the name, so they each put in five hundred dollars and bought the factory. They had five or six sewing machines, a press, and a cutting table. My father was involved in the manufacturing process; the cutting, the sewing. That was kind of his responsibility. Irving did the patterns as well as the sales and marketing.

Later in life, he was famous for his vests. He produced thousands and thousands of vests. Work vests, out of assorted material—scrap.

Tata didn't have much education, but he was very

quick with numbers. He had a very good sense of logic. He was not an academic; it was common sense. Street smarts. That's how he was able to prosper: hard work with good common sense. He also passed onto the three of us a smart strategy: as owners, number one, work alongside your staff. That's where the whole family business attitude stemmed from. But also, from a strategic point of view, don't ask anybody to do something that you can't. Another important strategy—that probably came from the Holocaust—is the importance of knowing who you can trust. Trust, for our father, was very, very thin. By being immersed in the operations and working alongside his staff, nothing could be happening behind his back. He wasn't an economist, he wasn't a social scientist, he wasn't a psychologist. He just knew what he had to do to survive.

Lorie used to tell people that he studied at the University of Charles Goldfinger. He wanted him to learn the business from the bottom up, and he did. Everything from cutting and sewing to running the production, how to work all the machines, how to repair the machines. Tata did a lot of that work himself. When he was working in the back, was he sewing? He was sewing. Was he cutting? He was cutting. Was he packing? He was packing. This is a lesson that we all learned. Also, to treat people with respect. Our father had every nationality in the factory. It was like the United Nations.

Tata came to work until he was ninety-eight. Virtually every day. He only stopped when our mother got sick. He died in 2016 and he was driving and working up until that year. Cutting and sewing, until 2015. We worked seven days a week for many, many years. It wasn't until the late 1990s that we transitioned into five days a week, when each of us worked every third Saturday. But it was his work ethic. And we asked him, "How can you work seven days a week? Full tilt, day after day, week after week?" He replied, "Compared to what I went through in the concentration camp and during the war, this is a cakewalk. It's a pleasure."

His work ethic was inspiration for all of us. It was survival. He had no choice. In Poland, he came by it honestly. It wasn't just because of the war that to make ends meet, the standard of living was much less. In order to survive, in order to prosper, you had to work long hours. Obviously, in the concentration camp, there was no time for rest. And really, he didn't.

When our father first arrived in Canada, there were other people with the same background, other survivors, so there was a close network. And then, he immediately joined a synagogue and it became his network. His world was very much part of the Jewish world. He didn't really have non-Jewish friends. The trust had been broken. The people he knew were very close to their families and the immediate sphere of people who had come to Canada under similar circumstances.

Our mother was a special lady, a very special lady—when she entered the room, you knew she was there. Both our mother and our father were bigger than life. Our mother wrote her memoirs in phonetic Polish in about 1970. Jan Grabowski, a professor of Holocaust studies at the University of Ottawa, got it translated into proper Polish and had it published with two other testimonies in Poland.

Our parents wanted us to be educated. Both Howie and Ralph have master's degrees. They didn't want us to go into the factory; they wanted us to have a better life. They didn't feel that we should work seven days a week or work long hours, that we should make a better life for ourselves.

Lorie finished his BA in psychology, but when our parents split up with their business partner, he came into the business. Our mother said, "Look. Your dad's all by himself now. He just bought the business. Help him out. You're not going back to school this year." He was going to apply for an MA the following year because he wanted to take a sabbatical and work in psychology, but there was nothing available. So, he said "Okay. I'll stay for a year." He hasn't gone back!

Howie swears that our father wanted him to be a rabbi. Up until the age of twelve, we did go to religious school. Howie used to wear a kippah and a tzitzit, the ceremonial shawl. Instead he got his master's degree in environmental studies, although originally he went to Israel to study the social organization of the kibbutz. Then afterward, he worked for the Social Planning Council of Toronto. After working for a consulting firm, doing all sorts of surveys and what-have-you, Lorie approached him about coming into the business.

Ralph studied economics, taking a lot of MBA courses; every MBA course except for OB, organizational behaviour.

Tragically, our oldest brother, Marvin, developed paranoid schizophrenia when he was sixteen or seventeen years old and never recovered. He passed away at fifty-three years of age. That affected our parents a great deal.

One thing that had a huge impact on our lives is that we didn't have any cousins. Ralph's wife probably has about seventeen first cousins. We grew up with no grandparents, no cousins, nothing. There might be the odd relative tucked away somewhere in New York or New Jersey. For us, that was normal. But when you meet other people who have maternal grandparents, paternal grandparents, cousins, it's like a different world that's difficult to understand. We grew up just a nuclear family. That was it. In their final years, our parents provided for their family not only a home and education but a place to work and flourish within the garment industry. Our nuclear family has grown from our parents to a family of twenty-five, with seven great-grandchildren, eight grandchildren and spouses, ourselves, and our wives.

HARRY GOLDFARB

Based on interviews with his wife, Helen Goldfarb.

I think it is it important to talk about this because it's history. It's good for the next generation to know what people went through.

I MET MY HUSBAND, Harry Goldfarb, in Kirghizia [now Kyrgyzstan], while I was working in an office. The Jewish people who had escaped into the Soviet Union from Poland were put to work digging canals and he was in charge of the people who were doing the digging. He had to make sure that they were doing their job and not just standing around. I was working in the office and he had to come in every day to hand in the list of people who were working. If you worked, you got a pound of bread; if you didn't work, you didn't get any bread. Anyway, he came in one evening with a book and asked me if I wanted to read it. I accepted, of course. Then he came in the next day and asked if I liked the book and wanting to know how much of it I had read.

After a few months, he said, "You know what? We don't know when we're going to go home and I'm getting old." He wanted to get married and I told him that he would have to talk to my parents. "I have nothing to say," I said. So he went and talked to my parents and they said, "Bring your parents. We want to meet your family, then we'll talk about it." He had a very nice family and they accepted. There was a Jewish guy there who was like a *shammash*, who performed various religious duties. He cut the chickens, he gave *kiddushin*, performed ceremonies. He did everything, whatever we needed. When somebody had a baby, he did the circumcision. Everything that we needed. So we had a *kiddushin*, a wedding.

My husband was from a small village in the northeast of Poland called Saranac. He was born there on August 24, 1913, and before the war he had apprenticed as a tailor. His father, Ainuch Goldfarb, was a baker and his mother, Leah Peya, looked after the home and their three children. When Germany was about to invade Poland, Harry was called up to the Polish army and posted to the artillery. He was good at math, so he

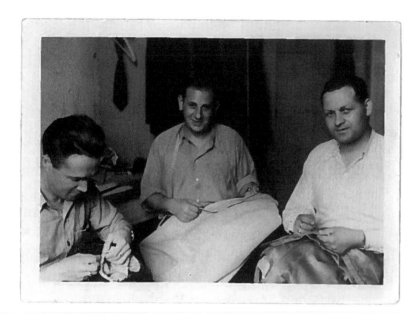

Harry Goldfarb (left) in the Goldkopf DP camp, in the American Zone of Germany.

did the calculations to help them know where to fire the cannon. The Polish army fell very quickly, however, and he was briefly taken prisoner. But they didn't realize that he was Jewish—he spoke Polish very well—and he managed to escape. He first went back to Saranac, but by then his parents had already fled to the part of Poland that was occupied by the Soviet Union, so he kept going until he got to Siemiatycze, near the eastern border of Poland. He knocked on the door of a house, and when they let him in, he asked if they would give him a change of clothes so he could take off his army uniform.

My family lived in Siedlce before the war, about eighty kilometres from Warsaw. It was a city with a large Jewish population. My father was a shoemaker there. Life in Poland was very hard—we didn't have any running water in the house, so there were no washrooms; you had to go to an outhouse in the backyard.

My father's sister had married a man from Siemiatycze, on the other side of the Bug River, the dividing line between the German-occupied territory and Soviet-occupied territory at the start of the war. When the war broke out, this auntie sent a man with a letter telling us to come and stay with her until the fighting stopped. So my mother made two big bags from our velvet blankets and packed in whatever clothes, bedding, pillows, and other things that she could. And we went to Siemiatycze, to my auntie. My mother had four sisters. They all stayed behind. I tried to get somebody else to come with us, but her mother-in-law wouldn't let her go. Some people just thought the war would be over soon. They had no idea what the repercussions would be and they stayed in their town.

We all thought the war in Poland would be over in a few weeks, so my auntie rented a room for us. We lived in that room—my mother, my father, my sister, and my brother—for about nine months. Then the Soviet soldiers came at twelve o'clock at night to every house where Jewish refugees were living and banged on the doors, saying, "Get ready. You only have fifteen minutes to pack up whatever you can to take with you." They took us to the train station and put about fifty people onto each cattle car. When my auntie woke up and heard the news, she came to our room and saw that it was empty. She ran to the train station to find us and brought us sugar and butter and a big loaf of bread so we would have food for the journey.

We travelled in those cattle cars for four weeks, until we arrived in a labour camp in Siberia. There, we had to work in the forest, cutting trees and stripping off the branches. When the trees were clean, they used horses to drag them to the lake. The Russians told us we'd be there forever. They told us to make a home and try to live the best we could. There was nothing around us but forest; there was nothing to do except work. If they told you to do something and you refused, they sent you away. One time, they wanted me to take a job and I told them I wouldn't do it. So they took me away—I was only sixteen—and my parents didn't know where I was. The other labour camp they took me to wasn't far, but you needed a horse to get there. They gave me a job cutting wood for outhouses.

I was away from my family and they took me to stay in a barracks, one very long room where all the other people staying there were men. They showed me where to get a cot for them to set up and I started crying. "No!" I said. "I'm a girl, a young girl. I don't want to sleep in a room with all these men." I went outside and walked around until I saw a man standing by a little wooden hut. He turned out to be a Jewish man—it turned out that he was from my husband's shtetl, although I didn't know my husband then. I told him what my situation was and he said that I could sleep on a shelf in the hut. He was a mechanic and the hut was his shop, where he fixed bikes. He told me that he would lock the door at night so I would be safe and come in the morning to let me out. So at night, he left and locked the door behind him. He was a very nice man, who saved me from having to stay with all the men. I worked in that camp for four weeks. After that, the Russians said that I could go back to my parents. There, they gave me the job of looking after a cow, but I was afraid to go near it. Finally, they told me I could tend the vegetables growing in the garden.

While we were in Siberia, the Russians gave my father the job of looking after a horse, but he had no idea how to handle it. So my brother, who was only a little boy, five years old, took a stool and harnessed the horse. I don't know how he knew what to do. When the horse was brought back from pulling the logs to the river, he removed the harness and looked after it.

After eighteen months in Siberia, they took us away from there, first to the Kazakh Republic, but after a month, the people there said they didn't want us, so they took us to Kirghizia. We were in Kirghizia for five years. The conditions were terrible—there was no floor in the small room where the five of us lived. No stove, no running water, nothing. The water ran in canals through the backyards and some people washed in it, some people took the water to drink, some people washed diapers. There were local people living there, but mostly it was Jews who had come from Poland.

All the local women there always wore high boots, so my father went to the market, bought some leather, and started making boots. When they were finished, my sister took them to the market and sold them. There weren't many goods there; no stores to buy what you needed. Some people were speculators, working in the black market, bringing things back from big cities in Soviet Union and selling them. One time, a very rich Jewish guy speculated on the black market. Two men took him out, killed him, and took away everything he had.

We didn't feel threatened in Kirghizia; the local people there showed us a lot of respect. I was put to work digging the six-foot-deep canals for the water to get to every house. But I got sick and when I went to the hospital, they told me that I couldn't do that kind of labour. Still, as before in Siberia, I wasn't allowed to refuse, so my father did my work for me. One day, a city official—like a mayor here—came by on her horse while my father was digging. I told her that I was sick—that was why my father was doing my work—and showed her the paper from the hospital. She asked me in Kyrgyz if I could write and I said yes. Then she asked me if I could do arithmetic and again I said yes. So she said, "Come with me." I walked beside her horse as she took me to her office. When we got there I said, "Give me a pen and a paper and tell me what you want me to write." She gave me some numbers and asked me to do some sums, to add and subtract. I did as she asked and she said, "From now on you will work in the office. Let your father do the digging and you come here." I was very happy to get the job in the office. And then, of course, that's where I met my husband. We got married in 1943 in Osh, Kirghizia.

At the end of the war, the Soviets started sending all the Polish refugees back to Poland. We were sent by train to Szczecin, a centre for Jews being "repatriated" from the Soviet Union. In one building, there were lists of the names of Jewish people who had survived and people went there to search for family members.

We didn't stay very long in Poland. We didn't find any of our family on those lists from the Red Cross. No one in our family who had been in Poland when the war began had survived. All of my family, from both my mother's side and my father's side, who had remained in Poland and the part of the Soviet Union overrun by the Nazis were gone. And word started coming back to us about Jews who had tried to go back to their home towns in Poland. We were told that some of their former neighbours had moved into their homes and did not want to give up what they had taken, and that some Jewish people had been killed. Our house was a fourplex and we heard that it hadn't been damaged. My father wanted to go back to Poland to sell it, but people told him that the moment Jews got off the trains, they were being killed because the Polish people didn't want to give back what they had taken from them. I was afraid to go out. We decided that we had to get out of Poland, to get across the border to the American Zone where there were displaced persons camps.

Bricha, the Jewish underground organization that was helping Holocaust survivors get out of Eastern Europe and smuggling them to British Mandate Palestine, had a base in Szczecin. If you paid them money, they would smuggle you in buses and trucks to DP camps in the American occupation zones in Germany and Austria, and then ultimately to Palestine. We paid money for the transport and Bricha smuggled us across the border. Our truck had no problem, nobody stopped us. But in the second truck, the one right after us, there was a man who was a jeweller. They stopped that truck and they took away all his jewellery. If you were lucky, nothing happened; otherwise, the Russians would take away whatever you had. By this time, I had my son—I was the only one with a child and I was holding him in my arms. The smugglers told me that if he cried on the truck they would have to smother him. People were so afraid.

Finally, we made it into the American Zone, to a DP camp called Goldkopf. When we were there, deciding where to go next, my husband said that he didn't want to go to Israel because he figured it would be filled with tailors. He read a lot and he was always talking politics. He wouldn't be able to make a living, he thought, because so many of the Jewish tailors were going to Israel.

Then, some people from Canada came to the DP camp and wanted to know who was a tailor. They had a sewing machine and asked the people who said they were tailors to make a pocket. Once a person made a pocket, then they would know he's a tailor. So my husband went in and made a pocket. He was a very good tailor. An excellent tailor. So that's how we got accepted right away to go to Canada. We were in a place called Butzbach for a whole month before we could go to Canada. Every day, they took us for special medical tests. I remember they put spray in my hair in case I had lice. It was a full month before they let us go.

We always stuck together, my whole family. When my husband went to make a pocket, he also helped out my brother-in-law. My sister and my brother-in-law were able to come six months after us and my parents came after a year. As soon as I got to Canada, with my husband and my little son—he was by this time four years old—I went to the Canadian Jewish Congress (CJC), to fill out the papers to bring my parents here. I needed to have at least five hundred dollars in the bank and a paper showing that I had a place for them to live. Rabbi Kelman (the brother of the rabbi of Beth Emeth) loaned us five hundred dollars and then two other men, who were friends of Harry, also loaned us five hundred dollars—one gave me two hundred and the other gave me his bank book with three hundred dollars. He gave me the whole book and told me that I could take all the money and I was able to get the paper showing that I had more than five hundred dollars in the bank. And I had friends, and they had friends who bought the first house at Euclid and College. They gave me a paper offering the second-floor flat to my parents. It was very nice of them. And that's how my parents and my brother came here. It took a year. By working hard and saving, we were able to pay back all the money that was loaned to us in good time.

We came to Canada in 1948 on the RMS *Scythia*. When we landed, they wanted to send us to Winnipeg, but I said that I had family in Toronto, which I did—my father's cousin had a printing shop on Spadina. I told them and they let us come here, to Toronto. And because I came here, I brought my sister and her family here as well as my parents and my brother. The CJC first rented a room to us on Dovercourt Road. My husband was given a job right away and started work the day after we arrived in Toronto. He went to work in a factory for Posluns Sportswear on Spadina. They had a man there, a supervisor, who was harsh. The workers suffered a lot from that man. He always rushed them—my husband used to come home with his whole shirt wet from rushing around doing the sewing. The conditions were very difficult. My husband worked there for ten years.

After ten years, we decided that since Harry was so good at tailoring and doing alterations, we would buy a dry-cleaning business. There was a man—also named Harry—who owned a shop on Queen Street West near Roncesvalles, and who had to move to the United States because his wife had family there. So, my Harry said, "My wife will stay here and watch for a while. If the business is doing as well as you say it is, I'm taking it." I was there for two weeks, learning how they ran the business. It was as good as he said and after the two weeks were up we bought the dry-cleaning business on Queen Street. We were there for twenty-five years. My husband did all the alterations and I worked at the counter—taking in the clothes, covering them up after cleaning, making out the bills, and getting everything ready for the people to pick up. In those days, the paper bags to wrap the clothes in hung on a wire from the ceiling. I would have a terrible pain in my back by the end of the day, just from reaching up to grab the paper all day. But after a few years, the plastic bags came out and we had a rack with special plastic bags for pants, for suits, and for coats and dresses. That was much easier.

When we first came to Toronto, I had also gone out to work and my first job was at the Health Bread Bakery on College Street. I worked there until I got pregnant with my daughter in 1949—actually, when I got pregnant, they made me stop working. After the bakery, I worked in a butcher shop—taking the orders, making out the invoices, and wrapping the parcels to send out. Then I went into the business with my husband. The children went to school and I cooked every morning, so supper would be ready soon after we got home. All my life, I shopped, cleaned, and cooked, and I worked—all my life.

As I said, the first house we lived in was on Dovercourt, but we were only there for a short time because I wasn't well. We lived on the third floor and my heart couldn't stand all the walking up and down the stairs. There was no running water and no washroom on that floor, so I had to carry the water, taking the clean water up and bringing the dirty water down. I couldn't do it; I was always short of breath. A volunteer—I don't remember her name, but her husband was a doctor—took me to the old Mount Sinai Hospital in Yorkville. They told me that I had to live in a main floor apartment so I didn't have to walk up and down steps. My heart was too weak.

The CJC had bought houses where they could provide accommodations for two or three families. They had a house on Beatrice Street and they rented the main floor to us. When my sister came to Toronto, she and her husband and child joined us on the same floor. So they had a bedroom, Harry and I had a bedroom, and we shared the kitchen. On the second floor was a family with three kids, and on the third floor was a family with one child. The second floor had a kitchen, but the third floor didn't; they used a little oven. We all managed because we were used to hard conditions. We didn't have those things in Poland—there was no water, no electric stove. We had to make fire with wood, putting on a little bit of kerosene and then, when the fire heated up, putting on a little bit of coal. It wasn't an easy life. We had to bring in water from the pump and had a barrel in the kitchen to put the clean water in. Then we had a pail for the dirty water. It was very hard. And when you had to do laundry, oh, boy; how many times we had to bring in water!

From the money we made doings alterations, step by step, we were able to save up. First, we had a house on Ossington; we paid down one thousand dollars and we bought the house. We had a mortgage from the author Mazo de la Roche.

We had a lot of friends in Toronto. They were all from Poland, from different cities and some of them from my city. We were five couples and we played cards every Saturday night, the men in the kitchen, the women in the dining room. Every Saturday night—it was a must! We never skipped. We played thirteen-card rummy.

We weren't very religious but for the New Year, we'd always go to shul. When we lived downtown, we used to go to Bais Yehuda—before they merged with Beth Emeth, Bais Yehuda was on Dovercourt Street. And we lived on Ossington, so we walked there every Friday night.

We shut down the dry-cleaning store in, I think, 1983. After that we didn't know what to do with ourselves. Harry decided to work part-time, doing tailoring for a nearby cleaners. We used to go to the Jewish Community Centre. I learned swimming, I learned crocheting. I started crocheting for everybody—blankets, afghans. Now I go to a seniors' club at B'nai Brith.

I have two children, a son and a daughter, who are university-educated professionals. My son is an information technology consultant, and my daughter is a lawyer. Both are retired now. I have four wonderful grandchildren and a very sweet great-granddaughter. I'm very proud of all of them.

LOUIS TABACHNICK

Based on interviews with his sons Sol and Phil, and with his grandson Jeff.

We and our people, we know the stories because we grew up with the stories.

—SOL TABACHNICK

OUR FATHER AND MOTHER and their three sons were all born in the town of Bendin—Bendin in Jewish (Yiddish) and Będzin in Polish. Bendin was a fairly large city in southwestern Poland near the German border, not far from Kraków, and close to Oświęcim, or Auschwitz as it's better known. Bendin had a strong and vibrant Jewish community before World War II; they made up more than 60 per cent of the town's population.

Our father, Eliazar Joseph (later Louis) Tabachnick, was born on June 28 or 29, 1909. Our mother, Chaia-Bayleh (or Helen) Grossman, was born on January 1, 1912. Phil, the eldest son, was born on November 20, 1931. Next was Moishe (Morris), who was born

November 1, 1933. Sol is the youngest, born Shloime (Solomon, Sol, or Solly), on December 26, 1935.

Our maternal grandfather, Pinchas Lazar, left Poland for Toronto in 1912 or 1913 to work, hoping to bring his family—his wife and children, including a baby daughter, my mother—to Canada. But he died of the Spanish influenza and was buried in Toronto. Chaia-Bayleh was two years old when he left and her mother, Malka Grossman, who was very religious, never remarried.

We grew up in a very nice apartment in Bendin. Our extended family all lived within walking distance of one another and we celebrated all the holidays together.

Our parents were both tailors and, on our father's side, tailoring was the family business. Our paternal grandfather, Shmuel (or Shmiel) Tabachnick, was a tailor. And there were several sewing machines in our apartment because our father—a tailor like his father—had four or five people working for him, producing men's and women's wear. Our mother, who was also a very talented tailor, sometimes helped Dad with sewing in addition to being a homemaker.

Tabachnick family in Leninabad, Tajikstan, in 1945. Left to right: Sol, Morris, Phil, Helen, and Louis (Leiser) Tabachnick.

We generally got along well with the gentiles in Bendin before the war, but we experienced our share of antisemitism. As far as I'm concerned, Poland was a very antisemitic country. Do you remember *Fiddler on the Roof*—with the pogroms? That's what it used to be like. We were aware of what kinds of things were going on in Germany from day one. When the Germans invaded Poland, our family, along with aunts and uncles and cousins and our maternal grandmother, were on vacation in the beautiful countryside around Otwock. Two or three days after the Germans invaded Poland in 1939, there were rumours that they would round up all the men, so our dad and uncles took off with some of the other men. They returned a few days later to get us, though, realizing that they had left us unprotected. Phil and Moishe were eight and six; Sol was only four.

We left Otwock by horse and buggy, heading east. Everybody piled into the buggy—our parents, grandmother, uncles, aunts, and cousins—and when we got to Białystok, we went across the border to the Soviet side of Poland, which had been divided between the Germans and the Soviets. We had to walk across the border to Lvov because there were no trains or anything. We walked. A German soldier let us go through. From Lvov, we got on a train and travelled through Kiev and wound up, in 1940, in a city called Kursk, where we stayed for about two years. Dad got a job working as a tailor in a factory there and eventually became the manager.

The Germans invaded the Soviet Union on June 22, 1941, and by that time we started hearing stories about how the Nazis were treating the Jews in Poland—not all the details—not about the death squads and the gas chambers—just that things were getting very bad for Jews in Poland. Before that happened, our mother's brother, Shmiel, who was very religious, got upset because there was no synagogue in Kursk. So he, his wife, and their children returned to the German side and, sadly, they were eventually murdered. Our mother's sister, Shaindel, was not well, so she and her husband couldn't continue on with us when we decided we had to flee again. They perished too, as did my grandmother. Everyone in my mother's family died. Our father's family all perished as well, except for one sister, Laicha (Lola). After the war, she wound up in Costa Rica with her husband, who had relatives there.

When the Germans invaded, Dad was drafted into the Soviet army. He was sent up to Kamchatka on the Bering Sea and, from there, he was shipped to Smolensk, the site of two major battles in World War II; in 1941 and 1943. When they were marching on Smolensk, however, Stalin gave orders to release all the foreigners because they weren't trained as soldiers.

While our father was in the army, the three boys stayed with our mother, who worked as a tailor to support us. From Kursk, we continued to travel east, away from the fighting. We travelled by train through

Kazakhstan and finally arrived in Tashkent, the capital of Uzbekistan, not knowing where else to go. There were other Jewish people with us, but none of them were relatives. As the Germans kept pushing further into the Soviet Union, we kept moving back. By the time we stopped, we were nearly at the Chinese border, at the Amur River.

One day, while we were in Tashkent, Phil, Moishe, and Sol were playing by the railway tracks with some other kids when all of a sudden we saw, in the distance, a man coming toward us in a Soviet soldier's uniform. It was our father! He had had some idea where to look for us—the plan had always been to move east into Central Asia—but still, it was really lucky that he found us. We spent a few months in Tashkent. Then, in 1942, the Soviet government sent us to Leninabad (now Khujand) in Tajikistan because they needed labourers to work in the cotton fields.

Things were tough in Tajikistan, where we lived on a *kolkhoz*, a collective farm. Our work was hard. Even as little guys, we all had to pick cotton. At the end of the day the only food we got was some pieces of mushy black bread. All we had with that was a cup of boiled water. It was horrible. Sol nearly starved to death he was so weak. We didn't see real bread for six or eight months. We'd pick up whatever bits of vegetables and fruit we could, wash it, and boil it. We even picked up the stuff that was left over from harvesting the corn and

wheat. We'd shake out all the pieces of stems and leaves and our mother would make soup out of it. We would eat soup that was made of straw and grass and leaves. We were so hungry. When they could get work, both our parents did bits of tailoring in Tajikistan as well.

Phil had his bar mitzvah while we were in Tajikistan. There was a rabbi who used to travel around to different communities. Our mother covered the window of our little hut and somehow found the ingredients to make a sponge cake. It was all done quietly, with no show.

Phil went to the local Russian school. According to him, the school was okay, but it was all about teaching the Soviet way of life. They said, "This is the way it is and that's it." What they were teaching in school truly was the way people think about socialism—everybody being equal, living free and all of that—but it wasn't. People were afraid to say one word against the government. If somebody snitched on you, you got arrested, and you went to Siberia.

When the war was finally over, we made our way back to Poland, the five of us travelling west from Tajikistan in cattle cars. There was no problem crossing the border out of the Soviet Union; the Soviets just let people out. We hadn't realized how bad things had been in Poland until we got out of the USSR. People had talked about it. There had been rumours, but nobody really knew. Almost all of our parents' siblings had stayed in Poland. Once the Germans occupied the whole country, they had no choice. Between our two parents, they had twenty-three siblings. Only three had survived—our mother, our father, and our father's sister Lola. He found her by chance in Germany after the war. He was on the streetcar and saw her walking down the street. She had survived the concentration camps.

By the time we got back, in 1946, Lola had married and was living in Wrocław. We stayed there with her and her husband, but our parents wanted to go back to Bendin to see who was left. Of course, there was nobody left. They only went back for one day and saw right away what was going on with the Poles. They said that all the stones in the cemetery had been laid down on the ground to walk on. There was no Jewish community left. And they were still killing Jews in Poland, even after the war.

Our parents had actually wanted to go to Palestine with Bricha, the Jewish underground organization set up to smuggle survivors out of Europe. To make our way to Palestine, we would have to cross into Czechoslovakia. Once we got together the money we needed, we went by train to Wałbrzych, near the Czech border. We were instructed to stay there for a day or two, then leave at nine o'clock at night to cross the border into Czechoslovakia. We actually walked across the border and kept walking until we got to Prague. We were told to sit near the huge circular fountain and wait for the people from Bricha. The Czech police in the area would have apparently been "looked after"—bought off. After we met up with the people from Bricha, we went by train to Vienna.

We stayed in Vienna for a couple of days and then we were transferred to the British sector—Germany and Austria had been divided into zones administered by the British, the French, the Americans, and the Soviets—to a DP camp in a place called Admont, a small town in the beautiful, picturesque Austrian Alps. There were maybe a thousand people in the DP camp, Jews from all over Europe, living in former military barracks. There was one room per family. We stayed there for about two and a half years. The UNRRA, the United Nations Relief and Rehabilitation Administration, managed the camp and supplied the food. Our father and some of the other men were volunteer firefighters and the young people went to school. We weren't treated the way that the Germans would have treated us, that's for sure, but the British Zone was not as good or friendly as the American Zone.

Phil, who had learned to play the violin in Tajikistan—he was very good—joined with others who could play instruments and formed an orchestra. They played all kinds of music, in concerts, at weddings, and in plays. Austria felt like freedom, like breathing fresh air. But we still wanted to go to Palestine. We travelled to different consulates, trying to get visas. But the British weren't making it easy; Jews who tried to immigrate there were being held in detention camps in Cypress.

In 1947, about a year after we arrived in Admont, some people came from Canada looking for tailors, so our parents registered. They were interviewed in Graz and our mother said to the interviewer, in Yiddish, "Panye Mister, I have cousins in Toronto, Sam Wasserman, maybe you know him?" He was writing down things and didn't even look up. Eventually he looked up and said, "Neyn, ikh kon nisht aza man." (I don't know anyone by that name.) Strangely enough, when we came to Toronto, our father wound up working as a tailor for the Posluns family, who were distant cousins of my mother's. Although my parents didn't know it at the time, it turned out that Samuel Posluns himself was the man who had interviewed them in Graz. And Sam—Shmuel Wasserman, our mother's cousin—was working for him as well.

When we couldn't go to Palestine, we had actually wanted to go the US, but, because our parents were tailors, we came to Canada. Canada was very little heard of, at the time. Everything was about America, the United States. We knew nothing about Canada.

Anyway, the Canadians gave our parents a sewing test to see if they were really tailors. They gave each of them something to sew—my father could do both men's clothing and women's clothing, and my mother could do kids' clothes, everything. They took the test on the same day, lining up with others to take it. Some people couldn't go for the test because they weren't tailors.

Needless to say, our parents both passed the sewing test, but then we worried about the health test. Everyone had to take a health test and if you had tuberculosis, they wouldn't let you in. They looked at your lungs, in your throat and your ears, all that. They told you right away if you passed. We all did.

Finally, everything was in order and, in 1948, we got on a train to travel from Austria to Italy. We travelled all through Italy to Genoa, and from there we took a boat to Canada. Getting on that boat was already freedom! We were out of Austria. We were kids. It was terrific! We were on a boat ride! It was a Greek ship, the SS *Nea Hellas*. The food on board was wonderful and there was so much of it! But as we sailed across into the North Atlantic, the weather turned nasty and cold, and water came up over the deck. It was rough. The trip took about eight days and we landed in Halifax in April.

In Halifax, we got on a train to Montreal, where we lived for three months. Our father and mother had jobs waiting for them there. The factory was owned by Rabbi Felder's father and he took good care of us. His son, the rabbi, lived in Toronto. All the families who came over were placed with elderly Jewish widows. We stayed with a Mrs. Yellin, a very old lady. We lived with her for a few months, but our mother wanted to come to Toronto because her father had gone there. So we moved because of him, even though he was long dead by this time. Our mother had never really known him.

When we got to Toronto, the Canadian Jewish Congress (CJC) helped us find out that our mother's father was buried in Roselawn Cemetery. The three boys would sometimes go with our mother to visit her father's grave before the holidays.

As we've said, our father went to work for Sam Posluns in Toronto. He worked there for many years. Tailors used to get tickets for the garments they did, what they were worth. When it was slow, they were able to live off of the tickets they accumulated. They wouldn't cash them every week. They could be cashed anytime. It was pretty difficult in those days because the manufacturing of clothing wasn't a year-round job. That's why they used to save the tickets from each garment they made. Actually, we all had to work when we got here. There wasn't too much formal education because it was tough times. By this time, we were in our late teens and we all went to work. At first, Phil went to work for Remington Typewriters.

Sol and Morris both got into lots of fights—both were young and strong and, taunted as DPs, had to defend themselves. It wasn't that easy here in Toronto, when we came over. They were just young guys and always had to fight. Our friends when we first lived in Toronto were what we called other greenies. Greenhorns. As a matter of fact, Sol still has friends from those days; they go out every Saturday night. We all used to play games at each other's houses every Wednesday. The girls

mostly played Scrabble and the guys played a little bit of cards. We were eight couples who had all become friends more than fifty years ago, before we got married. And we stuck together. We used to get together twice a week, on Wednesday nights and Saturday nights. We used to go on vacations together.

Eventually our parents got out of garment manufacturing and opened a store called Helen's Creamery, after our mother. They served bagels and breads and cream cheeses and fish, all kinds of stuff. Our mother did all of the cooking for the store. Cooking, plus she had help out in the front. She prepared homemade foods like *kishke*, *knishes*, and *leber knishes*. Customers came from all over southern Ontario to buy our mother's baked carp, gefilte fish, and strudels. She never wrote down the recipes. She would say, "A bissel dos un a bissel dos"—you put in a little of this and a little of that. There's nowhere now to get this kind of stuff. But the store was hard work—our parents worked long hours, seven days a week. They kept the business until they retired in the mid- to late-seventies.

We had a good life in Toronto because it was a free country.

Phil continued playing the violin, taking classes for a while at the conservatory. But it didn't last because we couldn't afford to pay for the lessons. He got into sales in different industries. Ultimately, he gravitated into the furniture industry. He had retail stores and was involved in manufacturing for many, many, years. And then, he went to work for other companies in the furniture industry. He and his wife, Joyce, got married in the early 1950s and had a two boys, Brian and Jeffrey, both happily married. One lives in Toronto, and the other in Spain. Joyce passed away a few years ago. Brian was in the car business, and Jeff ultimately went into the real estate business.

Sol went into the meat business, working as a butcher. He and his wife, Sandra, had three children, two boys and a girl. His oldest son is married, has a good education and went into the film industry, scouting locations. His daughter is staying with him right now, and his youngest son is in the furniture restoration business, making furniture out of wood from old wooden barns and so on.

Our middle brother, Morris, who passed away a few years ago, was always in sales. He was married a few times. He has a daughter who lives in Toronto and a son from another marriage, who lives in the US. Both are happily married with children.

Our father passed away in 1982, when he was seventy-three years old. He was a firecracker, very quick in his work. And our mother, she lived to ninety-six; she died almost thirteen years ago. She was like a magnet. She just attracted people. She always had a card game going, always. And she always had people, older friends, newer friends in a line coming up to see her.

We're going to be gone pretty soon. You have to pass the stories on to other generations. They have to know about it.

EAST AND WEST

BY OCTOBER 1948, twenty-seven ships had brought 1,643 tailors to Canada, comprising about three-quarters of the final number, and their division between cities followed the initial plans. About 55 per cent had settled in Montreal, 36 per cent in Toronto, 7 per cent in Winnipeg, and 2 per cent in Vancouver. Just over 60 per cent of the tailors were Jews and, of the total, only 339 were women. While some non-Jews in the program were sent to small communities like Moose Jaw, most of the Jewish tailors were destined for the big cities.[1] There were exceptions. One tailor settled with his family in the Jewish settlement of Hoffer, Saskatchewan, and one married couple went to Calgary. Eight single men, including Mendel Good, found jobs in Ottawa and five Jewish tailors were placed in Saint John, New Brunswick.[2]

The larger Jewish communities of Toronto and Montreal were appealing destinations for the survivors. As Walter Friedman wrote, "At the beginning it was rather difficult to convince some of these refugees about the desirability of settling in Western Canada, but more recently the happy reports of those who went there act as an inducement for others to join them."[3] The small Jewish community of Vancouver welcomed fifty survivors from the Tailor Project. The second contingent arrived in May 1948 as a group of seven men and three spouses. They were placed in private homes until rental housing could be found. The *Jewish Western Bulletin* reported that they were "a cheerful little group of travellers, with Henryk Gutowicz trying out his English, and Nusen Szredni hugging his violin." They were greeted by the local Canadian Jewish Congress (CJC) refugee committee chair, Sam Tenenbaum. "The refugees were amazed at many things in Canada, not the least of which was Mr. Tenenbaum's tie. It is a flamboyant silk affair, showing a gentleman in a loin cloth aiming a hefty arrow at a snarling leopard in a billowing tropical tree."[4]

There was nothing humorous about Vancouver's severe housing shortage, however. Temporary housing in family homes and the CJC building were yet another challenge for survivors anxious to settle into new lives. Just as they had in Montreal and Toronto, the National Council of Jewish Women created special programs to help acculturate the survivors. Jewish employers were also accommodating. A former partisan, who gave up his hopes of US immigration after waiting three frustrating years, had found his way into the Tailor Project. Struggling with one tailoring job after another, he was sent to work in a warehouse. Less than two years later, he was running his own business. The survivors who settled in Vancouver eventually found homes in Jewish neighbourhoods and moved quickly from working as low-skilled labourers to becoming skilled workers and entrepreneurs. Their aspirations matched the achievements of Vancouver's Jews, who operated clothing, furniture, real estate, foods, scrap, and pharmaceutical businesses.[5]

Winnipeg's lack of rental accommodations for families was so critical that they were initially housed in the former Jewish orphanage and billeted in run-down hotels. With no other options, the CJC bought an apartment house in 1949 to cope with the demand.[6] The DPs arrived in a city that, in 1948, had twenty-nine clothing factories employing more than 2,300 workers. Jews comprised half of the owners and managers in Winnipeg's booming garment trade and there was lots of economic opportunity for the survivors.[7] Like other employers who participated in the program, they were not really sure what to expect. The director of the Western CJC office had been skeptical about the project when he wrote to Hayes in September 1947. He was assured that the commission had been scrupulous in screening for "technical qualifications." Nonetheless, Heinz Frank wrote that

I have more than a mere hunch that we shall get at least a number of people whose previous experience in the needle trade will not go beyond the occasional sewing of a button to their jackets.… There is quite a bustle of activity going on among local Jews who urge people who are directly or indirectly connected with the selection of Needle Trade Workers to help their relatives to come to Canada. There is no doubt that some refugees will thus slip through without having the necessary qualifications, and I feel that, whether we like it or not, we must take into consideration that we are faced by more than a mere housing problem.[8]

Frank was not wrong. Camp survivor Philip Weiss, whose father had been a garment manufacturer, liked to say, "Never before in the history of the garment industry were so many coats and gloves sewn by workers educated at the finest schools in Europe."[9]

CHAIM APPLEBAUM

Based on interviews with his sons, Isaac and Ed Applebaum.

Our parents, all they really did was work. They didn't travel. Consequently, my brother and I didn't travel. We stayed in Winnipeg, living our lives. They worked.

—ED APPLEBAUM

OUR MOTHER SHARED more about her experiences than our father. We don't know a lot about him, about his early life and what happened in the war, because our father was not the kind of person to talk a lot. He was very shut down, very quiet. He didn't talk about himself. In fact, a lot of what we know about our father comes from our mother. What we do know, is that our father, Chaim Appelbaum, was born in Warsaw on May 3, 1912. We don't know anything about his education—just that, before the war, he thought of studying to become a rabbi. That's it, really.

Our mother, Chela Nagurna, grew up in Ostrolenka (Ostrołęka in Polish), a city about 120 kilometres northeast of Warsaw. She said that she had a good childhood there as one of the youngest of many siblings, seven or eight—she came from a big, substantial family. There was certainly some antisemitism in Ostrolenka. It was close to the Lithuanian border and that part of Poland was pretty bad. She didn't really focus much on any difficulties she had before the war. Her life there was pretty stable and not unusual for Jewish people living in a small Polish town.

Chela was only fifteen when the war broke out and the Germans invaded Poland. By the time the German soldiers reached Poland in September 1939, she was living in Warsaw, away from her family, taking care of an ailing uncle. She had apparently been sent to Warsaw for two main reasons. The first was that her mother's brother was very ill and at fifteen, Chela was already capable of taking care of a household, cooking and cleaning, and taking care of her uncle. The second reason was that she was a very attractive young woman, and her parents were worried that when the German

Chaim (Harry) Applebaum at the Bergen-Belsen DP camp, 1947–1948.

soldiers came into Ostrolenka, there might be trouble for her.

When the Germans established the Warsaw ghetto on October 12, 1940, it turned out that the uncle's house was within the ghetto boundaries, so they didn't have to move. The ghetto was seriously overcrowded, though—the whole Jewish population of Warsaw, which had the largest Jewish population in Poland, was forced into a tiny area of the city. As a result, people had to live wherever they could find some space. And, our mother told us, that's how she met our father: he was one of a number of people who ended up living on the roof of her uncle's home. They didn't have anywhere else to live, so they were living on the roof. One of the other people staying there was a rabbi. Our father was twelve years older than our mother when they met—by this time she was sixteen and he was twenty-eight.

Mum said that when the war started and the Warsaw ghetto was established by German decree, the ailing uncle could see what was happening. He saw there was no future for him and he died. That's what Mum said, "He just died!" So she was alone, living in the Warsaw ghetto, until she got together with Dad.

When the Warsaw ghetto was liquidated in 1943, our mother and father were both sent to the Majdanek concentration camp. Most people there were either sent on to Treblinka, which was a death camp, or to Auschwitz, which was both a forced labour camp and a death camp. We know that our father was sent to a number of camps before he was sent to Auschwitz, and we have a record of them in his war reparation claim statements. Both our parents were Auschwitz survivors, though. They both had numbers on their arms.

Our father was sent to a forced labour sub-camp of Auschwitz, and our mother was sent to do forced labour in the main camp, so they were separated. She didn't get into all the details of what kind of work she did in Auschwitz. She would talk anecdotally, dropping a new story every once in a while.

Our mother said that in the concentration camps, when someone in authority asked you how old you were, you said whatever you thought they wanted to hear. If you were thirty and it was better for you to be twenty or twenty-five, you would say twenty or twenty-five. The work was very hard; our mother started doing outside work, but just when she was starting to get sick, she was lucky enough to get an inside job. That helped her to recover. I think the inside work had something to do with repairing shoes, which meant that she actually got a decent pair of boots. To get a decent pair of boots was huge. She was able to keep that job for a period of time.

She also had a business in the camps. She would collect the cigarette butts that the German soldiers flicked away, unroll them, then make little pouches of tobacco that she traded to the Jewish men for food, a piece of bread or whatever. However, there was one good thing about getting an outside job in Auschwitz—you could steal food. If you walked by a garden or a field crop, the German soldiers would often turn their heads so you could run in and grab a potato or a rutabaga. Or, gather the stuff that fell off passing trucks.

Our mother was in Auschwitz until 1945, but our father was only there until March 1944 and then he was transferred to Bergen-Belsen, arriving there in April 1944—so they were separated. In January 1945, Mum was put on a death march when the Germans forced all the Jews out of Auschwitz because the Soviet Red Army was getting closer. In effect, the Nazis wanted to destroy all the evidence of what they were doing. The Jews themselves were literally evidence of the Nazi war crimes. The Germans marched them out, thinking that they would die on the long circuitous trek from Auschwitz to Bergen-Belsen. And thousands of them did die from starvation or were shot along the way.

Our parents were reunited in Bergen-Belsen in March 1945, about a month before they were liberated on April 15, 1945. When the camp was liberated, everyone went back to their hometowns, hoping to be reunited with family. Our parents did go back to Poland together, but nobody showed up. Neither of our parents had any surviving family members. No one in their families lived. So they decided to go back to Bergen-Belsen, which had now become the biggest refugee camp in Germany. It was the best place to be to get out

of Europe and our parents wanted out. They despised Europe because of what had happened there.

Isaac asked Mum why they didn't go to Israel. She said that the reason they wanted to come to Canada as opposed to going to Israel was that they had just come from a war and they didn't want to go back to another one. They knew that there was going to be a war in Israel. They wanted to get away from the wars, so they came to Canada.

In Bergen-Belsen, our parents were raising a toddler—Isaac was born in the DP camp in October 1946. The impression we got from our parents was that everybody was trying to restart their lives there. Trying to figure out what they were going to do, where they're going to go. Everyone was just…displaced. The allied governments didn't seem to care; they weren't going to help repatriate the refugees, or give them a new place to live. It fell on individuals to do that. This project, the Tailor Project, we understand, was really a private initiative—it didn't come from the governments. That tells you a lot. Our parents didn't have any family in Canada, so there was no other way for them to get here. There was nowhere else to go except Israel. The Tailor Project was the only way for non-sponsored people to come. If you didn't have a sponsor, you couldn't get into Canada.

In the Bergen-Belsen DP camp, our father essentially made a living as a trader. He didn't have a formal job, just traded this for that. Collected this or that. Not unlike our mother with her cigarettes. That was how people survived throughout Germany at that time. They would smuggle things from one sector to another, from the English-controlled area to the American-controlled area or the Russian-controlled area. If there was a shortage of something—like sugar or whatever—in the Russian sector, you might be able to get it in the American sector. You could smuggle it across, then sell it and make some money. Then you could use the money to buy something else and bring it back to sell. This was the business that many people engaged in.

We arrived in Canada in September 1948. Our parents never spoke about the boat ride over. Mum said that when people landed in Halifax and the immigration officer asked people how old they were, people didn't think of saying how old they actually were—to them, they were still living in the war. They said what they thought the official wanted to hear. If you thought that it was better for you to be younger, you would say you were younger. Or, if you thought it was better for you to be older, you would say that you were older. Many of these people ended up doing themselves out of some of their pension later because they tended to say that they were younger. When they got to be sixty-five, their Canadian documents would show that, for example, they were only sixty. They couldn't get their pensions until years after they should have.

You have to remember that these were people who had lived through such bad experiences. Things that would seem like terrible experiences to other people were just like another rainfall to them. They were used to it.

Our mother remembered arriving in Winnipeg through the Tailor Project. They'd been on a long train ride from Toronto and, by the time they got to Winnipeg, it was winter. It was freezing cold and there was lots of snow. She thought that she had arrived in Siberia because that was her image of Siberia. Coming from Poland, if you went on a long train ride, you ended up in Siberia. It's funny because, later in her life, she grew to love Winnipeg; she loved her life there. She would often joke about Winnipeg being "like her Florida" because everybody loved going to Florida; Winnipeg was her Miami. She rarely travelled. She stayed in Winnipeg because she was happy there.

At first, of course, Winnipeg was a real shock. The day after our parents arrived, Dad went to the factory. The next morning, 6 a.m., boom—he's off to the factory. That was it. They were taken to Winnipeg, taken to some accommodation—a Jewish woman rented them a couple of rooms upstairs—then, boom, get to work.

Another part of the story about Siberia is that when they got to Montreal from Halifax, the Jewish people they met told them that if they were going to Winnipeg, they were going to Siberia. So they tried to stay in Montreal, but the government said, "No, you have to go to Winnipeg." The next stop was Toronto where the

Jews also told them, "If you're going to Winnipeg, you're going to Siberia." They tried to stay in Toronto, but the government said, "No, you have to stay in Winnipeg for one year, then you can go wherever you want." So they ended up in Winnipeg. Even though they got there in early October, there was already a lot of snow. The nicest story about being in Winnipeg with the Tailor Project is that Dad would make us coats. He made several fur coats—he worked on both cloth garments and fur. In the cloth season, he made cloth garments, then in the fur season, he worked in the fur factories.

It wasn't like an office job, where you go in and you're doing the same thing all the time. He always said it was piecework—certainly the cloth garment stuff was piecework. Our father would come home and he would have all of these little "petacks," I think he called them, or petals. They were just little pieces of cloth or paper with numbers on them, in different colours. Each of them represented a different type of garment. Every week, or every two weeks, he would go to the kitchen and spread these things out on the table. He would sort them, putting the short blue ones with the long blue ones, the short pink ones with the long pink ones. Then there were the red square ones. All the different garments had different-sized little *petacks*, pieces. That was how he got paid. He had to hand them in, showing that this was what he had done over the past week or two. Ed remembers as a little boy having that bonding moment with our father, sorting these things with him on a Saturday or a Sunday afternoon when he was about six or seven years old. Isaac was much older and was off being a teenager. There's ten years between us.

After a few years in the factories, Dad tried to get another business going. Working as a tailor was what he knew, but he wanted more. He had no formal training or much of an education. And Mum had very little education. There was a market in Winnipeg, a food market in an area where there were little shacks and booths. Sort of like Kensington Market in Toronto. He bought a truck and would take things—pots and pans, knives and forks, and brassieres and underwear—out to farm country and trade or sell them for things that he could bring back to Winnipeg and sell to the market guys. He had a thing going with the country farmers and with the city merchants.

And chickens. He would bring home chickens and slaughter them in the backyard. When Ed was a little boy, he remembers opening the door of the fence, looking inside, and seeing our father with a big knife, whacking the chickens, killing them. Literally, seeing a chicken with his head cut off. Our father cut the bird, the chicken fell down and then started scampering around with no head. It scampered about five or six feet and then just plopped over.

Then, in 1963, our parents bought a corner grocery store. The income from tailoring wasn't enough to sustain them and he had sold the truck he used for the trading business. To their credit, they were more ambitious. Our mother ran the grocery store and our father again worked every day in the factories as a tailor. They were a two-income family, so to speak. They basically worked all day, seven days a week. Our mother never took a day off, except for the Jewish High Holidays. That would be it. They'd fudge the Jewish holidays. The ones that they had to stay closed, they would. The ones they could fudge, they fudged. Mum worked from nine in the morning until eight in the evening, seven days a week. In the summer they would stay open a little later because it was sunny quite late. That was common. That's the immigrant story. In those days, mom-and-pop grocery stores were everything. People would buy their weekly groceries at the corner store. They would buy everything, so it was actually a decent business back in the 1960s. Mum once told me an interesting story about jobs. I had asked her why Jewish people had the reputation of being cheap and she said that in prewar Poland, the income of a Jewish person was limited. There were many jobs and positions that Jews could not apply for. As a Jew, you could not control the amount of money you could earn but you could control the amount of money you would spend!

We lived above the grocery store. We had no living room. The living room was both a storage room and a living room. The kitchen was a kitchen and a storage room. Then we had two other storage rooms for the groceries. Three bedrooms upstairs; our parents' bedroom, and each of us had a little cubbyhole. We had little bedrooms and a washroom.

Dad eventually came up with the idea of buying a hotel. He found a partner, another survivor, and the two of them bought a hotel in a small town outside of Winnipeg, adjacent to a First Nations reserve. Neither of us ever went there. That was when Dad gave up the tailoring. Unfortunately, our father didn't take to the hotel work. Each of them, he and his partner, had to live out there for a period of time. He would be there for six weeks, and then he would come back and the other partner would go out there for six weeks. That took a real toll on him. He was never the same person after that.

The hotel was about 140 kilometres from Winnipeg, in Hodgson, Manitoba, near Fisher Branch. It was a very small town and was pretty rough. Some of the hotels in and around Winnipeg were owned by Jews and some of them had a reputation of being, essentially, drinking establishments. The hotels were originally founded by British people, then the next generation of immigrants, the Ukrainians and the Poles, bought them. Then the Jews bought them. These were places that basically sold alcohol to the First Nations people, that's what it was about. It was an ugly business. There was a lot of physical violence. Our father never talked about it with us, we never heard him talk about it, but his hair turned white during that time. It really aged him; it was hard on him. It was one of the things that killed him.

Dad started to drink then, and the partnership split up. The other partner stayed; he was tough as nails. He seemed to be able to handle the stress because he lived for many years after they dissolved the partnership. Plus, the business separated Dad from our mother. They were still married, but they were apart because Dad was in Hodgson and Mum was in Winnipeg. Our father needed her on a daily basis to stabilize him. To put food on the table and to take care of him. He needed that. Like a lot of men in that generation.

As we've said, our father never talked about his war experiences, but it was pretty clear to us that he went through some torture. In his war reparations claims, he tells a story about being put in a cattle car on a train when the Warsaw ghetto was liquidated. He said that after everybody was packed into the cattle car, a German soldier climbed on to the roof and threw hand grenades into the cattle car. Then the train took off. He said that by the time the train got to Majdanek, there were only ten to fifteen people still alive in the cattle car. Everybody else had died.

Dad had scars on his back from shrapnel wounds for his whole life. In the war reparations claims, he talks about the different people who helped him in Majdanek. There were no doctors—you had to cure yourself—but there were different people who helped him. Some of them even ended up in Winnipeg with them after the war. They vouched for the truth of what he was saying. That helped him in terms of getting more money from the Germans, but he wasn't happy with what they were offering. He didn't settle with Germany until the end, the last year or two of his life. It was a mistake. When he finally did settle, it was too late—he died a year or two later. It did give a pension, but only for a few years.

Our mother got $13,000 in her war reparation claims. That was enough in the mid-1950s to buy a small house. It was the war reparations that got our parents their first house, either as the down payment or it paid for the house. It got them started. Ed was born in that house in 1956. Our mum worked in the grocery store seven days a week for years, and, with our father doing tailoring, they eventually bought a house in the suburbs. They sold the first house when they bought the grocery store in 1963, and, in 1970, they bought the house in the suburbs. After they moved out to the suburbs, our parents kept up both the grocery store and the hotel.

Dad died when he was sixty-one and Mum died when she was sixty-four. Our parents had hard wars; these were people who survived Auschwitz. Our mother was a heavy smoker who died of lung cancer. And our father had developed liver damage in the war years. He had surgery in Winnipeg, which helped, but it didn't help enough. And here we are, both of us, about to out-live our parents. Of course, we had very different life experiences, but we also inherited their genetics. The people who actually survived the concentration camps, who lived through the war and made it to Canada, had to be tough—they had to have survivor genetics.

My parents didn't associate too much with the Jews who had spent the war years in Canada. We were the *greene*, the new immigrants. The Jews who had spent the war years in Canada were the *gaylers*—the "others." Our parents' friends were at least 99.99 per cent Jewish survivors—they likely met most of them in Winnipeg. Like us, they were *greene*. Some of them had been in the concentration camps, like our parents, others had been hidden, and some had survived the war in the work camps in Siberia.

There were evenings when they got together and shared their experiences—and it often accelerated into very passionate exchanges. They spoke to each other in Polish until they figured we were asleep. Then they started speaking in Yiddish. They were full of emotion and very loud, getting their wartime stories out. That was their therapy. They exchanged stories about survival. It was cathartic for them. I think that's why they had to be intense, honest, and real, to tell stories from their guts. When these people came to Canada, they were provided with jobs through the Tailor Project, but they were not provided with any therapy; there was nobody

that they could tell their stories to except each other and their kids. They were getting the trauma out, but not in a way that could satisfy them. The stories kept being repeated. There were no psychiatrists to help them at that point. The Jewish community didn't realize that it might be helpful for these people to be able to speak in a group with a therapist and get their stories out. Instead of telling their stories to their children, with the children finally saying, "Enough!" Isaac got a load of stories right out of the womb because he was born at Bergen-Belsen. Our mother bombarded him with stories until he told her that he couldn't listen anymore. Ed heard them all later.

In today's world, we think of post-traumatic stress disorder (PTSD); we recognize that people suffer from that. There is all kinds of literature and research and thinking and therapy around it. And that's essentially what these people were struggling with, PTSD. But there was no help for them. What many of them had to cope with was unimaginable. The two of us had an amazing experience with our mother in Germany, when she went back for four days to testify at a war crimes trial in January 1979. We went back with her—Dad had died in 1973—and Isaac can remember seeing her on the witness stand giving testimony and hearing things from her about what she saw. You can't imagine. It was the trial of a woman who was a guard in the women's section in Auschwitz. Her name was Hildegard Lächert and the German press called her "Bloody Birgitta." She was being tried for the hanging of fourteen or sixteen women, and our mother was a witness to that. Lächert was sentenced to twelve years in prison.

There were so many stories. When our mother went to visit Ed in Israel, not long after the war crimes trial, she was reunited with two women she had been with in Auschwitz. They hadn't seen each other in at least thirty years. It was a really heartwarming reunion, all the more so when one of the women took Ed aside and told him, "Your mother, if it wasn't for your mother, I wouldn't be alive today. I would not have survived. There were so many times when I was ready to give up. When I just wanted to kill myself. Throw myself into the electric fence and just be done with it. Your mother saved me. She gave me the courage to keep going." That made him feel so proud, to understand how heroic some of these people were. It wasn't just about themselves; it was about the person they were sleeping beside. The nature of heroism for them was survival and helping others survive.

What our parents wanted for us was to just be successful; they wanted normal things for us. They wanted grandchildren. They wanted us to be happy and productive. They wanted us to be doctors or lawyers or engineers. For them, that's what it meant to be successful. For them success was making a good living, being safe and financially secure. They wanted us to be independent and to have good lives.

Our sense is that Mum had a better life in Canada than Dad did. She certainly had a longer life. Our mother was more good-natured. She had more of a positive outlook on life, she laughed more. She had a warmer personality. Dad was more depressive and angrier. He carried a lot more inside himself; our mother was better able to cope. She outlived him by fourteen years. But by age, the numbers were similar. Dad was sixty-one and Mum was sixty-four when they passed away.

We both left Winnipeg and came to Toronto. That was very common, a lot of people leave Winnipeg. They say that Winnipeg's biggest export is people. Isaac moved to Toronto in 1970, to go to Ryerson to take photography. He became an exhibiting artist and photographer. Ed stayed in Winnipeg until 1981 and then moved to Toronto to go to school, finish his degrees, and become an architect. Isaac has one daughter and Ed has two.

Isaac said that Dad wanted him to become a dentist, but he told him that he had no interest in dentistry. It never even occurred to him to become a dentist. He wanted to be a photographer, an artist. Our father said, "Photography is a hobby." Isaac told him that he had finally found something he cared about. "It excites me. It's what *I* want."

THE PASSAGE INTO NEW LIVES

IT HAD BEEN a quarter of a century since the Jewish community had absorbed such large groups of immigrants. "Their arrival presented a daunting challenge to the established community, which had to create an infrastructure that could absorb the newcomers." Despite the sincere efforts of the Canadian Jewish Congress (CJC), Jewish Immigrant Aid Society (JIAS), the Jewish Labour Committee (JLC), and masses of volunteers, they were unprepared and overburdened. This was complicated by several unique factors. Unlike previous arrivals, few survivors had relatives to turn to. If they did, they may have never met them or had been separated for decades. The traditional old-country institutions that had supported chain migration had declined or disappeared, and only the larger, establishment organizations were there to provide help with integration. Previous immigrants, whether they were still struggling economically or had some success, often resented the financial help given to survivors. The refugees took umbrage with their treatment as "greeners" (*greene*, greenhorns). They felt that they had been part of cultured, more advanced European Jewish societies than the more primitive ones that earlier immigrants from Eastern Europe had left behind.[1]

Canadian Jews and their community organizations expected the DP tailors to be grateful for their rescue, accept their lowly status as immigrants, and quickly assimilate. They also anticipated the arrival of survivors with some trepidation. The decimation of European Jewry, which included the loss of many of their own relatives, was impossible to comprehend. What kind of men and women could survive the kinds of horrors described by Sam Posluns in a speech to the Manufacturers Association?

> Who could understand the convulsions of the brain of those who stood on the brink of their own graves, with the general background of burning, shrieking and mad human beings, the savage crescendo of typhus and starvation and the upsets of gas chambers and crematoriums, the yelling and sobs and the shrieks of maddened women.... How can one understand, nor how can one put into words

Illustration from the United Jewish Appeal call for donations to "support the relief and rehabilitation and resettlement work of Joint Distribution Committee…United Palestine Appeal…United Service for New Americans."

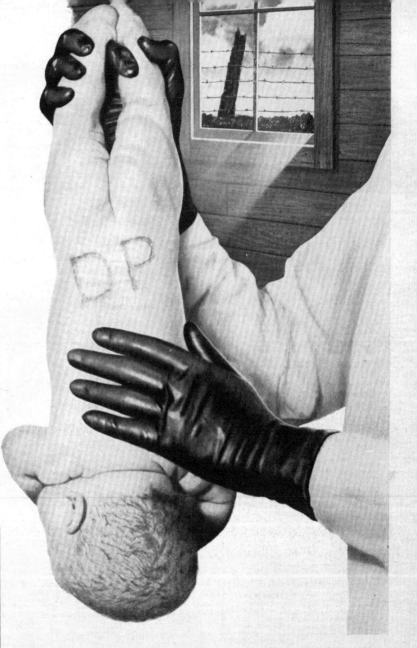

BORN BRANDED

THE room is cold. Outside, the wind howls and beats upon the wooden walls of the barrack. And here, in this room without heat, in this camp without hope, a child is born.

The jubilation is overshadowed by fear.

For as surely as if a hot iron were stamped into its flesh, this child is born branded.

The brand is D P. That stands for Displaced Person.

In this case, it stands for a new-born child whose parents have survived the hideous scourge of Hitlerism. The years in Belsen, Buchenwald, Dachau, Oswiecim. The gas chambers and the mass graves. The cold. The hunger. The sickness.

They have come out of the long night of terror, in which six million of their people were murdered. With your help they have survived. They still live.

What happens to them now?

In the cold room of the D P camp, the father looks upon the face of his new-born child. And the father prays . . .

"Dear God, let me work that I may build a future for my son.

"Dear God, lead me to a land that is home, to a piece of earth under the skies of freedom, where my son may grow without hatred and live without fear.

"Dear God, hold us together."

⸱ ⸱ ⸱

Out of the camps of Europe, comes a prayer for deliverance . . . an appeal to the conscience of the American people.

In this American land with its tradition of liberty and justice for all—shall that prayer for help go unheard, unanswered?

Look deep into your heart. You'll find the answer there.

⸱ ⸱ ⸱

This is a year of greater need, because...

1. UNRRA's impending liquidation has placed greater burdens on the agencies of the United Jewish Appeal.

2. The Jewish population of the D P camps has trebled in one year.

3. Rehabilitation efforts must be expanded to help hundreds of thousands in Hungary, Rumania, Poland and other countries.

4. Medical care and rehabilitation programs must be provided for the 170,000 surviving Jewish children, 26,000 of whom are in D P camps.

5. Palestine must be built up and developed with U.J.A. funds.

6. Many services, including special aid for child refugees, must be provided for displaced Jews who find a haven in the United States.

Give Them Life . . .

and Make it Worth Living

UNITED JEWISH APPEAL

FOR $170,000,000

To support the relief and rehabilitation and resettlement work of Joint Distribution Committee . . . United Palestine Appeal . . . United Service for New Americans

Henry Morgenthau, Jr.
General Chairman
342 Madison Avenue, New York City

when words have not yet been written into the English language to express the sufferings and the mass slaughtering of a people?

It was no wonder Canadian Jews were wary of the DPs.[2] Matthew Ram wrote from Germany that he had "heard unfriendly comments about the DPs." He realized that there were cultural and experiential chasms that made communication with Canadians difficult. "On the one hand," Ram realized, the survivors "expected to be received much more emotionally than they were; on the other hand Canadian Citizens expected that the new-comers would show their gratitude more than they do. The various responsible groups must attempt to do a better job of interpreting one group to the other."[3]

The thirty-year-old director of social services for Montreal's JIAS, Dr. Joseph Kage, undertook the task of easing survivors' passage into their new lives. An empathic and innovative social worker, Kage understood that survivors faced the added burden of "the traumatic experiences of the Nazi era of persecution and complete uprooting."[4] He had emigrated from Belarus as a young man and maintained deep connections with the migration process. Kage argued that Holocaust survivors faced the challenges of meeting basic needs such as housing and jobs, but also of overcoming "the psychological obstacles due to [their] traumatic experiences

overseas." Too often, Kage noted, "we are too sensitive when the newcomer breaks some unwritten laws, peculiar to our Canadian tradition." We "quickly and impatiently" withdraw our friendship or even conclude, erroneously, "that the immigrant cannot be assimilated and will remain a stranger."[5]

Kage created programs to address the "need for speedy, effective and comprehensive help to repair the damage wherever possible and to offer a programme of rehabilitation." He established Canada's first specialized social service programs designed specifically for immigrants and pushed for intensive programs of child and family welfare, vocational counselling, recreation, and, in particular, language education. JIAS evening schools held classes in English and, in Quebec, French, as well as citizenship education, and Canadian history and geography.

Kage envisioned the night schools as therapeutic as well as educational. He later wrote,

The conversations that occur are oft times related to the problems and difficulties encountered by the immigrant. The trading of experiences, the sharing of frustrations, the acceptance of one's problems without being belittled or unduly criticized, the presence of an atmosphere where emotional tension may be not only released but understood—all are

Mothers' and Babes' Summer Rest Home, Tollandale on Lake Simcoe, Ontario. Rose Dublin standing in centre with twins Anne and Max on either side.

elements operative in the classroom—elements which…permit the release of repressed emotional feelings that if not directed in the proper channels can become damaging to the individual, and to his future adjustment.[6]

Kage also promoted new methodologies for all workers who dealt with survivors. He encouraged them to become familiar with new practices in psychology that required them to have some understanding of survivors' experiences to help them feel safe sharing their painful memories.[7]

Not everyone who arrived as a garment worker took advantage of these programs. Even if they participated, the journey to their new lives remained filled with challenges. The Tailor Project and Jewish organizations provided them with some of the tools they needed, yet every newcomer created their own unique path. In November 1948, the Garment Workers Commission's coordinator, Walter Friedman, proclaimed,

> The tailors in practically all cases have proven themselves capable, willing workers. They have had to familiarize themselves with Canadian customs, adjust themselves in strange homes often under difficult conditions…. [T]hese newcomers have shown themselves most anxious to become useful and loyal citizens of our country. It does anyone's heart good to see their happy faces when after years of hardship and frustration they suddenly realize that they are again re-entering free society and can become useful members of the community.[8]

Along with their children, the tailors became part of a growing survivor community that would gradually reshape Canadian Jewish life.

CANADIAN OVERSEAS GARMENT COMMISSION

Room 33, 165 Spadina Ave.

TORONTO

WA. 7728   EL. 5746

Dear Friend:

Before you left Europe you were asked to sign an undertaking that you would accept employment in Canada in the tailoring trade as directed by the Minister of Labour for a specific period.

You have faithfully fulfilled the undertaking that you gave before your departure from Europe and it is now the pleasure of the Department of Labour to give you a certificate certifying to the completion of your undertaking.

We know you have been looking forward to this certificate for some time and with this in view we have arranged a public ceremony at which these certificates will be officially presented. The meeting will take place on Thursday evening, June 23rd, 8:00 p.m. in the Assembly Hall of the Central High School of Commerce at 570 Shaw Street (between College and Harbord Streets).

Officials of the various Government Departments - Federal, Provincial, and Municipal - have been invited and we know they will be interested in meeting you as new citizens and will be glad to pay their respects to you on this occasion. Mr. David Croll M.P. will be the guest speaker. There will also be persons from the different voluntary organizations who have been of assistance in this project and who will address you in your own language.

We know you will not want to miss this opportunity and will be sure to attend this meeting to receive your certificate. We would appreciate your being at the Auditorium at 7:30 p.m. prompt in order to arrange proper seating plan before the ceremony. PLEASE BRING WITH YOU YOUR LANDING PAPERS OR SIMILAR DOCUMENT OF IDENTIFICATION. Be sure to come and bring your friends and family.

With best regards,

Thomas Aplin

Thos. Aplin,
Co-Ordinator.

By the summer of 1949, most of the immigrant tailors had fulfilled the conditions of their contracts and were free to take other jobs. They were invited to receive their Department of Labour certificates at official ceremonies. Notices were posted in the ethnic press.

Z TORONTO, ONT.   **TORONTO**

The Overseas Garment Commission

organizuje

ZEBRANIE PUBLICZNE

na którym będą wręczone naszym nowym Imigrantom tak zw.
"Release Certificates" — zaświadczenia wykonania kontraktów
Główny mówca

DAVID CROLL

POSEŁ DO PARLAMENTU

Udział wezmą również przedstawiciele rządu federalnego, prowincjonalnego i miejskiego. — Zebranie odbędzie się w

CENTRAL HIGH SCHOOL OF COMMERCE
570 SHAW STREET

we czwartek, 23-go czerwca, o 8-mej wieczór

GOŚCIE BĘDĄ MILE WIDZIANI.

THE OVERSEAS GARMENT COMMISSION

устроює

ПУБЛИЧНІ СХОДИНИ

зполучених з виданням звільняючих свідоцтв
для наших нових імігрантів

Головний бесідник: ДАВИД КРОЛ, К. Р., Ч. П.

Представники федерального, провінціяльного і міського
урядів будуть присутні.

CENTRAL HIGH SCHOOL OF COMMERCE

570 SHAW STREET

ЧЕТВЕР, 23 ЧЕРВНЯ   ГОД. 8-ма ВВЕЧІР

Запрошується все громадянство.

די „אָווערסיעז גארמענט קאָמישען"

פרעזענטירט

אן עפענטליכע פאַרזאַמלונג

צו פרעזענטירן צו אונזערע נייע אימיגראנטן, באפרייאונגס סערטיפיקאטן
גאסט רעדנער:

דייוויד קראָל, קיי. סי.. עם. פי.

פארטרעטער פון די פעדעראלע, פראָווינציעלע און מוניציפאלע רעגירונגען
וועלען זיין אנוועזענד.

פלאַץ: סענטראל הייסקול אוו קאמערס,
570 שאו סטריט.

דאטע: דאנערשטאג, יוני 23-טען, 8.30 אווענט

אלע זייגען געלאדען

You are invited to attend a

Public Presentation

of Release Certificates to Garment Workers

on Thursday, June 23rd, 8.00 p.m.

at the Central High School of Commerce
570 Shaw St., Toronto

—

Guest Speaker:

David Croll, K.C., M.P.

Representatives
of Federal, Provincial
and Municipal Governments
will be present

 ⑦

Canadian Overseas Garment Commission

CONCLUSION

LOOKING BACK at his involvement with what he described as an almost biblical mission to be "our brothers' keepers," Max Enkin situated the Tailor Project as an undertaking "unique for the times." The Canadian Jewish community came together on every level to "rescue" these men and women and their young families from languishing indefinitely in Europe's DP camps. The Canadian Jewish Congress (CJC) and the Jewish Labour Committee (JLC) overcame old hostilities to join in a fight against the anti-immigrant attitudes of the labour movement and antisemitic elements in government. Factory owners worked hand-in-hand with unions, joined together organizationally and personally in a common cause. They devised an avenue to squeeze open Canada's doors for the first significant number of Jewish immigrants in more than twenty-five years. The five men on the selection team returned to Canada with a heightened passion to do all they could for their fellow Jews who had suffered so grievously. There were limits to their success. As David Lewis of the Cooperative Commonwealth Federation (CCF) wrote to his father, Moishe, at the JLC, it was patently unfair that so small a proportion of the DPs were Jews. "Justice," he wrote, "is never a complete monarch in the present immoral world."[1] For the survivors who made Canada their home, the Tailor Project was transformative. They were given a new lease on life and, like Philip Weiss, were forever grateful.

> I came here as a tailor, that was the only way I could come to Canada. We didn't have relatives, I didn't have where to go…. I lost my youth in Europe but I think that I came here as a newborn person entirely. I had to adapt myself. It wasn't easy. I had to embrace a new culture, become a different man, think differently, do things differently but I thank God that I found myself in Canada.[2]

Morris Dublin with his daughter Helen in an Austrian DP camp, 1947.

MORRIS DUBLIN

Based on interviews with his daughter, Anne Dublin.

When we got our first house on Manning Avenue in Toronto, Dad set up a little workshop in the basement. There was a long table and an ironing board, one of those small ones. Of course, he had an industrial sewing machine, too. I remember going down there as a young girl, often on Sunday, to watch my father pin and baste and press the fabric for whatever he was sewing. I remember being fascinated by the work he did. And while he worked, he would often tell stories about his family and his home back in Poland, or he would sing songs, or I would listen to the silence as he worked. I remember how the colours of the thread entranced me. I remember the smells of the very, very heavy iron that he used. He would wet a strong linen cloth and a natural sponge and everything would steam up.

MY PARENTS STARTED telling us stories about their experiences when I was seven or eight years old. Of course, they didn't tell us everything at that point. But every time they told a story, they would add another detail. Then, when they were both getting on, when they were in their seventies and eighties, they were interviewed a few times. So, I heard these stories again and again. I think my parents needed to tell their story, to share what happened, just for their own psychological well-being. They were quite traumatized by the war and they needed to share. They needed to know that these stories and the people in them would not be lost, and they wanted us to know where we came from. In those days, people didn't go to psychiatrists or psychologists. If you had post-traumatic stress disorder (PTSD), some people clammed up, they wouldn't talk at all, and other people just had to tell the stories.

My father's name was Morris Jacob Dublin, or in Yiddish, Moshe Yaacov Dublin. He grew up in a small city in southwest Poland called Sosnowiec. His father, Mordecai, was a shoemaker, and the family was very poor. There was quite a space between my father and his three older sisters, so he was pampered and coddled by his mother and his older sisters. He had a rather peaceful boyhood.

Sosnowiec was an industrial city in a coal-mining area. Most of my grandfather's customers were coal-miners who came to get their boots repaired or to buy new boots. The Jewish population was about thirty thousand—a sizeable community. It was not a shtetl; it was a city—a city with paved roads and good sidewalks. My father grew up in what we would call a traditional home. They were not ultra-Orthodox, but most Jews in those days followed the traditional ways.

Yiddish was their first language. It was spoken at home and spoken within the Jewish community, but because my grandfather, Mordecai Dublin, had non-Jewish customers, he could also speak very good Polish. My father learned Polish as well. He went to a cheder, a religious school for boys, until he was about seven or eight years old and then he decided that he wanted to go to a Polish school. He wanted to learn other things. I think that even then my father was a bit of a rebel. His mother didn't want him to go to the Polish school, so my father went to the school by himself and stood in the hallway until the principal came along and said, "Little boy, what are you doing here?"

My father replied, "I want to go to this school." The principal found out where his parents lived and asked them, "What is this boy doing at our school all by himself, without any parents?" To make a long story short, he ended up going to that Polish school until he was bar mitzvahed, until he was thirteen years old. Then he had to go to work to help support the family. As I said, they were very poor.

First, my father considered learning the shoemaking trade, but somehow it didn't appeal to him. So instead, he was apprenticed to a tailor. He learned his trade over the next five or six years, until he could set himself up with a sewing machine. It wasn't really a shop—he managed to get a sewing machine, he put it in the room where he lived, and started making a little money. Around that same time, when he was eighteen or nineteen years old, he met my mother, Rose Gail Kornhandler. They fell head over heels in love and got married in January 1939. My mother had already lost her parents, but she had an older brother named Fischel who took care of my mother and her two older sisters.

My father never spoke about any conflict between the Jewish community and the rest of the population in Sosnowiec before the war. From his experience, it was a fairly peaceful place. There may have been an incident here or there—as there was all through Poland—but from what he said, it was a good place to grow up. I guess it was because there were so many Jews there and most of them lived in the same neighbourhood. They felt a real sense of community. If they saw the war coming, and even if they knew about Nazism, most people said to themselves, "It'll be like World War I—that was terrible, it was awful, but we will survive in the same way that we survived the first war." Very few people could imagine what was to come. Very few people could imagine that genocide would be committed in such a systematic way.

But soon after the Nazis invaded Poland on September 1, 1939, my mother's brother, Fischel, was rounded up with a number of other young men, taken to the river, and shot. My mother, horrified and devastated, said to my father, "We have to get out of here. If they can do that to such a fine young man, a married man with children, they'll do anything." So, my mother persuaded my father to run away, to escape. They went with my father's youngest sister, Pola, and her husband. The two couples left, travelling—partly by train, partly by wagon, and partly on foot—to the east, to the Soviet Union, along with thousands of other Polish Jews. There were thousands who left in those early days when the border was still somewhat open. How easy it was to cross the border depended on where you went and which border crossing you used. At some of the border crossings, the Soviet soldiers shot at the Jews trying to cross the border; at other ones, they helped the Jews. A Soviet soldier actually helped the two couples cross a river and get to the other side.

My parents told us quite a bit about their experiences in the Soviet Union and there are two stories in particular that I'll tell you. One is from the early days, when my parents were living in a small industrial city in the Ural Mountains called Sverdlovsk. This was before the Soviet Union went to war with Germany, before 1941. These were two years of relative calm. The couples had been separated at this point. My father's sister, Pola, and her husband were immediately sent to Siberia, and my parents were on their own. A lot of Polish Jews who didn't want to be sent to the interior of the Soviet Union were suspected of smuggling or black-market activities and were sent to Siberia right away. My parents were willing to go where the authorities wanted to send them and so they went to Sverdlovsk.

My father somehow managed to get a sewing machine there. Not an electric one—the kind with a hand wheel to make the needle go up and down. My mother would do the turning while my father did the sewing. So, it was a project for both of them. My father would put the sewing machine in the little window of their room to let people know that if they needed any sewing done, they could knock on the door.

The second story happened later, when the Germans broke the Non-Aggression Pact in 1941 and the Soviet Union and Germany went to war. All the young men were drafted into the Soviet army, millions of them, and my father was one of them. He was sent to work in a brick factory. It was hard labour, but it wasn't combat. One day, a Soviet officer came along—a Jewish officer—and struck up a conversation with my father, asking him, "Don't you have a trade? Why are you working as a common soldier?" My father told him that, yes, he did have a trade, that he was a tailor. The officer replied, "Don't worry. I'll find a better place for you." A few weeks later, my father was transferred behind the lines, into a tailoring workshop with other tailors. I'm sure that saved his life because, for one thing, he wasn't in the line of fire anymore, and, for another, he could sometimes do extra work for the officers. Sometimes he was able to barter for an extra potato or an extra piece of bread, and other times he made a little money to send to my mother, who was back home with a baby already, my first sister, Deborah. Mom was also working—women were already doing all kinds of work in the Soviet Union in those days. My mother was a crane operator—she was very proud of being able to say that she used to operate a crane. But they still needed all their skills and all their wits to help them survive the horrendous conditions. As far as I know, my father stayed working in that tailor shop until the end of the war.

My mother had managed to move closer to where my father's workshop was, but the baby became sick and there was no medicine. Deborah passed away at about seventeen months old, before my father left the army. My father—this breaks my heart—had tried to arrange to give his own blood for a transfusion for the baby, but it didn't work. They ended up having to bury the baby by the side of the road. There was no Jewish cemetery, there was no rabbi; that's all they could do.

My next sister, Helen, was born in January 1945. When the war was drawing to a close, my parents decided to go back to Poland to see if there was any family left. The whole time that they had been in the Soviet Union, they had no idea what was happening in Poland. All they knew was that after 1941 there was no more mail. Between 1939 and 1941, mail could still go back and forth—I understand that the family back in Poland sent them parcels of food and clothing for the baby. But after 1941, everything stopped. Deep in the interior of the Soviet Union, with all news embargoed because of the war, they had no idea what was going on. They had a sense that something bad was happening, but no one—according to them—knew the extent of the genocide.

Right after the war ended, the Soviets no longer wanted the Polish Jews to stay and strongly encouraged them to leave. There was no problem crossing the border back into Poland—it didn't shut again until later. Since Sosnowiec is, as I said, in southwest Poland, my parents, my sister, and my aunt Pola had to travel through much of Poland to get back to the city, which is closer to Germany than to the Soviet Union. They had to go through Lwów (now Lviv, Ukraine) and Kraków before arriving in Sosnowiec. When they got there, it was to find that their homes were gone. Their families were gone. Polish people had taken over their homes, their businesses, and their properties, and they didn't want to give them back.

My parents never talked about what happened when they went back to their hometown. All I know is that they went there, they saw that everybody was gone, that nothing was there for them. I believe that they then went back to Kraków, where there was an organization to help Jewish survivors. Kraków is a bigger city than Sosnowiec, so there was more help for them, and I think that they didn't want to be so close to Germany. They wanted to get further away from the border.

After all the trauma they'd gone through, a lot of Polish Jews wanted to stay in Poland. The Bund, the General Jewish Labour Bund in Poland, a Jewish socialist party, was encouraging people to stay. The Bundists weren't Zionists—they believed that Jews could and should make a home wherever they were. They should find work there and become citizens of the country. The Bundists and the Zionists were always fighting each other because Zionists believe that the only place for Jews is Israel, their homeland. A lot of Polish Jewish survivors did want to stay. After everything they'd gone through,

they couldn't face going to a new country, with a new language and customs. But after the Kielce pogrom in July 1946, in which forty-two Holocaust survivors were killed, the Jews—including my parents—understood that there was no place for them in Poland. Word of the brutal pogrom, in which soldiers participated and the police just stood by, got out very quickly and after that there was a huge exodus. So, my parents arranged with the Bricha—the organization that helped Jewish survivors escape postwar Europe and that I call the "Jewish underground railroad"—to get across the various borders to a displaced persons camp in Austria.

My father was a strong Zionist. During his teenage years, he was a member of Hashomer Hatzair, a leftist Zionist organization. My brother and I also belonged to Hashomer when we were teens and went to Camp Shomria for one year. My father loved Hashomer Hatzair. He wanted to go to Palestine, but by the time my parents had the opportunity to go, in 1948, they had three young children. Even if they could have gone legally, my father knew it would be a very, very hard life with three young children. My twin brother, Max, and I were only a year and a half old and Helen was three and a half years old then. They had no money, no resources. So that's why they ended up going to Canada instead, where my mother had an aunt in Toronto.

One of the DP camps they were in was Riedenberg, near Salzburg, Austria. Life there was terrible. They lived

Morris Dublin in the doorway of his
dry-cleaning store in Toronto.

in one room in what had been soldiers' barracks. One room, one bed, a table, and, I think, a chair. Terrible conditions. My father's sister, Pola, had joined them when they were still in the Soviet Union, after she lost her husband and two children there. So, there were six people in one room. We all stayed there for about two years.

In every camp, there was a community centre or something like that, where people could post news items or different announcements. My father probably heard about the call for tailors in Canada there, by word of mouth. He never actually talked about "the Tailor Project." He always just said, "I was a tailor and that helped me come to Canada."

We all came to Canada in September 1948, on the ship SS *Samaria*. When we first arrived in Toronto, we lived on Huron Street, between College and Dundas. Once again, there were six of us in one room. But they were at ease there because they were with other people like themselves. As I said, my parents chose to come to Toronto because my mother had a married aunt there, but that connection was unfortunately the reason that they ended up living in such cramped quarters. As soon as they got off the train, my mother's aunt and uncle said that they had a place for them. They took them right away to a single room in their house on Huron.

We stayed in the room on Huron Street for about a year and a half. Then my parents and my aunt Pola scraped together enough money for a mortgage on a house on Manning Avenue. We lived on the first floor of that house and they rented out one flat on the second floor and one flat on the third floor. There was one bathroom for everyone. We had only three rooms for the six of us—my parents, three small children, and my aunt Pola—but we managed.

Fortunately, my father was able to start working as soon as we arrived in Toronto, at Lloyd Brothers custom tailors, making men's wear. He did tailoring there, not the cutting or the pressing. Dad sewed the jackets. Then, after about ten years, he left Lloyd Brothers and bought a little dry-cleaning store on Dufferin Street and we lived above the store. He moved the sewing machine that he had had in the house to the store and would do all sorts of repairs. When I took home economics at school, he helped me sew the first blouse I ever made. Once in a while, he'd make a piece of clothing from scratch, but mostly he did alterations. He called it the "schmatta" business. He was quite a go-getter and liked his independence. He sold new pants in the front of the store and would hem them for the customers. I think he mostly made money with the tailoring, with the alterations, not with dry cleaning. He liked being his own boss, though. A few years after he bought the store, my parents bought our first home in North York. In the house, there was a basement where we kept the sewing machine that Dad still used to pick up extra jobs.

In Toronto, my parents found friends and community among other, as we say, *greene* (greeners, greenhorns), other newcomers. They mostly made friends with people from their *landsmannschaft*, a group of people who came from the same area in Poland, which in their case was the Zaglembier Society. As long as my father was alive, he was a member of the Society. Once a year, we would go to the Bathurst Lawn Cemetery for the Yizkor service, the Jewish memorial service for the dead, between Rosh Hashanah and Yom Kippur. Holocaust survivors, their children, and their grandchildren would attend, but after my father passed away, they wouldn't let me be a full member of the Society—only of the Ladies' Auxiliary. I didn't like this policy, so I never joined up. But my parents are buried in the Zaglembier Society section, as is my sister, Helen. Their connection to the Society was very strong—it took the place of family and created a sense of community for my parents.

My father worked in the dry-cleaning store until he sold it in his sixties. But even after he retired, he got a job working at another dry-cleaning store a couple days a week—he just missed it, somehow. After that, he volunteered in the tailoring workshop at the Baycrest Centre for a few years, until he finally said, "Okay, I've had enough."

My parents never talked about their aspirations for their children. I think it was implicit. Get an education; for the girls get married and have children. Be a mensch. They wanted my brother to have a profession and they didn't really understand much about higher education or the arts, which my brother and I adored. There were quite a few battles in the house when we wanted lessons and they refused. Each of us in our own way rebelled, but at the same time, we all went to university and beyond. We all managed to make a living. We all ended up teaching and getting an education way beyond what our parents ever got. Helen became a high school English teacher in Toronto and was beloved by her students. Max got his PhD in sociology of education from Harvard, and I became an elementary school teacher and a librarian. Now I write books for young people.

We respected our parents. They had a hard life and worked hard to make a decent home for themselves and for us. I think they left a remarkable legacy. I'm not talking about material goods. I'm talking about the love of Israel, the love of Judaism, the sense of community, the sense of wanting to give back to people, to be a *mensch*.

That old sewing machine moved with us from house to house. In his last few years, my dad lived with me in my bungalow. The sewing machine was put in my basement, and he used it there for a couple years. As time went on, though, he couldn't see very well and he couldn't make it down the stairs, so he had to stop sewing. I think that was one of his great sorrows. I still have the machine and use it from time to time. If it breaks and I need to get it repaired, I bring it to a man from Portugal. He always says to me, "Don't sell this machine. They don't make machines like this anymore."

Morris Dublin's sewing machine.

The five members of the Garment Workers Selection Team, likely at Bergen-Belsen DP camp, with officials and displaced persons, 1947. In the middle, from left to right, David Solomon, Sam Posluns, Max Enkin, Bernard Shane, and Sam Herbst.

RECAPITULATION

Details re Tailors who arrived on first 27 boats
and compiled on Oct.24th, 1948.

	Total Tailors	Jewish	Non-Jewish	Male	Fem.	Total Persons	Jewish	Non-Jewish
	1643	953	690	1304	339	3171	1974	1197
MONTREAL 55%								
Entitled to receive	904	524	380	717	187	1744	1086	658
Number allocated	848	505	343	659	189	1680	1065	615
Over or short	-56	-19	-37	-58	⁄2	- 64	- 21	-43
TORONTO 36%								
Entitled to receive	591	343	248	470	121	1142	711	431
Number allocated	558	326	232	442	116	1104	691	413
Over or short	-33	-17	-16	-28	-5	- 38	-20	-18
WINNIPEG 7%								
Entitled to receive	115	67	48	91	24	222	138	84
Number allocated	149	69	80	126	23	265	138	127
Over or short	⁄34	⁄2	⁄32	⁄35	-1	⁄43	0	⁄43
VANCOUVER 2%								
Entitled to receive	33	19	14	26	7	63	39	24
Number allocated	58	35	23	49	9	79	52	27
Over or short	⁄25	⁄16	⁄9	⁄23	⁄2	⁄16	⁄13	⁄ 3
OTHER CITIES ALLOCATED	⁄30	⁄18	⁄12	⁄28	⁄ 2	⁄43	⁄28	⁄ 15

Other cities where tailors sent -

Fredericton, N.B.	1 Non-Jewish	Female	1 person
Newcastle Ont.	1 Non-Jewish	Male	4 persons
Lethbridge, Alta.	1 Non-Jewish	Male	1 person
Hoffer, Sask.	1 Jewish	Male	4 persons
Ottawa, Ont.	8 Jewish	Males	8 persons
Ottawa, Ont.	2 Non-Jewish	Males	2 persons
St. John, N.B	5 Jewish	Males	8 persons
Calgary, Alta.	1 Jewish	Male	2 persons
Cornwall, Ont.	4 Non-Jewish	Males	4 persons
Prince Albert, Sask.	1 Non-Jewish	Male	1 person
South Rock Falls, Ont.	1 Non-Jewish	Male	1 person
Windsor, Ont.	1 Jewish	Female	1 person
Windsor, Ont.	2 Jewish	Male	5 persons
Moose Jaw, Sask.	1 Non-Jewish	Male	1 person
TOTAL	30 Tailors	TOTAL	43 Persons

Summary of over and short in tailors		2500 Tailors - Project 65% complete	
Montreal	- 56	Winnipeg ⁄ 34	% Jewish tailors Approx.59%
Toronto	- 33 89	Vancouver ⁄ 25	% Jewish Persons Approx.62%
		Other Cities ⁄ 30 89	

By the autumn of 1948 the project was winding down, though tailors continued to arrive in Canada through 1949. This chart, showing how many tailors came and where they went in Canada, does not include family members. At its completion the Tailor Project had resettled some 2,500 European Jews in Canada.

The Tailor Project   225

AFTERWORD

I have been asked frequently why I was interested in this project.

Let's begin with the circumstances and events of 1947–48.

The war was over, and knowledge of the Holocaust was fully evident, yet Canada, along with other countries, maintained the prevailing antisemitism while countless Jews languished in the DP camps of Europe. Pre-state Israel did not have the open policy Jews now enjoy, and only five thousand Jewish refugees were permitted to enter Canada from 1933 to 1947.

I was active in the Jewish community as president of Holy Blossom Temple Youth and part of the Toronto Jewish Youth Council. It was a period of strong emotions for the youth of Canada as we faced antisemitism at home and the hope for a new state in Israel. The antisemitism we faced included legislative and legal constraints, and certain rights to property and occupations were restricted.

Leaders in the Jewish community took note of an opportunity to bring Jews to Canada. With the support of the Canadian Jewish Congress, they helped organize the labour unions and manufacturers of the men's and women's clothing industry, to present the Canadian government with a proposal to ease the labour shortage of tailors in the industry, as the government had done for the logging industry. This proposal was accepted.

A team representing the unions and the manufacturers was sent to the DP camps of Europe to select the tailors. My father, Max Enkin, was one of this team. They, in turn, elected him as chairman. The team included the messrs. Posluns, Solomon, Herbst, and Shane. (The families of Solomon and Posluns have helped us in the Tailor Project book.)

While at a stopover in England, my father was taken aside and told there could be no more than 50 per cent Jews accepted under this program (a decision of the government). Heartbroken, they still continued, but personal notes and observations from my father record the stress this put the team under.

Originally, the program was to bring over 2,500 tailors and their families, and because of health and other reasons, far more were interviewed than arrived.

Max Enkin and his son, Larry Enkin.

As my father reported on his return:

I met a young girl in Salzburg—she was only about 25, but looked considerably older—she was extremely nervous and said, 'You know that this is a very memorable day for me. On the 28th of October, 1944, I was lined up with my mother in Auschwitz. My mother was directed to the left, and I remained on the right, and that was the last I heard from her.' Throughout that winter, she slaved in labour camps without shoes. Her head was shaved. Eventually, she was made to walk from one camp to another. Do you think you can leave a young person like that in Germany and expect her to live a normal life again?

In late 1947, speaking to Holy Blossom congregation on what he saw in the DP camps, my father said, "Most of us are children of immigrants to this country…. Hospitality and looking after the homeless is or was an age-old tradition of our people. Let us copy and follow their example."

In the 1960s, I had the experience of meeting a tailor visiting our factory, who, seeing my father, recognized him as having selected him at a DP camp. My father said, "Tell me, of all the people who came, you are about the only tailor left in the industry." A brief pause—"But, Mr Enkin, I was a tailor." This lingered in my memory.

About a year and a half ago, I was at a book launch at the temple. The author Anne Dublin, in introducing herself, mentioned that her father had arrived in 1948. I told her that story, and she said, "Well, now you know two. My father was also a tailor."

I am now at a point in life where memories of the past are lost to current generations, yet I am sure there are lessons still to be learned. The Azrieli Foundation recently found that more than half of Canadian adults did not know that six million Jews were killed. After so many years, I think there is value in knowing about the actual tailors who arrived, what had happened to them previously, what was their life in Canada like, and now about their children. We will see they have made a valuable contribution to Canada and to the Jewish community, validating this enlightened immigration.

My own memories of antisemitism and restrictions on immigration in Canada are still fresh. It was a lesson Canada has learned well, with such moments as the recent Syrian immigration a sign of our strength. But, a report from the UN refugee agency indicates we are now witnessing the highest levels of displacement on record. An unprecedented 68.5 million people around the world have been forced from home. I hope Canada will continue to make every effort to support easing the plight of these people, both through immigration and by enabling their lives in their home countries to be more valued. I hope Canada will also be vigilant about the rise of antisemitism.

I also want to acknowledge the important role Impakt Corp. has played in bringing the stories of the tailors to light.

Larry Enkin
June 8, 2020

ENDNOTES

Abbreviations used in notes

CJA Alex Dworkin Canadian Jewish Archives
LAC Library and Archives Canada
OJA Ontario Jewish Archives, Blankenstein Family Heritage Centre, UJA Federation of Greater Toronto

INTRODUCTION

[1] Prime Minister Mackenzie King in Canada House of Commons, *Debates*, May 1, 1947, 2644–47.

[2] Charles Alexander Magrath, *Canada's Growth and Some Problems Affecting It* (Ottawa: Mortimer Press, 1910), 85.

[3] Clifford Sifton, Canada House of Commons, *Debates*, April 7, 1902, 2991.

[4] Dominion Bureau of Statistics, *Canada Year Book, 1922–23*, (Ottawa, 1924), 215.

[5] Barnett R. Brickner, as quoted in Joseph Kage, *With Faith and Thanksgiving* (Montreal: Eagle Publishing, 1962), 80.

POSTWAR CANADA

[1] Blair Fraser, "They won't go home," *Maclean's*, November 1, 1946.

[2] Rabbi Nathan Sanger in Emberg, Germany to Bernard Shane, "In search of tailors: Impressions gained during a recent two month journey through the continent," *Canadian Jewish Chronicle*, February 20–April 16, 1948, LAC.

[3] Irving Abella and Harold Troper, *None Is Too Many: Canada and the Jews of Europe, 1933–1948* (Toronto: Lester and Orpen, Dennys, 1982), 17.

[4] Abella and Troper, 35.

[5] Carine Wilson to J.A. Glen, Minister of Mines and Resources, January 16, 1946. Alex Dworkin, CJA ZA 1945 6 87.

[6] Abella and Troper, 230; Brief presented to the Standing Committee on Immigration and Labour of the Senate of Canada, July 3, 1946, CJA ZA 1945 6 87.

[7] Abella and Troper, 230.

[8] Abella and Troper, 241–42.

MAX ENKIN

[1] Rabbi Yael Splansky, speaking in honour of the Tailor Project, Holy Blossom Temple, Yom HaShoah, 5779–May 1, 2019.

[2] Beverly Stern, "Max Enkin has long been a leader in the community," *Canadian Jewish News*, August 23, 1981.

[3] Harvey Hickely, "Misery of DP Camps rends Canadian's heart," *Globe and Mail*, November 29, 1947.

[4] Max Enkin speech, "What I saw in the D.P. Camps in Europe," 1948, Larry Enkin private collection.

THE BULK LABOUR SCHEMES

[1] Irving Abella and Harold Troper, *None Is Too Many: Canada and the Jews of Europe, 1933–1948* (Toronto: Lester and Orpen, Dennys, 1982), 217–18.

[2] CJC report to Senate standing Committee on Immigration and Labour, May 7, CJA 1947, ZA 1947 6 41.

[3] Abella and Troper, 247–50.

[4] Franca Iacovetta, *Gatekeepers: Reshaping Immigrant Lives in Cold War Canada* (Toronto: Between the Lines, 2006), 4.

[5] For several years, Labor-Progressive MPP Salsberg was the only elected Communist in North America.

[6] Gerald Tulchinsky, *Joe Salsberg. A Life of Commitment* (Toronto: University of Toronto Press, 2013) 96–97.

[7] Joe Salsberg to Saul Hayes, December 12, 1947, OJA F70 f4 i002.

THE DISPLACED PERSONS CAMPS

[1] This and other references in this paragraph are from David S. Wyman, *DP: Europe's Displaced Persons 1945–1951* (Ithaca: Cornell University Press, 1989), 134–36.

[2] Dan Stone, *Liberation of the Camps: The End of the Holocaust and Its Aftermath* (New Haven: Yale University Press, 2015), 169.

[3] Max Enkin speech, "What I saw in the D.P. Camps in Europe," 1948, Larry Enkin private collection.

[4] "Children from Europe," *Canadian Welfare* 25, 1–2, in Franca Iacovetta, *Gatekeepers: Reshaping Immigrant Lives in Cold War Canada* (Toronto: Between the Lines, 2006), 2.

[5] Blair Fraser, "They won't go home," *Maclean's*, November 1, 1946.

[6] Bernard Shane, "In search of tailors: Impressions gained during a recent two-month journey through the continent," *Canadian Jewish Chronicle*, February 20–April 16, 1948, LAC.

[7] Enkin speech, 1948.

[8] Allan Bronfman to Saul Hayes, October 12, 1947, Larry Enkin private collection.

SAM POSLUNS

[1] This quotation and the following quotations in this section are from two of Sam Posluns' speeches to the Men's Clothing Manufacturer's Association of Ontario, c. November 1947, and Sam Posluns, speech, c. April 1948, OJA F70 f10 i001.

THROUGH THE EYE OF A NEEDLE

[1] Louis Rosenberg, *Canada's Jews: A Social and Economic Study of Jews in Canada in the 1930s*, Morton Weinfeld, ed. (Montreal and Kingston: McGill-Queens University Press, 1993), 175–78.

[2] Gerald Tulchinsky, *Branching Out: The Transformation of the Canadian Jewish Community* (Toronto: Stoddart, 1998), 87–91.

[3] Ruth A. Frager, *Sweatshop Strife: Class, Ethnicity, and Gender in the Jewish Labour Movement of Toronto 1900–1939* (Toronto: University of Toronto Press, 1992), 211–17.

[4] Tulchinsky, 92–93.

[5] An example of this would be my father, Darrell Draper, who was born in Canada in 1922. At the age of twenty, he graduated with an engineering degree from the University of Toronto. During the war he realized that he would never be hired as an engineer, so he anglicized his name and went to law school.

[6] Carmela Patrias, "Race, employment discrimination, and state complicity in wartime Canada, 1938–1945," in Bryan Palmer and Joan Sangster, eds., *Labouring Canada: Class, Gender, and Race in Canadian Working-Class History* (Toronto: Oxford University Press, 2008), 270.

[7] Ruth A. Frager and Carmella Patrias, *Discounted Labour: Women Workers in Canada, 1870–1939* (Toronto: University of Toronto Press, 2005), 71.

[8] Morris (Moishe) Lewis was the secretary of the JLC; his son David was the national secretary of the Co-operative Commonwealth Federation (CCF) and a key architect in the formation of the New Democratic Party, which he served as national leader from 1971 to 1975. Moishe's grandson, Stephen Lewis, became leader of the Ontario NDP from 1970 to 1978.

[9] Alan Borovoy, Canadian lawyer and human rights advocate, once described Kaplansky as the "zaiydeh" (grandfather) of the Canadian human rights movement. Fran Cohen, "The story of Athenia story of my father, too," *Toronto Star*, September 16, 1999.

MENDEL BEKIER

[1] From Mendel Bekier's Shoah Foundation testimony.

THE GARMENT WORKERS BULK LABOUR PROGRAM

[1] Memorandum of the Jewish Labor Committee to the Canadian Jewish Congress, July 11, 1946, LAC MG 28V75 vol. 16.

[2] "Sh'erit ha-Pletah," surviving remnant, is the biblical phrase (Ezra 9:14) that survivors adopted to refer to themselves and their communities.

[3] Irving Abella and Harold Troper, *None Is Too Many: Canada and the Jews of Europe, 1933–1948* (Toronto: Lester and Orpen, Dennys, 1982), 257.

[4] Abella and Troper, 257–59.

[5] David Dunkelman to Humphrey Mitchell, April 23, 1947, LAC RG27 box 278 f I-26-5-1.

[6] Franklin Bialystok, *Delayed Impact: The Holocaust and the Canadian Jewish Community* (Montreal and Kingston: McGill-Queen's University Press, 2000), 56.

[7] Joint brief on behalf of the Ladies' Cloak and Suit Industry to the Minister of Mines and Resources, March 18, 1947, LAC MG28 V75 vol.16.

[8] Max Enkin to Charlie Foster, July 22, 1947, OJA; Abella and Troper, 260–61. For a discussion of whether the industry had a legitimate need for thousands of new employees, see page 259 n.

[9] Employment agreement, Men's Clothing Manufacturer's Association of Ontario, OJA F31 f1 i00.

[10] Memorandum of the Conference held by the Industrial Team and the Representatives of the HIAS and the AJDC British Zone, September 21, 1947, OJA F70 f1 i003.

BERNARD SHANE

[1] I. Grosman, "Bernard Shane (Alav HaShalom): The man and his work as labour leader," *The Jewish Eagle* (*Keneder Adler*), November 7, 1975.

[2] See Rose Pesotta, Bernard Shane, and Les Midinettes, ILGWU Headquarters 1933–1939, Museum of Jewish Montreal, http://imjm.ca/location/1250.

[3] This quotation and following in this section, Bernard Shane, "In search of tailors: Impressions gained during a recent two-month journey through the continent," *Canadian Jewish Chronicle*, February 20–April 16, 1948, LAC.

THE SELECTION TEAM

[1] Franklin Bialystok, *Delayed Impact: The Holocaust and the Canadian Jewish Community* (Montreal and Kingston: McGill-Queen's University Press, 2000), 51–52.

[2] Memorandum Re Meeting at Ottawa May 30, 1947, at the Office of the Commissioner of Immigration, F31 f2 i009, OJA.

[3] David Solomon, personal notes on the Tailor Project while in Europe, 1947, Solomon Family collection.

[4] Abella and Troper, 262–63.

[5] Telegram from the High Commissioner for Canada in Great Britain to the Secretary of State for External Affairs, London, August 1, 1947, LAC Rg27 box 278 fI-26-51.

[6] Letter from J.J. Spector, August 6, 1947, Larry Enkin private collection.

[7] Memorandum re Meeting with Dr. A. MacNamara, Deputy Minister of Labour, Norman Genser and J.J. Spector, K.C. concerning Immigration of Displaced Persons for the Needle Trade Industry held at Ottawa on Thursday, August 14, 1947, Larry Enkin private collection.

[8] Abella and Troper, 264–65.

[9] Max Enkin interview with Phyllis Platnick, April 13, 1986, OJA AC 113 & 114.

[10] Norman Genser to Max Enkin, August 19, 1947, OJA.

[11] Max Enkin to Norman Genser, September 16, 1947; Norman Genser to Max Enkin, September 20, 1947; Larry Enkin private collection.

[12] Abella and Troper, 263–64.

[13] Max Enkin to Norman Genser.

DAVID SOLOMON

[1] David Solomon to Max Enkin, November 24, 1947, Larry Enkin private collection.

[2] David Solomon, Writeup #1, September 23, 1966, Solomon family private collection.

[3] David Solomon reminiscence, September 1966, Solomon family private collection.

[4] David Solomon, letter to family, October 1, 1947, Bucholz Camp, Solomon family private collection.

[5] David Solomon, "Things I remember," undated, Solomon family private collection.

SAMUEL HERBST

[1] Allan Levine, *Seeking the Fabled City: The Canadian Jewish Experience* (Toronto: McClelland & Stewart, 2018), 189.

[2] Samuel Herbst to Max Enkin, November 26, 1947, Larry Enkin private collection.

NEEDLES AND THREAD

[1] Unless otherwise noted, this section is based on personal letters and documents provided by the David Solomon and Max Enkin families; documents provided by Sam Posluns' family to the Ontario Jewish Archives (F70), Platnik's interview with Enkin (AC132, OJA) and these articles by Bernard Shane: "In search of tailors: Impressions gained during a recent two-month journey through the continent," *Canadian Jewish Chronicle* February 20–April 16, 1948, LAC.

[2] *Vochenblatt*, n.d., Larry Enkin private collection.

[3] Josef Rosensaft later became president of the World Federation of Bergen-Belsen Survivors. His son, Menachem Rosensaft, became the founding chairman of the International Network of Children of Jewish Survivors.

[4] Shane's comment is a powerful indication of how little understanding even the most sympathetic North American Jews had of the Holocaust. For every Jew who was alive at the end of the war, their survival was a miracle.

[5] Sam Posluns, speech, c. April 1948, F70 f10 i001, OJA.

[6] Bernard Shane to Moishe Lewis, October 4, 1947, LAC MG 28 V 75 vol.7.

[7] Bernard Shane to Moishe Lewis.

[8] Alfred Zimmerman to Abe Zaitlin, March 20, 1947, CJA ZA 1947 10 127.

[9] Abella and Troper, 266.

[10] This quotation and the following ones in this section are from the letter from Bernard Shane to Moishe Lewis, October 4, 1947.

[11] David Solomon reported upon his return that they had examined 5,048 DPs at a rate of 187 a day in the thirty days between September 30 and October 31, 1947. They had approved 3,162 and rejected 1,886. In total 1,309 non-Jews and 1,853 Jews had been approved. Solomon report, November 19, 1947, CJA CA 31 300t 004.

JOSEPH KLINGHOFFER AND MAX ENKIN

[1] Joseph Klinghoffer interview with David Aronson, 1988, Sarah and Chaim Neuberger Holocaust Education Centre; Max Enkin interview with Phyllis Platnick, April 13, 1986, AC 113 & 114, OJA.

WELCOME TO CANADA

[1] Memorandum, Canadian Clothing Workers Project, November 18, 1947, Larry Enkin private collection.

[2] Saul Hayes to Max Enkin, December 2, 1947, Larry Enkin private collection.

[3] Joe Salsberg to Saul Hayes, December 12, 1947, OJA F70 f4 i002.

[4] C.E.S. Smith to Norman Genser, December 6, 1947, OJA F70 f4 i005.

[5] Memorandum of meeting with departments of of immigration and labour, Ottawa, December 5, 1947, OJA F70 f 4 i004.

[6] Max Enkin to David Solomon, December 17, 1947, Larry Enkin private collection; David Rome, CJC's publicity director, saw this setback as an opportunity. He wrote to Hayes that the arrival of the first ship, sans Jews, "offers us certain opportunities to nail down the fact that the project as a whole is not an all Jewish one. From this point of view it might be advisable to inform the press of the landing of this ship and to get from them the greatest possible coverage. I would highlight the Christian element of the group by having Greek orthodox priests as well as Roman Catholic welfare workers there. These Greek orthodox are usually bearded and colourful and should be good for a lot of publicity." David Rome to Saul Hayes, December 8, 1947. CJC CA 31 300t 003, CJA.

[7] Irving Abella and Harold Troper, *None Is Too Many: Canada and the Jews of Europe, 1933–1948* (Toronto: Lester and Orpen, Dennys, 1982), 268.

[8] Matthew Ram, "Report from Germany," ZB Posluns, *Congress Bulletin* 5(8) (November 1948), CJA.

MATTHEW RAM

[1] Max Enkin to O. Cormier, November 1, 1947, Larry Enkin private collection.

[2] Matthew Ram, "Report from Germany," ZB Posluns, *Congress Bulletin* (November 1948).

[3] Matthew Ram to Max Enkin, November 18, 1947, CA 31 3001 003, CJA.

[4] Matthew Ram, "Report from Germany."

[5] Matthew Ram, "Report from Germany."

SETTLING IN

[1] Franca Iacovetta, *Gatekeepers: Reshaping Immigrant Lives in Cold War Canada* (Toronto: Between the Lines, 2006), 5; "Could this be prejudice?" *Toronto Star* editorial, February 7, 1948; "Aliens seized in Toronto on illegal count lose deportation plea," *Globe and Mail*, February 5, 1948, 30; "Oust D.P.'s, admit Vichy men 'revolting,' declares rabbi," *Toronto Star* October 16, 1948, 35. De Bernonville eventually fled to sanctuary in Brazil.

[2] "The issue resurfaced with a vengeance in the 1970–80s, mostly due to the outrage of survivors who now had the ear of CJC. The result was the Royal Commission on war criminals in Canada (Jules Deschenes) which in turn resulted in little action and much anger and frustration among the survivor community." Gerald Tulchinsky, *Branching Out: The Transformation of the Canadian Jewish Community* (Toronto: Stoddart, 1998), 328.

[3] Blair Fraser, "Houses, houses, where are the houses?" *Maclean's*, March 1, 1949.

[4] H. Frank, CJC Western Division, to Saul Hayes, September 25, 1947, CJC CA 31 300t 003, CJA.

[5] Phone interview with Max Enkin, Vienna, Austria, October 28, 1947, CJC CA 31 300t 003, CJA.

[6] Max Enkin speech, "What I saw in the D.P. camps in Europe," Larry Enkin private collection.

[7] Eva-Lis Wuorio, "We can't go back" *Maclean's*, June 1, 1948.

[8] JIAS Record, August 1948, in Joseph Kage, *With Faith and Thanksgiving* (Montreal: Eagle Publishing, 1962), 183.

[9] https://pier21.ca/walls/Honour/Meta-Echt-and-Marianne-Ferguson; Adara Goldberg, *Holocaust Survivors in Canada: Exclusion, Inclusion, Transformation, 1947–1955* (Winnipeg: University of Manitoba Press, 2105), 51.

[10] Kage, With Faith and Thanksgiving, 239,184.

[11] Walter Friedman, "Step by step with the immigrant tailors," *Congress Bulletin* 5(8) (November 1948), CJA ZB Posluns.

[12] Canadian Overseas Garment Commission, Toronto Program, April 1949, OJA F17 s 47 7 f1.

[13] A. Solkin to Latch, January 29, 1948, JIAS F9 s5-3 f18 1 i002, OJA.

[14] Canadian Overseas Garment Commission, Toronto Program, April 1949, F17 s 47 7 f1, OJA.

[15] Re: Immigration of Tailors, OJA f31 f2 i008.

MONTREAL

[1] Joseph Kage, *With Faith and Thanksgiving* (Montreal: Eagle Publishing, 1962), 187.

[2] Adara Goldberg, *Holocaust Survivors in Canada: Exclusion, Inclusion, Transformation, 1947–1955* (Winnipeg: University of Manitoba Press, 2105), 56–57.

[3] Walter Friedman, "Step by step with the immigrant tailors," *Congress Bulletin* 5(8) (November 1948), CJA ZB Posluns.

[4] Case file, Shmul G., JIAS Social Service, box 42.

[5] Case file, Shmul G.

TORONTO

[1] Enkin interview OJA; Jack Lipinsky, *Imposing Their Will: An Organizational History of Jewish Toronto, 1933–1948* (Montreal and Kingston: McGill-Queen's University Press, 2011), 243–44; Solkin to Simpson, January 28, 1948, OJA s5–3 f18–1 001.

[2] Canadian Overseas Garment Commission, Toronto Program, April 1949, OJA F17 s 47 7 f1; Lipinsky, 246.

[3] "Smooth adjustment marks Tailor Project as community assists," CJC *Bulletin*, October 7 1948, CJA.

[4] Lipinsky, 246; Joseph Kage, *With Faith and Thanksgiving: The Story of Two Hundred Years of Jewish Immigration and Immigrant Aid Effort in Canada (1760–1960)* (Montreal: Eagle Publishing, 1962), 188.

EAST AND WEST

[1] "send a tailor should be able to speak german as well as polish or ukrainian tailor should not be over thirty five years old," telegram from Joe Lix to Garment Commission, January 24, 1949, UJRA Dc2.01 49 scythia 36, CJA.

[2] "Recapitulation," UJRA Dc 20.1 48 Samaria 22, CJA; "About a dozen Holocaust survivors made their way to Saint John after the Holocaust. Some came with sponsorships extended by cousins living in the city, others came for professional reasons, such as medical professionals and tailors. Most of the survivors became involved in the life of the Saint John Jewish community, but there were some who felt somewhat isolated because of their wartime experiences."

Katherine Biggs-Craft, "Documentation of the Holocaust in the Maritimes," *Canadian Jewish Studies* 24 (2016), 183.

[3] Walter Friedman, "Step by step with the immigrant tailors," *Congress Bulletin* 5(8) (November 1948), CJA ZB Posluns.

[4] *Canadian Western Bulletin*, May 6, 1948.

[5] Jean Gerber, "*Opening the Door: Immigration and Integration of Holocaust Survivors in Vancouver 1947–1970*" in Paula Draper, Richard Menkis, eds., "New Perspectives on Canada, the Holocaust and Survivors," *Canadian Jewish Studies* Vol IV–V (1996–1997): 63–86; Jean Gerber, "Immigration and integration in post-war Canada: A case study of Holocaust survivors in Vancouver 1947–1970," unpublished MA thesis, Department of History, University of British Columbia, September 1989.

[6] Adara Goldberg, *Holocaust Survivors in Canada: Exclusion, Inclusion, Transformation, 1947–1955* (Winnipeg: University of Manitoba Press, 2105), 58.

[7] Gerry Berkowski, "The Winnipeg garment industry 1900–1955," *Economic History Theme Study*, 1987, Henry Trachtenberg, editor, 1989.

[8] H. Frank, CJC Western Division, to Saul Hayes, September 25 1947, CJA CJC CA 31 300t 003.

[9] Allan Levine, *Seeking the Fabled City: The Canadian Jewish Experience* (Toronto: McClelland & Stewart, 2018), 226.

THE PASSAGE INTO NEW LIVES

[1] Franklin Bialystok, *Delayed Impact: The Holocaust and the Canadian Jewish Community* (Montreal and Kingston: McGill-Queen's University Press, 2000), 57.

[2] Undated Sam Posluns speech, c.1948, OJA F70f10i002.

[3] Matthew Ram, "Report from Germany," CJC *Bulletin*, CJA 07 10 48.

[4] Joseph Kage, *With Faith and Thanksgiving* (Montreal: Eagle Publishing, 1962), 180.

[5] Joseph Kage "Immigration and social service," *Canadian Welfare* 24 (3) (January 1949), 3–8, in Franca Iacovetta, *Gatekeepers: Reshaping Immigrant Lives in Cold War Canada* (Toronto: Between the Lines, 2006), 55.

[6] Kage, *With Faith and Thanksgiving*, 180, 228–9.

[7] Joseph Kage, "The Jewish Immigrant Aid Society of Canada," *Social Worker* 18 (February 3, 1950), in Iacovetta, 67.

[8] Walter Friedman, "Step by step with the immigrant tailors," Congress Bulletin 5(8) (November 1948), CJA ZB Posluns.

CONCLUSION

[1] Enkin interview, OJA; David Lewis to Moishe Lewis, July 8, 1948, MG 28 V 75 vol 16 f 7, LAC.

[2] Interview with Phillip Weiss by Josh Freed, Holocaust Documentation Project, 64, Winnipeg, January 21, 1982, CJA.

PHOTO CREDITS

page 11: Alex Dworkin Canadian Jewish Archives.

page 14: Ontario Jewish Archives, fonds 70, file 5, item 4.

page 18: Ontario Jewish Archives, fonds 70, file 4, item 2.

page 22: Courtesy Faye Kieffer

page 24: Ontario Jewish Archives, fonds 70, file 5, item 44.

page 28: (left) Ontario Jewish Archives, fonds 28, series 6, file 200.

page 28: (right) Ontario Jewish Archives, fonds 70, file 15, item 3.

page 32: Courtesy Leibgott family

page 40: Ina Fichman collection, Alex Dworkin Canadian Jewish Archives.

page 44: Courtesy Bekier family

page 48: Courtesy Bekier family

page 50: CJC Bulletin 07 10 48, Alex Dworkin Canadian Jewish Archives.

page 56: Who's Who in Canadian Jewry, 1967. Alex Dworkin Canadian Jewish Archives.

page 60: Courtesy Judy Cohen

page 62: Courtesy Judy Cohen

page 68: Courtesy Judy Cohen

page 76: Courtesy the family of Max Greenholtz and Ella Birnbaum

page 82: Courtesy the family of Max Greenholtz and Ella Birnbaum

page 86: Ontario Jewish Archives, fonds 70 file 5, item 3.

page 88: Larry Enkin collection

page 92: Solomon family collection

page 96: Ontario Jewish Archives, fonds 70, file 5, item 4.

page 98: Courtesy Faye Kieffer

page 101: Ontario Jewish Archives, fonds 70, file 1, item 1.

page 107: Ontario Jewish Archives, accession 1985-12-5.

page 110: Courtesy Mendel Good

page 115: Courtesy Mendel Good

page 120: Courtesy Faye Kieffer

page 132: Courtesy Nayman family

page 136: Courtesy Nayman family

ABOUT THE AUTHORS

ANDREA KNIGHT has been a writer and editor for more than thirty years. In addition to her focus on Holocaust history, she currently works with the Feminist History Society, documenting the history of second-wave feminism in Canada. She co-founded the New Jewish Press at the University of Toronto and, for a number of years, was managing editor of the Azrieli Series of Holocaust Survivor Memoirs. During this time, she also served as a member of the National Task Force on Holocaust Education, Remembrance, and Research. She has an MA in history from the University of Toronto and lives in Toronto.

PAULA DRAPER PhD is a historian and educator specializing in memory history. She served as vice-president of the Association of Canadian Jewish Studies and has been involved in a multitude of Holocaust-related projects, including the Royal Commission of Inquiry on War Criminals in Canada, the second trial of Holocaust denier Ernst Zundel, and as Lead International Trainer for Steven Spielberg's Shoah Foundation. Dr. Draper has published widely on the topic of Canada and the Holocaust and is now researching the post-war experiences of Canadian Holocaust survivors. She lives in Toronto.

NICOLE BRYCK was the Social Program Manager at Impakt Labs, an organization that creates storytelling-based advocacy materials about social issues. This was her first experience doing Holocaust research and she found it very moving to hear about the incredible and awe-inspiring lives of these survivors.